12⁰⁰

some
underlines

BY L. G. SHREVE

The Phoenix With Oily Feathers
(a novel)

Tench Tilghman

TENCH TILGHMAN

Tench Tilghman.
Miniature on ivory by Charles Willson Peale.
Courtesy: Frick Art Reference Library.

TENCH TILGHMAN

The Life and Times

OF

Washington's Aide-de-Camp

BY

L. G. SHREVE

TIDEWATER PUBLISHERS
Centreville, Maryland

Library of Congress Cataloging in Publication Data

Shreve, L. G., 1910-
    Tench Tilghman, the life and times of Washington's aide-de-camp.

    Bibliography: p.
    Includes index.
    1. Tilghman, Tench. 2. United States—History—Revolution, 1775-1783—Campaigns. 3. Soldiers—United States—Biography. 4. United States. Army—Biography. 5. Washington, George, 1732-1799—Friends and associates. I. Title.
E207.T57S57   1982   973.3′092′4 [B]   82-60330
ISBN 0-87033-293-7

Manufactured in the United States of America

First edition

To the memory of
ROSALIE TILGHMAN SHREVE
1846-1920

Contents

PART THREE

PEACE — AND A
NEW ENVIRONMENT : 1783-1786

PART FOUR

EPILOGUE : 30 NOVEMBER 1971

APPENDICES

List of Illustrations

Preface

Then as now, it was hard to contemplate the events of the bicentennial year of 1976 and the inspiring celebration of 19 October 1981 marking the two hundredth anniversary of the surrender of the British under Cornwallis at Yorktown without succumbing to the romantic view that all of our national ancestors were heroes. We tend to picture them as endowed with superhuman courage, iron determination, unshakable loyalty, and wisdom stemming from the direct intervention of God. Moreover, in any study of the era of the American Revolution we are struck by the pervasiveness of the forces that propelled that age and formed the crucible from which emerged the greatest nation in the world.

Consequently, when I undertook to document to the fullest possible extent the life of Tench Tilghman, I was faced with a formidable task. I tried to rid my mind of every preconception, to start my study as if I had never heard of him. While there is no scarcity of source material on Tilghman's all-too-short life and while his accomplishments have been documented in poetry as well as prose, it has been more than a hundred years since the appearance of the only book devoted solely to him. Based on Tilghman's diaries and correspondence then in private hands, its publication was timed to coincide with the celebration of the American Centennial in 1876. It had the virtue of being accurate and the vice of being too brief. Dealing primarily with the war years, it presented only a narrow vision of the man himself, a barebones outline of his life span, with no amplification of his individuality or of his attainments in relationship to his times. In all fairness to the author of that century-old volume, it should be noted that research facilities available to scholars today were then essentially lacking. A somewhat more comprehensive article length study appeared in the *Maryland Historical Magazine* in June 1947. As this book goes to press yet another engaging study of this interesting eighteenth century man has appeared in the same periodical.

Since 1876 literally thousands of books have been written on every aspect of the American Revolution plus scores of biographies of its principal participants, statesmen as well as soldiers, on both sides. The bibliography in this volume lists over two hundred titles of primary and secondary source material which I have examined, much of it in detail. In almost every instance Tilghman's participation in the service of his country is mentioned, if not fully discussed. Of great significance was the discovery of a cache of Tilghman's letters lost from public view for eighty-three years. From this amalgam new aspects of Tilghman's life emerge, as well as a fresh glow on familiar figures, scoundrels as well as heroes. There seem to have been no dull characters among Tilghman's acquaintances, and he was directly or indirectly involved in a number of well-known events. Benedict Arnold's treason, for example, had highly personal overtones for Tilghman since Peggy Shippen, Arnold's second wife, was Tilghman's first cousin. He was called upon to testify at the court-martial of the irascible General Charles Lee, fought bitterly against the slanderous attacks on Washington by the Conway Cabal, and was deeply immersed in the Asgill Affair.

While Tilghman was never a principal actor in the unfolding drama of the American Revolution, his supporting role was such that he was on center stage at all times. His constant companions—in addition to privation, hardship, and danger—were the towering figures of the struggle. For the greater part of seven years, unless absent from headquarters on Washington's direct orders, he never left his chief's side. Lafayette trusted him to such a degree that, under specified circumstances, he would allow no one but Tilghman or Gouvion to translate dispatches written in French for Washington's eyes alone. He was in daily contact with Henry Knox, Alexander Hamilton, James McHenry, Nathanael Greene, Baron deKalb, "Mad Anthony" Wayne, Count Rochambeau, and Ben Lincoln—not to mention that trio of malcontents, Horatio Gates, Charles Lee, and Thomas Conway.

Washington never failed to refer to Tilghman in the most glowing terms; his devotion to him was absolute and after his death "none mourned him more." Tilghman's repudiation of his family's Loyalist background and of his father's restricted political views, his utter commitment to the cause of liberty, and his selflessness during the war give him the right to a well-deserved but too little recognized place of honor in the annals of the country which his sacrifices helped form.

Tench Tilghman's reputation, even in the harsh light of modern historical scholarship, remains remarkably unblemished. Because of this, and because no detractor has appeared to shake the ground on which his reputation rests, I have had to guard against presenting a static, uncritical portrait. Indeed I have tried to describe the whole man and to put him in the context of his truly exciting era. I leave to the reader the measurement of my success.

L. G. SHREVE

Baltimore
July 1982

Acknowledgments

Without considerable help from scholars, archivists, librarians, curators, genealogists, and interested friends—ever on the lookout for helpful information of whatever kind in their own peregrinations through the research libraries of the United States, France, and England—the writing of this book would have been impossible. It is with gratitude, therefore, that I list the names of the following, to all of whom I am indebted in many different ways.

Mrs. Guilliam Aertsen III, Mrs. William B. Bagbey, Ms. Ruth M. Blair, Manuscript Cataloger, Connecticut Historical Society, Mrs. John Nicholas Brown, Mr. Joseph Bryan III, Mr. C. F. W. Coker, Manuscript Division, Library of Congress, Mr. Stiles Tuttle Colwill, Gallery Curator, Maryland Historical Society, Dr. Jacob E. Cooke, MacCracken Professor of History, Lafayette College, Ms. Lynn Cox, Prints and Photographs Librarian, Maryland Historical Society, Mr. Francis James Dallett, Archivist, University of Pennsylvania, Mr. Rodney G. Dennis, Curator of Manuscripts, Houghton Library, Harvard University, Dr. Brice M. Dorsey, Mr. John Goldsborough Earle, Mr. P. William Filby, former Director and now Consultant to the Maryland Historical Society, Mrs. L. McLane Fisher, Mr. John Frazer, Jr., Mr. Tench Frazer, Mr. Thomas L. Gaffney, Curator of Manuscripts, Maine Historical Society, Mrs. David F. Gearhart, Mr. Nicholas Tilghman Goldsborough, Mr. Richard B. Harrington, Curator, Anne S. K. Brown Military Collection, Providence, Rhode Island, Mr. James N. Haskett, Chief Park Historian, Yorktown National Historic Park, Mrs. Wilma Pitchford Hays, Ms. Alexis D. Henry, The Library Company of Philadelphia, Mr.

Bruce Henry, Assistant Curator, Americana Manuscripts, The Huntington Library, Mr. Steven H. Hochman, Assistant to Dr. Dumas Malone, Alderman Library, University of Virginia, Mr. Bryden Bordley Hyde, Mrs. Jocelyn Pierson Kennedy-Taylor, Mr. Richard M. Ketchum, Mr. John Dwight Kilbourne, Director, Anderson House Museum, The Society of The Cincinnati, Ms. Susan A. Kopczynski, Park Historian, Morristown National Historical Park, Mr. Douglas W. Marshall, Curator of Maps, William L. Clements Library, University of Michigan, Mr. Paul Mellon, Mrs. Phillipus Miller V, Dr. James E. Mooney, Director, The Historical Society of Pennsylvania, Mrs. Malcolm N. Oates, Dr. Edward C. Papenfuse, Director, Hall of Records Commission, State of Maryland, Ms. Linda J. Pike, Assistant Editor, The Papers of The Marquis de Lafayette, Olin Library, Cornell University, Mr. Joseph F. Reed, Executive Vice President, Valley Forge Historical Society, Dr. Edward M. Riley, Director of Research, The Colonial Williamsburg Foundation, the late Mary-Carter Roberts, Ms. Eleanor Merryman Roszel, Mr. Joseph Rubinfine, Mr. Michael D. Schaffer, Assistant Editor, The Charles Willson Peale Papers, National Portrait Gallery, Ms. Eleanor Shannahan, National Geographic Society, Mr. Richard K. Showman, The Rhode Island Historical Society, Mrs. Arthur L. Shreve, Jr., Mrs. Dortha H. Skelton, Reference Librarian, The Earl Gregg Swem Library, The College of William and Mary, Mr. Richard Tilghman Smyth, Mrs. Romaine S. Somerville, Director, The Maryland Historical Society, the late Mrs. Arthur N. Starin, Curator, Maryland Room, The Talbot County Free Library, Mr. Robert G. Stewart, Curator, The National Portrait Gallery, Mr. James R. Sullivan, Superintendent, Yorktown National Historic Park, Mr. Benjamin Chew Tilghman, Dr. R. Carmichael Tilghman, Dr. Tench Francis Tilghman, Mr. W. H. DeCourcy Tilghman, Mr. Michael F. Trostel, Restoration Architect, The Orangerie, Mount Clare Mansion, Mr. Ronald von Klaussen, Mr. Frank C. Wachter, Mrs. William D. Waxter, Jr., Dr. Harry E. Whipkey, Director, Bureau of Archives and History, Pennsylvania Historical and Museum Commission, and Mrs. Mary Hill Goldsborough Willson.

In a departure from the widespread but no less genuine thanks expressed to the above, I would like to extend an added measure of gratitude to Dr. Tench Francis Tilghman and Mr.

ACKNOWLEDGMENTS

John Frazer, Jr., great-great-great grandsons of Lieut. Colonel Tench Tilghman, for their reading of and subsequent corrections to portions of the manuscript dealing primarily with Tilghman family matters, and to Dr. R. Carmichael Tilghman, a great-great-great grandnephew of William Carmichael, for the same assistance regarding his ancestor and the latter's importance in the recruitment of Lafayette in the American cause.

Lastly, it has been often said that a medal should be struck to commemorate the encouragement, love, and unrestrained patience demonstrated by the families of those who write books requiring long periods of research, frequent travel, and hours of solitary confinement while transcribing the harvest to readable material. To my wife, Barbara, who has been in the front lines of this engagement for five or more years, goes the first impression.

L. G. SHREVE

Calendar of Events
in the Life of Tench Tilghman

1744 25 December	*Born at Fausley, Talbot County, Maryland.*
1747	Robert Morris arrives in Oxford, Maryland, from his birthplace, Liverpool, England.
1755 17 July	Anna Maria Tilghman, future wife, born at Bay Side, Talbot County, Maryland.
1756 12 August	Brother William born, later to be Chief Justice of Pennsylvania.
1760 11 June	Margaret "Peggy" Shippen, a first cousin, born.
1761	*Graduates from the College and Academy of Philadelphia, now the University of Pennsylvania. Enters business in Philadelphia as a merchant.*
1762	Father, James Tilghman, moves to Philadelphia.
1767 29 January	Father appointed Provincial Councillor of Pennsylvania.
1771	Brother William graduates from the College and Academy of Philadelphia.
18 December	Death of mother, Ann (Francis) Tilghman.
1774 5 September	First Continental Congress convenes in Philadelphia. Matthew Tilghman, uncle, chosen head of Maryland delegation.
26 October	Continental Congress adjourns.
1775 19 April	Battles of Concord and Lexington.
10 May	Second Continental Congress convenes at Philadelphia.

14 June	Congress authorizes a Continental Army.
15 June	George Washington chosen Commander in Chief of the Continental Army.
17 June	Battle of Bunker Hill.
19 July	Congress appoints Commissioners to negotiate treaties with the Indians.
July	Brother Philemon joins the British Navy.
July	*Joins the Pennsylvania "Ladies Light Infantry."*
5 August	*Appointed Secretary to the Indian Commission, German Flats, New York.*
23 August	By proclamation, George III declares the American colonies to be in open rebellion.
5 September	*Returns to New York City on conclusion of service with Indian Commission.*
1776 10 January	Thomas Paine's *Common Sense* published in Philadelphia.
4 July	Signing of the Declaration of Independence.
July	*Joins the Flying Camp; commissioned a captain.*
14 August	Matthew Tilghman elected President of the first Maryland Constitutional Convention.
August	*Joins Washington's official family as aide-de-camp and secretary.*
27 August	Battle of Long Island. Continental Army suffers disastrous defeat.
16 September	Battle of Harlem Heights.
16 November	Battle of Fort Washington. Another disaster— 2,800 men surrendering to the British.
13 December	Major General Charles Lee captured by the British.
26 December	Battle of Trenton—the first significant American victory.
1777 3 January	Battle of Princeton.
6 January	Washington goes into winter quarters at Morristown, N. J.
13 January	Lafayette and deKalb land at Georgetown, S. C.

11 September	Battle of Brandywine. Washington out-maneuvered by General Howe.
4 October	Battle of Germantown. Washington's boldness in defeat surprises tacticians on both sides.
11 October	Beginning of the Conway Cabal.
17 October	Surrender of "Gentleman Johnny" Burgoyne, thus assuring French aid to the American cause.
3 November	General William Alexander, Lord Stirling, informs Washington of the Conway Cabal.
19 December	Washington goes into winter quarters at Valley Forge.
1778 6 February	Franco-American Treaty of Alliance signed in Paris.
18 June	British evacuate Philadelphia.
28 June	Battle of Monmouth. Washington saves the Army from near disaster.
4-12 July	*Testifies at court-martial of General Lee.*
11 December	Washington goes into winter quarters at Middlebrook, N. J.
1779 1 April	*Commissioned by Congress a Lieutenant Colonel in the Continental Army.*
8 April	Margaret "Peggy" Shippen marries General Benedict Arnold.
10 May	Arnold opens treasonable negotiations with British General Sir Henry Clinton in New York.
	Meets Anna Maria Tilghman, his future wife.
23 December	Benedict Arnold's court-martial convenes.
1780 26 January	Arnold found guilty of minor charges of abusing his authority as commander in Philadelphia in 1778-79.
2 May	French expeditionary force of 6,000 sails for America under Count de Rochambeau.
10 July	Arrival of Rochambeau's expeditionary force at Newport, Rhode Island.
3 August	Arnold receives orders from Washington to take command of West Point.

20-24 September *Accompanies Washington to first conference with Rochambeau at Hartford, Connecticut.*

25 September Arnold flees, his treasonable plans having been discovered.

1781 16 February Hamilton's celebrated quarrel with Washington. *Tilghman fails in attempt to bring the two together.*

11 March George Olney writes to Tilghman, relating details of Greene/Biddle/Washington incident.

29 April Admiral de Grasse's victory over British naval forces off Martinique.

18-24 May *Accompanies Washington to Wethersfield, Connecticut, for second conference with Rochambeau.*

10 June "Mad Anthony" Wayne reinforces Lafayette before Richmond. The resulting force of 5,800 includes some of the best troops in the Continental Army.

12 June *Refuses to intercede for his brother William in attempt to secure safe passage to England to study law.*

5 July French army of 4,500 under Rochambeau joins Washington's 6,000 Continentals above New York.

4 August Cornwallis occupies Yorktown and Gloucester Point on the York River, expecting reinforcements from Clinton in New York.

14 August Admiral de Grasse notifies Washington of intended move to the Chesapeake Bay.

19-26 August Washington and Rochambeau head for Virginia.

25 August French Admiral de Barras sails from Newport for the Chesapeake Bay.

2 September De Grasse sends 3,000 French troops under the Marquis de Saint-Simon to join Lafayette near Jamestown.

5 September De Grasse turns back the British fleet under Admiral Graves off Cape Henry in the Battle of the Chesapeake.

8 September *Accompanies Washington as the Commander in Chief makes his first visit to Mount Vernon in six years.*

10 September	De Barras and his French squadron arrive from Rhode Island to join de Grasse in the Chesapeake Bay.
17-18 September	*Accompanies Washington at conference aboard the French flagship* Ville de Paris *at mouth of the York River.*
30 September	Siege of Yorktown begins.
9 October	Bombardment of Yorktown begins.
14 October	Redoubts 9 and 10 outside Yorktown captured by French and American troops—the latter led by Alexander Hamilton.
19 October	Cornwallis surrenders.
20 October	*Leaves Yorktown for Philadelphia with dispatches for the Congress from Washington.*
24 October	*Arrives in Philadelphia with official news of the surrender.*
29 October	*Voted "a horse, properly caparisoned, and an elegant sword, in testimony of the high opinion of his merit and ability" by the Congress of the United States.*
1782 1 April	Washington establishes headquarters at Newburgh, New York.
12 April	Peace talks begin in Paris.
10 June	*Writes to his uncle, Matthew Tilghman, asking for the hand in marriage of his daughter, Anna Maria Tilghman.*
1783 23 March	Death of Charles Carroll, Barrister, married to Anna Maria's sister Margaret.
11 April	Congress proclaims the end of the war.
13 May	Formation of The Society of The Cincinnati.
9 June	*Marries Anna Maria Tilghman, Saint Michaels Parish, Talbot County, Maryland.*
13 June	The Continental Army disbands.
3 September	Treaties of Paris and Versailles signed.
25 November	*Accompanies Washington and Governor Clinton as they re-enter New York, the British having evacuated to Staten Island.*

26 November	Congress convenes at Annapolis, Maryland.
4 December	Washington bids farewell to his officers at Fraunce's Tavern, New York.
23 December	*Resigns his commission, at Washington's side, in Senate Chamber, State Capitol, Annapolis.*
1784 1 January	*Forms Tench Tilghman & Co., Baltimore, mercantile traders, with Robert Morris as his partner.*
	Lafayette visits Tilghman in Baltimore.
24 May	Daughter Anna Margaretta born, later to marry Tench Tilghman, son of Peregrine Tilghman and Deborah (Lloyd) Tilghman, of Hope, Talbot County, Maryland.
1786 18 April	*Dies in Baltimore. Buried in Old Saint Paul's Cemetery.*

POSTHUMOUS EVENTS

11 October	Birth of Elizabeth Tench, his second daughter and only other child, later to marry Colonel Nicholas Goldsborough, of Otwell, Talbot County, Maryland.
1787 15 May	Matthew Tilghman buys Plimhimmon from Thomas Coward. Gives it to his daughter Anna Maria, widow of Tench Tilghman.
1843 13 April	Death of Anna Maria (Tilghman) Tilghman.
1971 30 November	*Remains removed from Old Saint Paul's Cemetery, Baltimore, and reinterred at Oxford, Maryland, next to those of his widow.*

PART ONE

THE EARLY YEARS

1744-1776

CHAPTER 1

A Prelude to Victory

The Battle of Chesapeake Bay was one of the decisive
battles of the world. Before it, the creation of the
United States of America was possible;
after it, it was certain.
—Michael Lewis, *The History of The British Navy*

It is Tuesday, 18 September 1781. Shortly before noon the sloop
Queen Charlotte, a British prize captured by the French and used
as a tender, began navigating her way through the fleet of Francois Joseph Paul de Grasse, Rear Admiral of the French navy,
fresh from a victory over the British under Rear Admiral Thomas, Lord Graves, and that of Louis de Barras and his squadron
from Newport, both now anchored just inside the Virginia
Capes. Heading for the *Ville de Paris*, de Grasse's flagship, the
Queen Charlotte had on board General Washington, four other
generals, and two aides-de-camp, bound for a strategy session
with the French admiral. Entering the Chesapeake nineteen days
earlier de Grasse had brought with him the flower of the French
navy, including the mighty *Ville de Paris*. He had brought with
him also 3,500 French infantry, a contingent disembarked near
Newport News under the command of the Marquis de Saint-
Simon. Low-lying clouds were being driven in a southerly direction by a brisk northeast wind. Overhead, honking audibly, a
flight of Canada geese was winging toward the rice fields and
marshes of North Carolina in an early fall migration.

In keeping with her size and designation the *Ville de Paris* was
anchored on the outer fringe of the flotilla, beyond the *Bourgogne, Diademe,* and *Reflechi,* next to the *Auguste,* flagship of
Commodore Louis Antoine, Comte de Bougainville. Two hun-

dred and ten feet long with a sixty-foot beam, her normal complement was 1,200 sailors and marines. A gift from the people of France to their king, she carried 112 guns on three decks—one more than normally found on ships of the line. Her extraordinary equipment included a printing press. In the engagement with the British under Graves beginning 5 September and ending five days later, she had taken sufficient punishment to fill her sick bay with wounded and to keep the ship's carpenter and his mates busy with repairs to the moment of Washington's visit. On the gun decks the carronades, painted red to lessen the impact of the sight of blood, had been newly scrubbed and the decks sanded and washed down with salt water to remove the last traces of combat. "Her sides, covered with bright varnish, gave to this vessel a most brilliant and imposing appearance."[1] On the spar deck, where Washington and his party would be received, all was shipshape and in order for this first meeting between the French admiral and the commander in chief of the American armies.

Washington and his officers had boarded the *Queen Charlotte* at College Landing on the James River before dawn the day before. With him were the French generals Chastellux, Duportail and Rochambeau, General Henry Knox, his artillerist, and two aides, Jonathan Trumbull, Jr., and Lieut. Colonel Tench Tilghman. Tilghman's presence had its special significance. Long recognized as the steadiest of Washington's aides and the one most trusted by his chief, he was also one of only three of a total of thirty-eight who served on the headquarters staff in the entire course of the war who spoke French—Laurens and Hamilton being the others. Laurens was at headquarters, just back from an arduous voyage to France where he had been sent to plead—successfully, as it turned out—with Louis XVI's ministers for more aid. The impetuous Hamilton, out of favor with Washington since their notorious quarrel of seven months earlier, had joined a New York artillery regiment and was no longer at headquarters. Tilghman, moreover, had been at Washington's side at the Wethersfield conference the preceding May where Washington and Rochambeau had planned the strategy which now held the promise of paying off handsomely.

As the *Queen Charlotte* moved briskly along on a starboard tack she attracted every eye aboard the ships she passed. Conversely, Washington and his party were treated to the imposing sight of thirty-two French ships of the line, row after row of enormous floating gun platforms swinging in the tide, their thick hemp hawsers squeaking monotonously. Passing astern of the *Languedoc* moments before her guns boomed in salute, the *Queen Charlotte* hove to as the American contingent prepared to mount the boarding ladders permanently installed amidships on both sides of the triple-decked *Ville de Paris*. De Grasse, resplendent in his blue and red admiral's uniform, was on deck with his officers to receive them. Diagonally across his breast, topping the elaborate gold lace of his uniform, he wore the flame colored ribbon of the Order of Saint Louis. The story of the greeting between the two commanding officers has become legendary. De Grasse— tall, but not as tall as Washington—is reported to have embraced him with Gallic enthusiasm, kissed him on both cheeks, and exclaimed, *"Mon cher petit General!"* The American officers roared with laughter and the fat Knox dissolved in helpless mirth.

Following this brief greeting de Grasse and his guests retired to his cabin under the quarterdeck, astern, to conduct the business of the conference. In typical fashion Washington had his questions written out in advance. The French admiral's answers were taken down by Trumbull and Tilghman. A copy in French, written by Tilghman, was signed by de Grasse.[2] On the whole Washington got what he wanted, de Grasse agreeing to stay "upon these Coasts" until the end of October. After his victory over the British during the engagement off Cape Henry and the North Carolina coast during the period 5-10 September, de Grasse had informed Washington that he wished to return to West Indian waters no later than 15 October. Washington, ever apprehensive that Cornwallis would somehow escape the trap in which he found himself, had come aboard for the express purpose of persuading de Grasse to stay longer in his blockading position to insure that the *coup de grace* he was planning against Cornwallis would effectively seal his enemy's fate and secure the cause of American independence. Siege work would be new to the Americans; only von Steuben had ever participated in one. To the French it was one of the commonplaces of warfare; Yorktown would be Rochambeau's fifteenth siege.

A formal dinner ended the conference, followed by a tour of the flagship. The muffled sound of bilge pumps plus vapors generated by the burning of a combination of vinegar and turpentine to rid the air of the smell of pitch and wet gunpowder did little to dampen the enthusiasm of the inspecting group. There was general agreement that the *Ville de Paris* was the finest ship afloat. Back on the spar deck de Grasse's captains, summoned for the occasion, were presented to Washington and his party. Antoine Cresp de Saint-Cesaire, captain of the pavillion (meaning that he was the captain of the flagship from which de Grasse directed the operations of the fleet) of Admiral de Grasse came first, followed by Bougainville. Next came the Comte de Barras and then Joseph Desire, Marquis de Messeme, captain of the *Bourgogne*. From the *Protecteur* had come Gabriel-Francois de Mouchet-Battefort, Marquis de Laubespin, and from the *Victoire* Francois Sarret de Grozon and Albert de Saint-Hippolite. From the *Marseillais* came Henri Cesar, Marquis de Castellane-Majastres, a squadron commander. Clement-Joseph de Taffenel, Marquis de la Jonquiere, had brought with him his son Claude, who served with him on the *Reflechi*, to see Washington and his men. The Vicomte de Montemart and Jean-Marie du Bessey, Chevalier de Contenson, both lieutenants, were also present as was the Marquis de Pange who later went ashore to fight at the siege of Yorktown with a French grenadier regiment.[3] Once more cannon boomed in salute as the crews of the fleet manned the yards and tops in honor of Washington, who stood at attention until the *Queen Charlotte* had cleared the inner line of the flotilla.

Near noon on 22 September the General's party, cold and wet, entered College Creek and made its way to Williamsburg. Part of the return voyage was made in the frigate *Andromaque* after *Queen Charlotte* had run aground. The last thirty miles were spent in an open boat, laboriously rowed close to the shore line to escape the full force of an equinoctial gale. Six hours aboard the *Ville de Paris* with de Grasse had taken Washington from the army for four and a half days. There had been little movement on the part of the enemy, but Tilghman noted in his diary[4] that "Part of the advanced Fleet with the French Grenadiers and Chasseurs and American light troops[5] came up to College Creek." The pincers were tightening.

Cut off by land by the forces of the Marquis de Lafayette and by sea by the French fleet, Cornwallis, bottled up in Yorktown, had been looking in vain for relief from General Clinton and

Washington and His Generals at Yorktown. This painting depicts the meeting of the generals of the American and French armies at Yorktown, Virginia, after the siege and surrender of the British forces under General Charles, Lord Cornwallis, 6-9 October 1781. The men are, left to right: Marquis de Lafayette, General Benjamin Lincoln, General George Washington, Comte de Rochambeau, General de Chastellux, and Lieutenant Colonel Tench Tilghman. By Charles Willson Peale. Courtesy: Maryland Historical Society.

Admiral Graves, both in New York. Reduced to extreme measures, he had, at irregular intervals, dispatched at least three six-man crews in open boats—oarlocks greased to deaden any sound—to work their way through the French fleet in the dead of night to make the long voyage up the east coast to New York, rowing all the way except in those rare intervals when a favorable breeze might fill a jerry-rigged sail. He had no liking for his situation and had made it plain to Clinton, his superior, that relief would have to arrive momentarily to avert disaster.

But Clinton, inexplicably, appeared to be in no hurry to send either land or naval aid to his beleaguered subordinate. Finally on 1 September Admiral Graves moved south with nineteen ships of the line, a few frigates and other smaller vessels. Delayed by contrary winds, it was five days before the British sighted Cape Henry at the entrance of the Chesapeake. About eight o'clock in the morning de Grasse was alerted by lookouts that an unidentified fleet was approaching. Expecting de Barras and his squadron from Newport, de Grasse received the news with delight. Later, however, when the size of the fleet became apparent, de Grasse knew it was the British and immediately readied the French for battle. Four of his ships were upriver landing troops under Saint-Simon. He was also handicapped by having almost two thousand men away from the fleet gathering fresh vegetables.

Hampered by unfavorable winds and a high tide, it was almost noon before de Grasse could get his fleet moving out of the bay and nearly four in the afternoon before the battle was joined. Ships on both sides suffered severely. Worst hit of all was the British *Terrible*, of 74 guns. She had been leaking badly for days, and on 11 September Graves ordered her stripped and burned, the only vessel lost in the battle. The British suffered over three hundred casualties as against two hundred for the French. Though indecisive as an action, the encounter resulted in such damage to the British squadron that Graves put back to New York to refit. This was the same as victory for the French, for before another fleet could be sent from New York, Cornwallis's ability to continue the siege had been broken and he surrendered.

This one sea action, fought out of sight of land where the only eyewitnesses were the participants themselves, must rank as one of the most decisive military confrontations in the world's history. So tersely reported and so little noted save in detailed histories, it may have decided the fate of the whole North American continent because it eliminated the possibility of either the reinforcement or evacuation of Cornwallis's troops. Neither de Grasse nor Graves distinguished himself in the battle, which saw the British admiral confusing his captains with faulty signaling, flying flags for both line ahead and attack at the same time. A British victory would have meant the end of Washington's siege of Yorktown, and Sir Henry Clinton, who sailed from New York on 19 October with all his best regiments aboard all his best ships, might indeed have arrived in time. As it was he was too late—by five days. In the eyes of many, Graves, who should have been court-martialed, must forever bear the burden of the loss of the American colonies.

For Tilghman, as with others who had served Washington so faithfully, the momentous events of the war were almost over. Of the band of brothers who served as Washington's "Official Family," as the commander in chief so often and so fondly referred to his aides and others in his headquarters group, only the dashing Henry Laurens was not to survive the war, tragically losing his life in a minor skirmish on the Combahee River in his native South Carolina on 27 August 1782. The long war had begun at Concord Bridge five years and five months earlier. Beginning with the spring campaigns in and around New York in 1776, Tilghman had remained at Washington's side. From Trenton and Princeton, through the uncertainty and doubts of the Conway Cabal, across the Delaware and into the snows of Valley Forge, on to Monmouth and finally into the Southern Campaign; and now the long march was about to end. While two years would elapse following the collapse of British resistance at Yorktown before the Treaty of Paris would formally close the war, the real moment of triumph was close at hand—one which was to prove a fitting climax to Tilghman's dedicated service.

9

CHAPTER 2

The Tilghmans in England and America

I can eat my bread with thankfulness
and take my rest in peace . . .

—Richard Tilghman II, to his
cousin Abraham Tilghman
in England, 2 July 1734

The Tilghmans were an old English family, descendants of one Richard Tilghman who lived about 1450 at Holloway Court,[1] Snodland Parish, in Kent. From this point the Tilghman ancestry may be traced back through successive generations to a certain John Tilghman (Johannes Tylghmann), circa 1225.

By the end of the 12th century hereditary family names had become common in England although by no means universal. Historians generally agree that family names have occupational derivations. Thus a husbandman or "tillman" was one who tilled the soil; in short, a farmer. The motto assigned to the arms of William Tilghman of Holloway Court, as recorded at the College of Heralds in 1468,[2] *Spes Alit Agricolam* or "Hope Sustains the Farmer," gives added credence to this theory.

Changes in the spelling of the name may have been due to personal preference or simply to the inclination of registry clerks and others to spell a name as it sounded. This undoubtedly happened at the time of the second marriage of Oswald Tilghman in London in 1626 when he married Elizabeth Packnam. The record of his first marriage (to Abigail Tayler) gives his name as Tilghman, but his second marriage record lists him as Tilman.[3]

A Partial Tilghman Genealogy

from Dr. Richard Tilghman I to the Children of Lieutenant Colonel Tench Tilghman

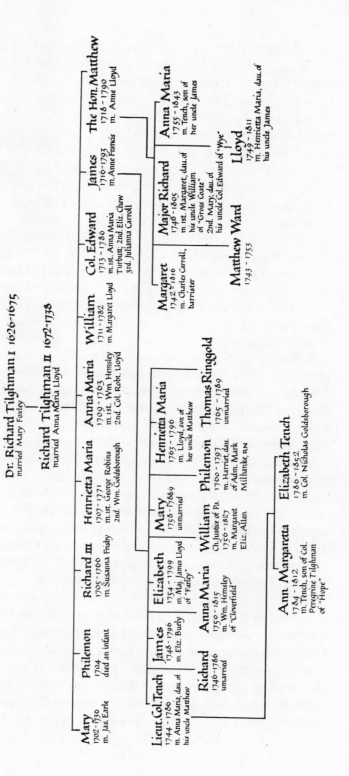

Dr. Richard Tilghman I 1626-1675
married Mary Foxley

Richard Tilghman II 1672-1738
married Anna Maria Lloyd

Mary
1702-1730
m. Jas. Earle

Philemon
1704
died an infant

Richard III
1705-1766
m. Susanna Frisby

Henrietta Maria
1707-1771
m. 1st. George Robins
2nd. Wm. Goldsborough

Anna Maria
1709-1763
m. 1st. Wm. Hemsley
2nd. Col. Robt. Lloyd

William
1711-1782
m. Margaret Lloyd

Col. Edward
1713-1790
m. 1st. Anna Maria
Turbutt; 2nd. Eliz. Chew
3rd. Julianna Carroll

James
1716-1793
m. Anne Francis

The Hon. Matthew
1718-1790
m. Anne Lloyd

Lieut. Col. Tench
1744-1786
m. Anna Maria, dau. of
his uncle Matthew

James
1748-1796
m. Eliz. Buely

Elizabeth
1754-1799
m. Maj. James Lloyd
of "Farley"

Mary
1758-1788
unmarried

William
Ch. Justice of Pa.
1756-1827
m. Margaret
Eliz. Allen

Henrietta Maria
1765-1796
m. Lloyd, son of
her uncle Matthew

Thomas Ringgold
1765-1789
unmarried

Philemon
1760-1797
m. Harriet, dau.
of Adm. Mark
Milbanke, RN

Margaret
1742-1816
m. Charles Carroll,
barrister

Major Richard
1746-1805
m. 1st. Margaret, dau. of
his uncle William
of "Gross Coate"
2nd. Mary, dau. of
his uncle Col. Edward of "Wye"

Anna Maria
1755-1843
m. Tench, son of
her uncle James

Lloyd
1749-1811
m. Henrietta Maria, dau. of
his uncle James

Matthew Ward
1743-1753

Richard
1746-1786
unmarried

Anna Maria
1750-1815
m. Wm. Hemsley
of "Cloverfield"

Ann Margaretta
1784-1812
m. Tench, son of Col.
Peregrine Tilghman
of "Hope"

Elizabeth Tench
1786-1852
m. Col. Nicholas Goldsborough

Oswald Tilghman, six generations removed from William Tilghman, was—according to his father's careful record—born on Sunday, 4 October 1579. He was baptized in All Saints Church, Snodland, on 11 October 1581, his godparents being Thomas Colepeper and Thomas Shakerly, "Gents," and Lydia Whetenhall, his aunt.[4] Married twice, his first wife was Abigail, daughter of the Reverend Francis Tayler, Vicar of Godalming, Surrey, whom he married on 13 January 1611/12, she then being in her twenty-sixth year.[5] By this marriage Oswald Tilghman had four children, only one of whom, Abigail, survived him. His second wife, Elizabeth Packnam, was married to him on 15 November 1626.[6] She and Abigail and a son Richard, born of his second marriage, are named in his will, proved 22 January 1628.

Around 1600 the Tilghmans had moved to London and had become not only a "family of ancient lineage"[7] but also people of substance. Oswald Tilghman was a member of the Grocers Company of London, one of the notable livery companies of that city. Moreover, through his maternal grandfather, Thomas Whetenhall, his ancestry now coursed back through the great families of Berkeley, Neville, Beauchamp (the Earls of Worcester), and Despencer (the Earls of Gloucester) to the Plantagenets and to William The Conqueror.[8] When Doctor Richard Tilghman came to the New World he brought with him a manuscript, still in the possession of a descendant, setting forth his ancestry to the thirteenth century.[9] Whether or not he was aware of his royal descent is a matter of speculation; certainly he left no evidence of it, as this Tilghman manuscript refers only to the Whetenhall marriage, not beyond. It is the very accurate Whetenhall manuscript (Harleian #1548, folio 121) in the collection of the British Museum, that defines the line of descent. Subsequent generations were either not as well informed on family matters as Doctor Tilghman or simply lost sight of them with the passage of time.

In 1649, when Doctor Richard Tilghman was twenty-two, Charles I was executed by the Parliamentarians and Oliver Cromwell became the ruler of a nominal republic during the interregnum. Doctor Tilghman, despite his then position as a chirurgeon (surgeon) in the British Royal Navy, appears to have signed, with other Roundheads, a petition "to have justice done upon Charles I."[10] Small wonder that upon the death of Crom-

well in 1658 and with the end of the protectorate in sight Tilghman decided that it would probably be expedient for him to leave
England and seek a more secure position in America. Moreover,
Doctor Tilghman might also have had aspirations for a life
beyond his reach in England.

In addition there was the close relationship—one which
apparently existed by inclination as well as by blood—between
Doctor Richard and Captain Samuel Tilghman, his first cousin.
Captain Tilghman was in Maryland waters on his trading ship
Golden Fortune as early as 1654[11] and as late as 1663,[12] if not later.
Captain Samuel Tilghman like his cousin was a man of spirit and
contributed in considerable degree to the settlement of early
Maryland. Doubtless he influenced his cousin to migrate to a
region where he found the country attractive and the government satisfactory to men of their outlook. It seems likely that the
two men were close from childhood, for Richard Tilghman was
but an infant at the time of the death of his father Oswald,[13]
whose will makes mention of Oswald's brother Whetenhall, the
father of Samuel, in a way which would seem to indicate that
Whetenhall (who lived to an advanced age) would reciprocate his
brother's generosity. Moreover, Captain Tilghman enjoyed a
favored and influential position with the Calverts, having been
created Admiral of Maryland by Lord Baltimore on 15 July
1658,[14] not only because of his navigational skill but because he
seemed to have been a principal champion of the proprietary. A
certain Vislanda Stone, in a contemporary letter to Lord Baltimore, stated, "Captain Tilghman and his mate Master Cook are
very honest men and do stand up much for your honor."[15]

For the seventeenth century Englishman looking for a place
to build a better life, free from outside influence, that part of
Maryland lying east of Chesapeake Bay was ideal. The region
was—and is—as much water as land, teeming with seafood and
wildfowl. Its soil was fertile, its white oak and pine forests provided excellent building material. And there was no government
to interfere. Compared to England where conditions were so
unstable, Maryland appeared a veritable paradise. Consequently, between 1652 and 1661 there were many who broke old ties
and, looking to new horizons, received grants of land on the
numerous tributaries of the Chesapeake Bay.[16] Calvert usually
granted landed estates on the condition that the grantee trans-

port to the colony twenty persons of British descent in return for 1,000 acres. Manpower was needed for the defense of the colony, and quitrents, annual taxes to be paid by the grantees either in commodities or money, were essential to the proprietor. On the other hand the grantee obtained a handsome start on the road to financial independence and political strength. For those who had enough land it was a good life, as good perhaps as the world had ever seen. It was a free life, too, self-contained and self-sufficient. And the grantees were quick to defend it against encroachments, first from Lord Baltimore's proprietary government, later against restrictions from England.

Being in a favored position to do so, Captain Samuel Tilghman was no doubt able to influence the Calverts in the matter of land grants for himself and his cousin. Whatever the circumstances, on 17 January 1659 both were issued patents in identical terms.[17] Doctor Richard Tilghman was granted Canterbury Manor and Captain Samuel, Tilghman's Fortune. Both grants were for 1,000 acres and both were located on the Tred Avon River, an offshoot of the Choptank River.

Having validated his patent by fulfilling the requirements of Lord Baltimore's terms, Doctor Tilghman embarked on the ship *Elizabeth and Mary* in 1661, bound for Maryland. In addition to his wife, the former Mary Foxley of London, he brought with him his two surviving children and eighteen indentured servants.[18] Whether or not Doctor Tilghman ever settled at Canterbury Manor in Talbot County is a matter of speculation; most historians think he sold the entire tract soon after his arrival in Maryland and that another plantation, The Hermitage, situated on the broad reaches of the Chester River, in Kent County, became the first real home of the American Tilghmans. Captain Samuel Tilghman did not settle on his grant, nor did he fulfill all the requirements to do so, being still engaged in trade—as previously noted—as late as 1663.

Doctor Tilghman prospered in Maryland, primarily as a planter, but at the same time he continued his practice as a physician and surgeon. Since existing roads could only be charitably described as terrible, nearly everyone traveled by boat or barge, and it was in this fashion that Doctor Tilghman visited his patients, resorting to horseback only when required. When trav-

14

eling by water, he is said to have used a small bateau, rigged with a leg o' mutton sail and rowed by slaves in the absence of a breeze.[19]

In the fourteen years between his arrival in the colony and his death in 1675, he sired three more children[20] and added enormously to his land holdings—over eight thousand acres in six more plantations. His initial purchase, made in 1663 from James Coursey, was known as Cedar Branch and consisted of 400 acres. Tilghman built a house, changed the name to The Hermitage and settled down for a life as an important member of the ruling class. His other lands he acquired by additional purchases or by subsequent grants from the proprietor in return for transporting additional indentured servants to the colony.

By 1669 Doctor Tilghman's economic and social position had risen to such a degree that Lord Baltimore appointed him High Sheriff of Talbot County, a post which he held until 11 June 1671.[21] As such he was in charge of levying and collecting quitrents—for the most part paid in tobacco—as set by the Lord Proprietor. That he went at his duties with enthusiasm there can be no doubt, as on 30 March 1671 a petition was presented to the House of Burgesses demanding his impeachment.[22] His accusers charged (1) that he had collected quitrents in excess of the rate and (2) that he had collected medical fees from the sick already paid by the county. Tilghman's defense was that he was in disagreement with the court as to the tax rate necessary to meet the county's requirements and that he had asked some taxpayers voluntarily to accept a higher rate, agreeing to reimburse the difference if the court overruled him. As to his medical fees, it was then the custom for individuals interested in the medical treatment of those for whom they were more or less responsible—such as an indentured servant—to give a physician or surgeon a bond in advance of treatment. After a complete investigation, the House of Burgesses dropped all charges against him on 18 April 1671,[23] finding that those making the charges were also the makers of such bonds and were simply trying to avoid their responsibilities.

At his death on 7 January 1675, Doctor Tilghman's estate included 187,289 pounds of tobacco,[24] no small part of which must have come from medical fees, George Robins having paid him 2,000 pounds of tobacco for board ("dyett") and funeral charges for the deceased Thomas Wilmer, and Colonel Thomas Hynson 4,621 pounds for "care and physick."[25] He was buried at The Hermitage where his gravestone may still be seen.[26]

Doctor Tilghman's only surviving son, most often referred to as Richard Tilghman II, was the principal beneficiary of his estate. Born on 16 February 1672, consistent with his station in life he continued the social and political ascent of the Tilghman family. In 1698, at the age of twenty-six, he was elected to the Maryland Assembly as a representative from Talbot County[27] and in 1711 was appointed to the Lord Proprietor's Council,[28] a post which he held until his death. In 1722 came additional honors when he became Chancellor of the Province and Keeper of the Seal.[29]

Colonel Richard Tilghman, so styled from his rank as head of the militia of Talbot County,[30] was active not only politically but also in support of the Episcopal Church, being a leading member and vestryman of Old Chester Church (St. Paul's Parish). When it became necessary to replace the old church in 1697, he volunteered to advance the funds for the new structure.[31] The vestry later reimbursed him. In 1723 he was named one of the Board of Visitors to establish the first public school in Queen Anne's County, "situated on the south side of the main road that leads from Queenstown to Chester Mills," on land purchased from Tilghman.[32]

At nearby Wye House lived the Lloyds, one of the most influential families in Maryland. On 7 January 1700 Richard Tilghman II married Anna Maria, daughter of Philemon and Henrietta Maria Neale Lloyd,[33] thus joining two of the largest landholding families in the province. Nine children resulted from this marriage, one of whom—James—was to become the father of Lieutenant Colonel Tench Tilghman.

Of the life of Richard Tilghman II much is known from his own hand, from letters preserved in the Tilghman family.[34] (See Appendix I: Tilghman Correspondence.) When Richard Tilghman II died on 23 February 1738 he had disposed of more than 10,000 acres of land to his younger children, leaving substantially more to his eldest son Richard than to the others.[35]

James Tilghman, the fifth of the six sons of Colonel Richard Tilghman II of The Hermitage and Anna Maria Lloyd, his wife, was born on 6 December 1716[36]. On 30 September 1743 he

James Tilghman, father of Tench Tilghman. Portrait by John Hesselius, from a private collection.

married Ann, daughter of Tench Francis, of Fausley,[37] Talbot County, Maryland, and Elizabeth Turbutt, his wife. Upon coming to Maryland, Tench Francis (born in Dublin in 1701) acted as attorney for Lord Baltimore in Kent County.[38]

Tench Francis's father was the Very Reverend John Francis, Dean of Lismore, County Wexford, and his mother the former Ann Tench.[39] Francis had arrived in Maryland as a youth and apparently went first to Kent County. Later he moved to Talbot where from 1726 to 1734 he was Clerk of the Court, a representative in the Lower House in 1734 and Deputy Commissioner in 1736.[40] In 1737 he moved to Philadelphia. He served as Attorney General of Pennsylvania from 1744 to 1752 and Recorder of Philadelphia from 1750 to 1754. As a result of his capabilities as a lawyer, he soon rose to prominence and made many close friends, among them Benjamin Franklin, with whom he joined in the establishment of the College and Academy of Philadelphia.[41] Indeed it is difficult to find a movement of importance during his residence in Philadelphia in which he did not play a significant part. He died in 1758. His son, Tench Francis, Jr., is said to have given five thousand pounds in support of the Revolutionary army.[42]

The marriage of James Tilghman and Ann Francis took place in Christ Church, Philadelphia. Following their marriage the parents of Tench Tilghman came back to Talbot County where James entered the practice of law. They undoubtedly moved into Fausley,[43] vacated by Tench Francis on his departure for Philadelphia, where the future Revolutionary figure was to be born on Christmas Day of the following year. James Tilghman later moved to Chestertown where he was elected to represent Kent County in the Lower House in 1762.[44] During the same year, following in the footsteps of his father-in-law, he too moved to Philadelphia, where he soon became well known. Called "Jemmy" by his friends, he was possessed of a sharp mind and was, to judge from several portraits which have survived him, rather portly in appearance. In common with other provincial gentlemen he was fond of out-of-door sports, particularly shooting,[45] but not to the detriment of intellectual or political pursuits. A close associate of Daniel Dulany, considered by many to have been the foremost lawyer in Maryland if not in all the colonies, James Tilghman became—in the years immediately preceding

Ann Francis Tilghman, mother of Tench Tilghman.
Portrait by Robert Feke, from a private collection.

the Revolution—a leading member of Maryland's luminescent bar. Others in this galaxy included three of Maryland's four signers of the Declaration of Independence, Thomas Stone, William Paca, and Samuel Chase, as well as James Hollyday and Edward Dorsey.[46] Governor Sharpe of Maryland, in a letter dated 8 May 1764,[47] refers to James Tilghman as "lately a Burgess for Talbot County & one of our first Rate lawyers but now settled in Philadelphia." Paca and Hollyday, even as Tilghman, were natives of the Eastern Shore. Governor Sharpe's letter is largely devoted to speculation on the authorship of a controversial pamphlet entitled *Remarks Upon a Messenger Sent by the Upper to the Lower House of Assembly of Maryland,* attributed by many to the joint efforts of James Tilghman and Daniel Dulany.

In 1767 Governor John Penn appointed James Tilghman to the Pennsylvania Proprietary and Governor's Council. Two years later he was asked to succeed William Peters as Secretary of The Land Office.[48] In 1768 he was also selected as one of the commissioners to negotiate with the Indians at Fort Stanwix[49] and in 1774 as one of two to treat with Lord Dunmore, Governor of Virginia, on the Pennsylvania-Virginia boundary dispute.[50] He also became private secretary to Lady Juliana Penn, widow of the late proprietor. At the outbreak of the Revolution Tilghman, like most officeholders of the day, remained faithful in his allegiance to the Crown, conscientiously believing that the maintenance of the royal authority and a continuance of the connection with England were proper. He did, however, believe that Parliament was making a great mistake in not repealing at once those acts which were so irritating to the colonists. Following his condemnation of the Boston Tea Party, his public position became more and more polarized and he soon became known as an outright Tory. The processes which led him to this position were no doubt painful because he was forced to resign his public offices and lose many of his friends.

In 1777 the citizenry of Philadelphia decided to rid the city of Tories[51] and drew up a list of those to be arrested or to seek parole. About thirty persons were affected, including Governor John Penn, Chief Justice Benjamin Chew, James Hamilton, Edward Shippen, Jr., and a Captain Gurney, all crown or proprietary officers. Not surprisingly, James Tilghman's name was also on the list. Nevertheless he appears to have been offended by this action, considering the parole with its many restrictions a reflection on his integrity. Charles Willson Peale, later to become well known as a portrait painter of exceptional ability but then a young military officer on duty in Philadelphia, had been befriended in a financial way by James Tilghman and sought permission to tell him he had to leave.[52] There seems little doubt that the permission granted Mr. Tilghman on 31 August 1777[53] to visit his family in Chestertown, Maryland, was due to Peale's good offices, thereby saving Mr. Tilghman much embarrassment and perhaps physical discomfort. Tilghman had planned to return within a month but the occupation of Philadelphia by the British prevented him from doing so and he remained in Chestertown. On 16 May 1778[54] he was discharged from parole. He spent the rest of his life in Maryland and died there on 24 August 1793.[55] He is buried in the graveyard at Saint Paul's Church in Kent County.

CHAPTER 3

Youth and Early Training

Youth, what man's age is like to be doth show:
We may our ends by our beginnings know
　　　　　　　—Sir John Denham, 1615-1669

Tench Tilghman was that fortunate amalgam of the aristocrat and the man of talent. His life well illustrates the proposition that a person is the reflection of his early years. The recipient of the finest education available in pre-Revolutionary America, Tilghman was culturally inclined, distinguished in appearance, and had a zest and wit about him which made him popular with men and women alike.

Articulate, he not only spoke with charm and grace but also wrote with precision and style—qualities much admired by Washington. His facility with the French language undoubtedly contributed to the high regard in which Lafayette held him, as well as making him doubly useful as an aide-de-camp. Added to these gifts was a capacity for hard work, sound judgment, discretion, and loyalty.

What of Tilghman's appearance and his personal characteristics? Portraits show him through the eyes of the painter—and who knows if the painter's eyes were to be trusted? However, one needs but to examine his uniform to know that he was rather small and slender, about five feet ten in height, and weighed approximately one hundred and fifty pounds.[1] He had a ruddy complexion, gray eyes, and auburn hair tied in a queue.[2] Contemporary accounts indicate that he was lithe and graceful. He had about him a low-keyed, even unconscious attitude of authority and competence. "His modesty gave to his bearing the reserve

of hauteur, and though repelling familiarity, he was never wanting in courtesy, while to his friends his manners were most
cordial."[3] His correspondence attests to his charm and wit, and
his gentleness flattered and persuaded. While his looks and ac-
tions belied the quality, Tilghman could be as tough as a keg of
nails. Time after time his physical courage withstood the acid test
of gunfire and cannonading. An excellent horseman, he rode a
black horse which made him a well known and conspicuous
figure on the battlefield.[4]

How did he become the man so respected by his contemporaries? What were the forces which molded his character? It will
be my aim in this and the following chapter to attempt to provide
answers to these questions. A close look will be made at the social
and economic conditions in colonial Maryland at the time of his
birth and early years, at the position of his parents and other
members of his by then influential family, and finally at the
education which he enjoyed, especially in the center of colonial
culture at that time—Philadelphia.

Tench, the eldest child of James and Ann (Francis) Tilghman, was born on Christmas Day, 1774,[5] at Fausley, on Fausley
Creek—now known as Glebe Creek—a branch of the Miles River, in Talbot County, Maryland, about two miles from the town
of Easton, then known as Talbot Court House. In 1752 a reform
of the calendar pushed all dates ahead eleven days. For example,
an occurrence on May 20th, 1740 was reckoned, subsequent to
the calendar reform, to have taken place on May 9th. It is unlikely, however, that Tench Tilghman ever changed the anniversary of his birthday, since the ceremonial date for the celebration
on Christmas remained unchanged. (Washington, clinging to
the old calendar, always claimed February 11 as his birthday.[6])
One of a family of twelve children, of whom six were brothers, he
was christened "Tench" in honor of his maternal grandfather,
thus becoming the first in a long line of Tench Tilghmans, a line
which has persisted to the present day.

All six of the Tilghman brothers became notable citizens;
some markedly so. Richard, younger by two years than Tench,
was born on 17 December 1746.[7] As a young man he was sent to
England where he entered Eton College on 10 July 1762. However, he soon returned home to study law under Daniel Dulany
in Philadelphia. His loyalist sentiments, which matched those of

his father and his brother William, may have been in part derived from this association. In June 1776, in company with Robert Eden, Maryland's last Provincial Governor, he was permitted to depart once again for England on the British sloop of war *Fowey*.[8] Through the influence of his relative Sir Philip Francis, the putative author of the *Letters of Junius*, Richard received an appointment to the civil service of the East India Company in Bengal, India; in fact Warren Hastings recommended him for the post of Attorney-General of India[9] but he died at sea on his way to India before he could assume either post.

The third brother, James Tilghman, was born on 2 January 1748.[10] He became a lawyer and settled in Maryland. Subsequent to 1790,when Maryland reformed its judiciary system, he became an associate justice of the Talbot County Court. He died 24 November 1796.

William, the fourth brother, achieved great prominence. He was born on 12 August 1756[11] and in common with his older brother Tench attended the College and Academy of Philadelphia, in the class of 1772.[12] However, when his father left Philadelphia, William withdrew from college and accompanied him to Chestertown where he completed his law studies under his father's instructions.[13] In 1783 he was admitted to the Maryland bar and in 1788-90 served in the legislature from Kent.[14] In 1791 he was chosen a State Senator for the Eastern Shore but resigned in 1793 to return to Philadelphia to practice law. In 1801 President John Adams appointed him Chief Justice of the United States Circuit Court.[15] In 1805 he became Presiding Judge of the Court of Common Pleas for the First District of Pennsylvania.[16] In 1806 Thomas McKean, as Governor of Pennsylvania, appointed William Tilghman Chief Justice of the Supreme Court of Pennsylvania, a post which he retained until a few months before his death in 1827.[17] In 1807 the University of Pennsylvania conferred the degree of Doctor of Laws upon him, and he also received a similar degree from Harvard in 1814.[18] From 1824 to his death he served as President of the American Philosophical Society.[19]

The fifth brother, Philemon, was born 29 November 1760.[20] Like his father, he remained a Loyalist and at fifteen ran away and joined the British Navy in which he was later commissioned. He married Harriet,[21] daughter of Admiral Mark Milbanke,

Royal Navy. After the war he came back to Maryland and joined his father at Chestertown. At his father's death in 1793 he moved to his farm in Queen Anne's County called Golden Square where he died in 1797. His wife and several children moved to England.

Thomas Ringgold Tilghman, the youngest brother, became a merchant but dying young attained no great prominence. He was born on 17 August 1765[22] and lived only twenty-four years. He went into business first in Alexandria, Virginia, but shortly moved to Baltimore where he assumed charge of the affairs of Tench Tilghman and Company after the death of his oldest brother and until his own on 29 December 1789.[23]

Of Tench's early education little is known. In his childhood Easton and Oxford on the Eastern Shore were little more than hamlets surrounded, if not by water, by forests and thousands of acres of cropland cultivated by an ever increasing number of slaves. Plantation life was all-pervasive and tobacco was king. Since tobacco served as money it became almost the sole crop except for corn and other foods. Plantations lined the banks of every major river and most of the creeks. In such a setting elementary education left much to be desired. In many cases wealthy planters kept a plantation school for their own and neighboring children[24] and employed tutors who were often educated Englishmen in distressed circumstances glad to come to the colonies as indentured servants in search of a new life. Such a system was considered the best means of preparing children for more advanced studies. The curriculum would begin with a simple illustrated hornbook, setting forth the letters of the alphabet, progressing to William Lily's *Short Introduction to Grammar*, a standard primer in use for at least a hundred years. Then came such basic texts as *Aesop's Fables*, followed by more difficult assignments from the Old and New Testaments. Simple arithmetic, Latin prose and verse, and, for young men, the practical lore of plantation husbandry that one day would be their chief concern. After a sound grounding in arithmetic, the lad who would have to keep records and write letters in longhand would progress to roots, algebra and trigonometry, surveying, and Italian bookkeeping. With the completion of such a course he would then be ready to take his place behind the desk of a countinghouse or enter college or read law. It is likely that young Tench attended a plantation school. He later received instruction from the Reverend John Gordon, rector of Saint Michaels Parish, "a gentleman of attainments."[25]

In the plantation society in which the young Tench received his elementary education, aristocracy was a strong and positive force. In Maryland, and to a lesser degree in Pennsylvania, where differences in wealth and social position were apparent on every hand, the inequality of man was an accepted fact. Only to the upper segment of society was the term "gentry" applied, and only the individual men who comprised it were spoken of as "gentlemen." Readily recognizable by his name, his manners, his speech and by the clothes he wore, an eighteenth-century Maryland gentleman could hold his own not only in the sophisticated society of Annapolis but in Williamsburg, Philadelphia, or London as well.

Political patterns, too, were being formulated. Long before the Revolution an affinity had been established for government by the rich, the wellborn, and the able, and planters and lawyers dominated the political scene. The House of Delegates was a remarkably unchanging body and in election after election the same delegates, or members of the same family, were regularly returned to Annapolis. From Talbot and Queen Anne's counties members of the Tilghman, Lloyd, Chamberlaine, and Goldsborough families, all holders of large properties, became "the self-conscious and unquestioned leaders of every phase of the growing life of the province, so their principal forum, a duly elected assembly, achieved a corresponding vitality. Political energy, drawn from such roots, would not fail to challenge whatever opposed the theory and practise of self-government."[26]

Since its early pioneer days the pattern of social dynamics in Maryland had progressed significantly, especially between 1740 and the outbreak of the Revolution, aptly called the Golden Age. The blood sports of England, fox hunting and cock fighting, were directly imported as was horse racing. The Church of England made the transatlantic crossing without change in litany or doctrine. While forms of transportation were still crude, for at least half the year the water crossing between Talbot County and the provincial capital of Annapolis could be a pleasant one, and planters from the flatlands of the Eastern Shore entered into the town's growing cultural and social life with unbridled enthusiasm. The Tilghmans were often in Annapolis as the requirements of James Tilghman's law practice or his duties as a delegate from Kent made him a frequent visitor. Young Tench, as his eldest child, must have known the town well. Like Williamsburg in Virginia, Annapolis was Maryland's epicenter. Established fortunes were growing larger and new ones made, and warm hospitality was the order of the day. The streets of Annapolis radiated from two circles, Church and State, and on the river side of handsome residences along Duke of Gloucester Street terraced grounds and gardens ran to the water's edge. Everybody dressed for dinner and slaves in livery drove light carriages, a rare indulgence in consideration of the crudity of most streets and roads. Visitors from the Eastern Shore sometimes stayed all winter. Artisans had their places of business in modest structures along Cornhill Street, leading to State Circle, but the style and substance of the little Georgian town stemmed from the imposing residences of the Carrolls, Taskers, Dulanys, Lloyds, Chases, Harwoods, and Stewarts on the broader streets. All manufactured goods, even boots and shoes, were imported, and factors, who for the most part represented the great English mercantile firms, were kept busy with purchases to meet the growing demands of a vibrant New World society.

There had been a somewhat irregular mail service between Annapolis and Philadelphia since 1695, but in 1710 the newly formed postal office set up by the British government offered regular weekly service at nine pence per letter,[27] a step that did much to increase communication throughout the provinces of Maryland and Pennsylvania. A single letter could be sent to London for a shilling, or for one weighing an ounce, four shillings. *The Maryland Gazette*, published in Annapolis from 1727 to 1735, disappeared from view temporarily but was resurrected in 1745 to increase the little capital's reputation as a glittering social center and to spread news and advertisements of all sorts.[28]

William Eddis, whose *Letters from America* were published in London in 1792, was surprised to find the pronunciation of Marylanders accurate and elegant and was equally surprised at the quality of horses run at Annapolis in four days of racing staged by the Jockey Club for purses of fifty or one hundred guineas, noting that few meetings in England were better attended or where finer bloodstock could be found.[29] When the courts or the Assembly were in session prominent people gathered from the farthest corners of the province, packing Reynold's, The Ship, and other well-known taverns, or dancing the night away at balls and assemblies. *The Gazette* for 2 July 1752 announced that a series of eight plays, including *Richard III, The Beggar's Opera, Cato* and *George Barnwell* would be performed for the enjoyment and edification of all.[30]

Nevertheless, Maryland was not England and Annapolis was not London. A Tilghman or a Lloyd might wear English clothes, read English books, order Madeira by the pipe, and maintain ties of friendship and blood with the mother country, but the culture of eastern Maryland was based upon the plantation system, attaining its individuality from the relative isolation of plantation life, attention to the raising and marketing of tobacco, and to the ownership of slaves. As a culture it remained fundamentally American, molding attitudes and a collective state of mind which was to find nourishment and strength in the doctrine of Thomas Paine in his *Common Sense*, a pamphlet appearing in the early days of 1776 with widespread and far-reaching impact.

In this milieu Tench Tilghman spent his first fourteen years, until 1758 when his grandfather Tench Francis brought him to Philadelphia to further his education at the College and Academy of Philadelphia. By 1754 the fledgling college, later to become the University of Pennsylvania, had attracted at least one hundred students from Maryland. Faced with the prospect of sending their sons south to the College of William and Mary, to a northern institution, or across the seas to Oxford or Cambridge, Marylanders by the dozen had responded to advertisements in the *Maryland Gazette*,[31] pointing out the advantages the College and Academy of Philadelphia offered. In consideration of already existing family ties in Philadelphia, the decision by James Tilghman to acquiesce in a generous father-in-law's offer to sponsor his grandson's higher education is readily understandable.

CHAPTER 4

The Education of a Revolutionary

> Our Academy flourishes beyond expectation.
> We now have about one hundred scholars,
> and the number is increasing daily . . .
> —Benjamin Franklin to Jared Eliot,
> 12 September 1751

Philadelphia, built in a period when the restoration of London was captivating the imagination of all England after the devastating fire of 1666, was regarded as the first renaissance city in America. Invariably, visitors to the town rising between the Delaware and Schuylkill rivers compared it to London. When William Penn founded Pennsylvania, he arranged it to suit himself, giving instructions that all highways should be built in a straight line from point to point; accordingly, Philadelphia streets were laid out in a checkerboard plan, all at right angles to each other. The houses were well built of brick, and many were surrounded by gardens. There were sidewalks, street lamps, and numerous planted trees, as Penn wished to have "a green country town,"[1] like those with which he was familiar in England. High (now Market) Street became a thoroughfare of fashionable residences.

In the early 1700s the Quakers held a firm rein on social affairs, but by midcentury a more liberal life style began to appear. Benjamin Franklin, the founder of the College and Academy of Philadelphia, set the pace in providing additional cultural facilities with his Library Company of Philadelphia. Literature, music, art, medicine, and science were all cultivated avidly; Philadelphia became, in the last quarter of the eighteenth century, the chief center of colonial culture. Nowhere was this more apparent than in architecture, as indicated in the rise of the style known as Philadelphia Georgian, featuring Palladian windows, ornate dormers, the Doric entrance door, and flattened arches.[2] In every respect the city was becoming more and more cosmopolitan. In 1749 the Philadelphia Assembly was formed, adding a sophisticated note to the city's social life.[3] In the beginning the dances were simple affairs, starting at six and ending at midnight, and many members of Quaker families joined.

Moreover, many of the great families in Maryland were being drawn to Philadelphia for cultural and social leadership. Subtle changes were taking place in the lowland counties on the Eastern Shore of Maryland, a region which had reached the height of its early prosperity in the two decades just prior to 1750. The area was experiencing a change if not a gradual decline. The principal crop was no longer tobacco but grain for which a voracious market existed in Pennsylvania. Much magnificence and plantation wealth remained in Maryland, but the glittering society of Philadelphia where money and position were spawning had immense attraction.[4]

Less exuberant than Virginia and considerably more informal than New England, life in Philadelphia was full of enjoyment and substantial comfort. Fashionable clothes were much in vogue, and nowhere in America was the love of color more apparent. Even the Quakers were yielding to such impulses, carrying gold headed canes and wearing silver buttons on otherwise drab coats and handsome buckles on their shoes. Food and feasting reached manic proportions, undoubtedly because gourmandizing to the point of gluttony was one way in which the Quakers could enjoy themselves without breaching the simplicity of their religious practices. As an adjunct, the era saw the rise of dozens of social clubs devoted to the pleasures of the board, including the "Schuylkill Fishing Company of The State In Schuylkill," founded in 1732, where the "Fish House Punch" became legendary.

Midcentury also saw the birth of the fire companies to protect the city against a disaster such as had struck London. The "Hand-in-Hand" was founded in 1742, the "Brittania" about 1750 and the "Hibernia" in 1752, with an aggregate membership of 225, employing eight engines, 1,055 buckets and 36 ladders.[5] Membership in these companies was composed largely of the most prominent citizens, lawyers, merchants, physicians, and the clergy: in the "Hand-in-Hand" were four signers of the Declaration of Independence—George Clymer, Francis Hopkinson, Benjamin Rush, and James Wilson—as well as Chief Justice William Tilghman, Bishop William White, Provost William Smith of the University of Pennsylvania, Chief Justice Edward Shippen, Governor Thomas Mifflin, Benjamin Chew, Sr., Attorney General of the Commonwealth, Thomas Willing, Colonel Lambert Cadwalader, James Biddle, John Swift, and Tench Coxe.

Adding to Philadelphia's lustre as the colonies' leading cultural center was the American Philosophical Society, founded in 1744. A number of distinguished physicians were members, and the proceedings were to an appreciable extent devoted to medical discoveries. John Morgan, a front runner in medical education, was a member as were Benjamin Rush, William Shippen, and Thomas Bond. Among the Philadelphia scientists who were later to become famous were the ornithologists John J. Audubon and Alexander Wilson and the botanist John Bartram.[6] Later the fox hunters established a beachhead in New Jersey, just across the Delaware River from Philadelphia, with the formation in 1766 of the Gloucester Fox Hunting Club, carrying on in the best tradition of Charles Brooke, of Patuxent, Maryland, who had brought the first foxhounds into America nearly a hundred years earlier. Tench Tilghman, an accomplished horseman, was a subscriber right after his graduation from college, as were his uncles Turbutt Francis and Tench Francis, Jr.[7]

This, then, was the Philadelphia which Tench Tilghman discovered when he arrived to further his education in 1758. Although he was taking temporary leave of his parents (James Tilghman and Ann Francis Tilghman did not move to Philadelphia until four years later), Tench's family connections, through his maternal grandparents, the Tench Francises, and through his aunts and uncles by both blood and marriage, were sufficient to catapult the young student—in whatever time he might be allowed away from the spartan life of "the College, Academy and Charitable School of Philadelphia in the Province of Pennsylvania," to give the college its full incorporated name—into the uppermost ranks of Philadelphians. His mother had been one of nine children, eight of whom married, producing an aggregate of forty-nine children among them, thus supplying Tench with forty-eight first cousins on the Francis side alone. Through these various marriages he became related to the Willings, the Coxes, the Lawrences, the Shippens, the Mifflins, the Burds, the Allens, and the Chews. Tench Coxe, later a prominent Philadelphia merchant and banker, was one of his first cousins as was Margaret ("Peggy") Shippen, later to become the second wife of General Benedict Arnold. Moreover, the Robert Morrises, the Bordleys, Cadwaladers, and Dickinsons, Marylanders all and family friends as well, had settled in Philadelphia.

Tench Francis, who had been one of the most active and useful of the group of founders of the College and Academy, died on 16 August 1758. Even in an age when young men matured fast and were expected to assume measurable responsibilities when scarcely out of their teens, the death of his grandfather must have been a serious blow to young Tench Tilghman. Nevertheless his loss seems to have been quickly ameliorated by the abundance of other family relationships which gave substance to his life in his new surroundings. As shown in his earliest known letters, Tench was gregarious and funloving, fond of family and friends. No young man away from home for the first time could possibly want a more compatible atmosphere in which to advance his career.

The original building of Franklin's fledgling college Tench Tilghman was to attend stood at Fourth and Arch streets. That it was a wholehearted enterprise of Benjamin Franklin is indicated in a letter Franklin wrote to Jared Eliot, 13 February 1750-51. "It will be agreeable to you to hear that our subscription goes on with great success,"

> and we suppose will exceed five thousand pounds of our currency. We have bought for the Academy the house that was built for itinerant preaching, which stands on a large lot of ground capable of receiving more buildings to lodge the scholars, if it should come to be a regular college. The house is one hundred feet long and seventy wide, built of brick, very strong, and sufficiently high for three lofty stories. I suppose the building did not cost less than two thousand pounds; but we bought it for seven hundred seventy-five pounds, eighteen shillings, eleven pence and three farthings; though it will cost us three and perhaps four hundred more to make the partitions and floors, and fit up the rooms.[8]

Miss Margaret Shippen
daughter of Chief Justice Shippen

Margaret "Peggy" Shippen, later the wife of Benedict Arnold and
Tench Tilghman's first cousin. Pencil drawing by Major John André.
Courtesy: Yale University Art Gallery.

Tuition was set at five pounds four shillings per year. On the 12th of the following September Franklin wrote again to Eliot:

> Our Academy flourishes beyond expectation. We have now about one hundred scholars, and the number is daily increasing . . . We have excellent masters at present; and as we give pretty good salaries, I hope we will always be able to procure such.

In May 1755 the trustees were granted a new charter enabling them to establish a college with the authority to award degrees, the new incorporated name being that given above.[9]

By the fall of 1758, when Tench Tilghman matriculated under the sponsorship of his grandfather Tench Francis, a trustee at the time of his death in August of that year, Franklin's hope had been more than adequately fulfilled. Not only had the Old Building, as it was to become known, been renovated to meet the needs of the students, but a faculty assembled which by its excellence was to leave its mark upon those early graduates who studied under the individuals comprising it. The Rector was the Reverend Francis Alison and the Provost another Presbyterian clergyman, the Reverend William Smith, whose well-recognized contributions during his thirty-six years at the institution did much to pave the way for its transition into the University of Pennsylvania in 1780. Theophilius Grew, Professor of Mathematics during Tench's first year, died at the end of that year. His place was taken by Thomas Pratt. Dr. Alison taught Greek and Latin as well as Higher Classics and Metaphysics. Ebenezer Kinnersley taught Oratory and English Literature, William Creamer, French and German, and the Provost himself, Ethics. James Beveridge also taught Greek and Latin and the Reverend John Ewing, Ethics and Natural Philosophy. The Reverend Jacob Duché, a Church of England clergyman and eloquent preacher, doubled as a Professor of Oratory and Assistant Minister at Christ Church.

In keeping with the wishes of the trustees, and as might be expected from two such strong-minded men as Alison and Smith, study of the classics and religious education lay at the core of the curriculum. However, studies not so normally offered in other colleges of the day were available. This was particularly true of French which Tilghman must have studied assiduously

Tench Francis, Tench Tilghman's grandfather. Portrait by Robert Feke. Courtesy: Metropolitan Museum of Art.

because he became very proficient in its use. Students were encouraged, in "private hours," to read the *Spectator* and the *Rambler* for "the improvement of Style and Knowledge of Life," as well as Locke's *Essay Concerning Human Understanding*, Hutcheson's essays, and Varenius's *Geography*. The first year curriculum was devoted mostly to Latin and English exercises and reading from the classics, with the added specification that "Thro' all the years the French Language may be studied at Leisure Hours."[10] Second year students began studying moral and natural philosophy with such leisuretime reading prescribed as Dryden's *Essay of Dramatic Poesy*, Helsham's Lectures, and Newton's *Principia*. During the third and last year of the course, history, ethics, astronomy, and mathematics were studied, with supplementary readings from Fortescue on Laws, Pope's *Iliad* and *Odyssey*, Locke on Government, and Hooker's *Of the Laws of Ecclesiastical Polity*. A significant footnote to the third year curriculum made it known that "the HOLY BIBLE [is] to be read daily from the Beginning and now to supply the Deficiencies of the Whole."[11] Having warned parents that some students would require four or five years to complete the course, the trustees were of the stated opinion that graduates left the college with an education unsurpassed in any other institution of higher learning in North America.

In May of 1761 Tilghman graduated from the College and Academy of Philadelphia in an all-day commencement, attended in a body by the clergymen of the Episcopal Church, then in convention assembled in Philadelphia.[12] Graduating with him were his classmates William Fleming, Marcus Grimes, James Hooper, John Huston, William Kinnersley, the son of the Reverend Ebenezer Kinnersley, a distinguished early professor at the College, Matthew McHenry, Abraham Ogden, later a U. S. Commissioner to the Iroquois Nation and a founder of Ogdensburg, New York, Richard Peters, the nephew of Dr. Richard Peters, President of the Board of Trustees and one of the first, in later years, to mistrust Benedict Arnold,[13] Joseph Shippen, a first cousin of Margaret (Peggy) Shippen, Benedict Arnold's second wife, Henry Waddell, Alexander Wilcocks, who would later marry Mary, daughter of Benjamin Chew, Chief Justice of Pennsylvania, and thus become related by marriage to Tench and Mrs. Tilghman, and Jasper Yates, afterwards a Justice of the

Supreme Court of Pennsylvania. In 1767 Yates married Sarah Burd, a niece of Edward Shippen, whose wife Margaret was Tench Tilghman's aunt. Mrs. Yates's brother Edward Burd married his first cousin, Elizabeth Shippen, who was also Tench's first cousin. In this class of thirteen Tilghman was—to say the least—among his own kind.

A number of other individuals who were to achieve prominence in later life were members of classes two years ahead and two years behind Tench's—a group encompassing all students who attended the College while he was there, and a group small enough for all its members to have known each other well. Included were the Allen brothers, Andrew and James, sons of still another Chief Justice of Pennsylvania's Supreme Court, William Allen, both of whom married first cousins of Tilghman's, the former marrying Sarah Coxe, known as "the beautiful Sally Coxe," and the latter Elizabeth Lawrence. In May 1774 Andrew Allen accompanied Tench's father James when sent to Virginia by the Pennsylvania Provincial Council to induce Lord Dunmore, the Governor of Virginia, to unite in a petition to the King to settle the dispute over a shared boundary. As her second husband Mrs. James Allen married, in June of 1791, the Honorable John Laurance (no relation) of New York who had served as Judge Advocate at the trial of Major André[14] and was thus a wartime colleague of Tilghman's. William Paca, a signer from Maryland of the Declaration of Independence graduated at the end of Tilghman's first year of attendance, as did Philemon Dickinson, a fellow Talbot Countian, later to serve as a Major General in comand of New Jersey troops at the Battle of Monmouth and still later as a United States senator from New Jersey. The brothers Cadwalader, John and Lambert, sons of Dr. Thomas Cadwalader, a Trustee of the College, were nongraduating members of the Class of 1760. John Cadwalader served with both Pennsylvania and Maryland troops throughout the Revolution, twice declining a commission as a Brigadier-General in the Continental Army. An earnest supporter of Washington, he severely wounded General Conway, the leader of the cabal against Washington, in a duel fought on 4 July 1778 on which occasion Philemon Dickinson served as his second. Lambert Cadwalader served with equal distinction in the Revolution as a Colonel of the 4th Pennsylvania Continental Line. William Grayson, a rare Virginian in attendance at the College, was another nongraduate in the Class of 1760. During the Revolution he served as an aide-de-camp[15] to General Washington and was thus in close contact with Tilghman. Thomas Mifflin was there, the Quartermaster General of the Continental Army, later to be the President of the Continental Congress when Washington and Tilghman resigned their commissions at Annapolis in 1783. Another Eastern Shoreman in attendance was William Hindman, a nongraduate in Tilghman's own Class of 1761. He became the Secretary of the Talbot County "Committee of Observation" in 1775, a member of the Continental Congress from 1784 to 1788, and entered the United States Senate in 1800.[16] North Carolina was represented by Whitmel Hill, whose achievements were extensive. He served in the Continental Congress from 1778 to 1781.

The friendships and loyalties developed during these formative years were to serve Tilghman well for the rest of his life. Moreover, with such a significant number of early graduates of the College and Academy of Philadelphia espousing the cause of freedom when it came, it is not difficult to assess the impact of Tilghman's student years on his maturing political philosophy. There can be no doubt that the classical curriculum of this college brought out the best powers of mind and character—turning out as it did well-rounded men of strong intellect and political acumen.

Midway through Tilghman's college career, on 25 October 1760, George III ascended the throne of England and two years and four months later the Treaty of Paris put an end to the Seven Years War. Having struggled against the French for generations, the colonies had learned to cooperate against a common enemy, and many now thought of themselves as Americans as well as Pennsylvanians, New Yorkers, or Marylanders. When the French were finally ejected from the North American continent in 1763, the absence of a foreign threat and the subsequent lessening of the need for the protection of British arms reinforced that feeling. During the next decade when the Crown attempted to impose new means of taxation upon the colonies to help pay the home government's staggering debts, His Majesty's ministers managed to alienate the Americans to the point of rebellion—a rebellion which most certainly would have failed without massive help from a powerful ally. Thus the American Revolution could not have begun had the French not been driven from North America, and it would not have succeeded had the French not become the allies of the patriots.

In 1758 the British built Fort Stanwix where Rome, New York, now stands. Situated at the head of navigation of the Mohawk River, at the portage between that river and Wood Creek, it was intended as a strategic outpost in the struggle against the French and Indians. Subsequent to the signing of the Treaty of Paris the British, by act of Parliament, issued the Proclamation of 1763, establishing a line along the watershed of the Alleghenies as the temporary western limit of British settlement. Vigorously opposed in the colonies, it was intended to reduce Indian unrest stemming from colonial land frauds and westward expansion in territories recently won from France. Settlers beyond the "Treaty Line" were ordered out, and specific details were included to prohibit all future land acquisitions which could in any way be considered illegal or unethical. Other factors contributing to colonial opposition were that the act effectively restricted manufacturing, thus strengthening dependence on Britain, while at the same time confining the colonists to the eastern seaboard and denying escape over the mountains to debtors to British and American creditors.

In response to intense pressures—political as well as geographical—a relocation of the Treaty Line of 1763 was agreed to by the Iroquois Confederacy and the British government in 1768 in the Treaty of Fort Stanwix. In return for elaborate gifts, twenty boatloads full,[17] the Indians gave up claims lying west of the "Old Treaty Line" thus opening up vast tracts along the frontiers of New York, Pennsylvania, and Virginia for settlement. First called for July of that year, a resulting parley had to be postponed until September when distinguished colonials began assembling for the meeting. Governors William Franklin of New Jersey and John Penn of Pennsylvania had begun their journey up the Mohawk to Fort Stanwix, the latter accompanied by James Tilghman, who had been named to Pennsylvania's Provincial Council the year before, his brother-in-law, Colonel Turbutt Francis, and William Allen, Chief Justice of Pennsylvania's Supreme Court. As usual, the tribes were slow to assemble; Governor Penn and Chief Justice Allen left for Philadelphia on 15 October, before the official proceedings began.[18]

This journey by his father through the relative wilds of upper New York is significant in one aspect because it gives us a revealing and intimate glimpse of an emerging Tench Tilghman, then twenty-four years old, through a series of three letters he wrote to his father. Written from Philadelphia in September and October of 1768, they are the earliest of Tench's letters unearthed by the author in the course of his research. (See Appendix I.) Chatty and full of family news, two of these letters also mention horse racing, an indication of the importance the sport had assumed in Pennsylvania. More importantly, they reveal an acute awareness of the political climate of the day, and an understanding of political developments which might have run counter to family interests.

A little over three months after James Tilghman's expedition, Thomas Penn wrote from London[19] to Sir William Johnson, Indian Commissioner for the Crown, to thank him for

> having brought the Treaty with the Indians for a general boundry to a conclusion, and I have also received a more particular account of what relates to Pensilvania [sic], from Mr. Tilghman, who informs me how greatly my Family are obliged to you . . .

Having negotiated numerous land deals for the Penns, James Tilghman's contributions to the Treaty of Fort Stanwix must be considered as important, and certainly not open to the same degree of question as those of Sir William's, since the latter appeared not to have been able to separate his own interests from those of the Indians. Seven years later, in the late afternoon of empire, Tench himself became a central figure in further negotiations with the Iroquois Confederacy—negotiations undertaken by forward-looking colonists in the face of the gathering storm.

CHAPTER 5

The Mohawk Spawns Another Treaty

We think It Time For a Little Drink . . .
—Kanaghquaesa, an Oneida Sachem

We Now Form a Very Agreeable Society . . .
—Tench Tilghman's Journal,
25 August 1775

The uncertain era immediately preceding the Revolution saw not only the beginning of Tench Tilghman's business career but a decade of promising growth for the Francis-Tilghman Company, a mercantile enterprise Tilghman had formed with his uncle, Tench Francis, Jr., after graduation from college. Perhaps even before graduation, Tilghman had decided to become a merchant. His choice of a career was undoubtedly influenced by his observation of the success attained by another uncle, Philip Francis, in that field. The business connection between Tench Francis, Jr. and Tench Tilghman probably took place before 25 October 1765, since both signed the Non-Importation Resolutions of that date and continued thereafter to comply with all requests made of merchants, including a refusal to import any goods from England or Ireland. Other signers were Tench's father James, his uncle John Relfe, his cousins Andrew and John Allen, and Robert Morris. In light of his later position as a Loyalist, James Tilghman must have signed as a gesture of protest, intended to influence Crown authorities to repeal the Stamp Act.

Although subject to the interruptions and difficulties brought about by events leading up to the Revolution, the firm did prosper even though forced to dissolve in 1775. In a letter written years later Tilghman stated that it had enabled him to accumulate a modest competency. The business, like so many other mercantile ventures conducted with aggression and sound judgment, foundered on the rocks of the political storm of the Revolution—and for no other reason. In that trying period the manner in which Tilghman reacted was an early indication of his character. He had contempt for those who took advantage of public disturbances and the suspension of law for their own gain. In the letter written 10 June 1782 to Matthew Tilghman, by then his prospective father-in-law, with the principal intent of informing him of his engagement to the latter's daughter, Anna Maria, he discusses the closing of the firm and the fulfillment of his obligations as follows:

> I Made as hasty a close as I possibly could, of my commercial affairs, making it a point to collect and deposit in safe hands as much as would, whenever times and circumstances would permit, enable me to discharge my European debts which were indeed all I had, except about £——— put into my hands by Mr. R Senr in trust for my youngest Brother; but as a security for that I left and have yet a much larger sum in my Father's bonds. After I had happily collected & deposited the sum first mentioned, my outstanding debts began to be paid in depreciated money and as I never took the advantage of a single penny in that way I have sorely felt the pernicious effects of tenders Laws—I expect (and were I only to look forward to a provision for myself it would give me no uneasiness) to begin the World in a manner anew, with the consolation of having devoted the service of that time to my Country, which some others have spent in amassing fortunes upon its distresses . . .[1]

In these years close to the outbreak of the Revolution a number of other events took place that had equally far-reaching effect on Tilghman's life. In 1771 his mother, Anne Francis Tilghman, died, and on 4 September 1774 his Uncle Matthew— as ardent a patriot as ever graced the halls of any legislative body in pre-Revolutionary America—arrived in Philadelphia as Chairman of the Maryland delegation to the First Continental Congress. Whatever the fountainhead of Tench's quick response to the cause of independence, the influence of his uncle, Matthew Tilghman, cannot be discounted.

Matthew Tilghman, "the Patriarch of Maryland," uncle and father-in-law of Tench Tilghman. Portrait by John Hesselius.
Courtesy: Mr. John Frazer, Jr.

This period, too, saw Tench's first public service to his country as secretary and treasurer to the Indian Commission. In 1774 rumors of general unrest and confusion among the tribes of the Six Nations were heard in the colonies, even as the Indians were hearing rumors of impending war between the colonists and Great Britain. In April 1775 the Massachusetts Assembly, acting on its own to protect its borders, instructed the Reverend Samuel Kirkland, a Presbyterian missionary, to attach the Six Nations to the American cause or at least to keep them neutral.[2] Kirkland, a native of Connecticut, had been living among the Senecas and the Oneidas since 1764 and wielded great influence among them. Meanwhile, the British had promised to redress Indian grievances, thus precipitating the opinion that the Six Nations and other tribes would actively participate on the side of the British.[3]

The Iroquois, based in what is now central New York State, were the most powerful Indian group on the North American continent. The Six Nations Confederacy, or the League of the Iroquois, composed of the Mohawks, the Oneidas, the Onondagas, the Cayugas, the Senecas, and later the Tuscaroras, who drifted northward from Virginia and North Carolina, did not always work in perfect harmony, but their ties gave them security within their own territory. Outside of it they were nearly invincible.

For the purpose of securing the neutrality of the Indians along the whole frontier, the Continental Congress appointed, on 13 July 1775, three commissions to form treaties: one for the Six Nations and other tribes toward the north, a second for the Creeks or Cherokees toward the south, and a third for intervening tribes in the west. Appointed to the commission to deal with the Six Nations in addition to Tench were Philip Schuyler, Joseph Hawley, Oliver Wolcott, Volkert P. Douw, and Colonel Turbutt Francis (Tench's uncle, the probable source of his appointment). In serving with the commission, Tilghman found himself pursuing the same kind of mission his father had when the latter was instrumental in the formulation of the Treaty of Fort Stanwix. For the man who would be by Washington's side through virtually every battle of the Revolution and who would be remembered in history as the courier who carried from Yorktown to the Continental Congress at Philadelphia the dazzling news of the surrender of Cornwallis, it was as good a start as any. This experience obviously enhanced his acceptability when he volunteered his services to Washington.

By the Treaty of Fort Stanwix colonial settlement or land speculation in all territories between the Alleghenies and the Mississippi was barred and trade with the Indians restricted. Nevertheless, white settlers had continued to push westward in ever-increasing numbers as trade had become essential for both sides. The settlers and the frontiersmen primarily wanted pelts and skins; the Indians were more than anxious to exchange them for goods which had now become requisite to their rapidly changing way of life. Presided over by Sir William Johnson as Indian Commissioner for the Crown, the treaty was—according to one historian—a vast sellout.[4] In exchange for lavish presents the Six Nations ceded enormous expanses of land in central New York, Pennsylvania, and southward. The resulting boundary, running generally southwestward from Fort Stanwix, following the foothills of the Alleghenies as far south as the Tennessee River,[5] was ostensibly to protect the Indians from predatory whites. It was also greatly beneficial to land speculators, a principal one being Johnson himself.[6]

Sir William was a behemoth of a man with a gargantuan appetite for power, women, and high living. An Irishman, he had come to America at the age of twenty-three toward the end of the French and Indian War. An uncle, British Admiral Peter Warren, had purchased thousands of acres of land just south of the Mohawk River and Johnson was his uncle's choice to manage his American holdings. Thrown into close association with the Mohawks, he learned their customs and language, siring a number of half-breed children by various Mohawk women to whom he was probably married according to Indian custom. Ignoring any validity of these unions, he married, on her deathbed, Catherine Weisburg, his indentured servant by whom he also had had three children. His last Indian wife, Molly Brant—of whom Tilghman was to speak with respect and admiration in his journal—was the granddaughter of Chief Hendrick, a noted Mohawk sachem. She was the sister of Joseph Brant, another Six Nations chief called by the Indians Thayendanegea, a highly intelligent man who in later life became an ardent Christian. Molly Brant came from a prominent Mohawk family, later rising to the position of clan mother—the equivalent of a female governess of the nation. Undoubtedly Johnson's favorite, she lived with him for twenty years, bearing him several children. It was through her and her family connections that Sir William, knighted in 1756 for his services to the Crown, was able to manage the Six Nations so successfully.

On 11 July 1774, during the critical period that preceded open hostilities between Britain and her American colonies, Sir William died suddenly at Johnson Hall, the mansion that he had built on lands granted him north of the Mohawk. The first actual fighting was nearly a year away, but Johnson was already hard at work trying to keep the Iroquois loyal to Britain in the event of trouble with the colonies. His death came in the midst of a council with the Iroquois at Johnson Hall, with Johnson trying to quiet dissension within the Six Nations, whose chiefs were pressing him for an explanation of why the whites were not abiding by their former agreements and why they were cascading into Indian territory in the valley of the Ohio, pushing the Indians out. It was indeed an embarrassing question—one that proved to be too much for the old superintendent. He expired in the presence of the assembled Indians, leaving them in a state of stunned awe. Guy Johnson, who was both his nephew and son-in-law, immediately took his place and resumed the council the next day.

Meanwhile the Oneidas, always pro-American, had sent a delegation to Albany to confer with the New York Committee of Safety, urging that "the gate of Fort Stanwix be shut, that nothing might pass and repass to the hurt of our country,"[7] meaning that the then-abandoned fort be renovated and garrisoned. Moreover, in a direct appeal to Philip Schuyler, the Oneidas asked that the old council fires be rekindled so that the Six Nations might meet in friendship with the Americans. The Continental Congress, with Indian affairs much in mind, seized the initiative and set up the Indian Commission to secure the friendship of the Iroquois Confederacy. This was the body that gave Tilghman his first experience in diplomacy and which was to set the pattern for his wartime service.

In a letter to General Washington from Albany on 6 August 1775,[8] General Schuyler wrote:

> Congress has appointed Commissioners for Indian affairs. As one
> of them, I have ordered messengers to be sent into their country

to invite them to a conference at Albany. I have also requested the Caughnawagas of Canada to meet me at this place.

Schuyler was already in Albany, but the other commissioners, without Major Hawley, who was not able to make the journey, left New York on Monday, 7 August, bound up the Hudson. An earlier start on 5 August had to be abandoned because of head winds. Congress had appropriated $750 for entertainment and a speech to the Six Nations, subsequently delivered by Colonel Francis, had been prepared under the direction of Congress.[9] Tilghman's journal, in which he recorded daily the events of the mission, covers the four weeks beginning 5 August 1775 when the commissioners first left New York to 4 September when they returned. Designed for the amusement of his brothers and sisters at home, addressed to his brother Richard, and written in haste, the journal was certainly not for publication. Nevertheless, it contains many details omitted from the official report prepared as Secretary to the Commission for submission to the Continental Congress,[10] and is an extraordinarily valuable document. Apart from some very acute observations on the Indians, it contains graphic accounts of the country and the towns through which he passed as well as a revealing glimpse of social life at Albany. Its wit and humor present still another insight into Tilghman's character. Excerpts follow:

> The Jersey Shore is bounded by a perpendicular Ledge of Rocks about 50 feet in height which come close down to the waters edge, the N York shore is a gradual ascent on which is situated many Gentlemen's Seats and Farm Houses . . . The sailing thro' these mountains by moonlight was a most beautiful sight . . . on Wednesday morning 9th 6 o'clock a. m., found ourselves at half way Island. The Country now begins to grow less mountainous near the shore, but the distant prospect of the Kats-Kill or Blue Mountain has the most beautiful appearance I ever beheld.[11]

The ship arrived at Albany that same afternoon at 5:00 P.M. Tilghman described the town as consisting of

> about 400 Houses chiefly built after the old Dutch Fashion. There are two Dutch and one English Churches. On the Hill above the town is a Fort, now gone much to decay. At each end of the town are two very large and handsome houses, one belonging to Gen-

eral Schuyler, the other to M^r. Ransalear the Lord of the Manor of Ransalear at present a Minor.[12]

North of Albany the expedition turned west, up the Mohawk River, where the richness of the river valley so impressed Tilghman that he wrote:

> This Bottom is so extremely rich and valuable that I am informed it sells from £40 to £80 p Acre. A wealthy Farmer near Schenectady told me that his land had been in Cultivation 120 years successively and that there was not the least appearance of impoverishment.[13]

The Commission arrived at German Flats, the site selected for the preliminary conference, on Sunday, 13 August. The Flats ran along the south side of the Mohawk River at its confluence with Canada Creek, extending inland for two or three miles. At nine the next morning the preliminaries began with the smoking of a ceremonial pipe of peace when the Indians were informed of the purpose of the Albany meeting and invited to attend. The journal continues:

> Our interpreter[14] told them in a few words that M^r. Doer and Col^o Francis were two of the deputies appointed by the Continental Congress to hold a Treaty with the Six Nations & the Indians of Canada at Albany, but as the Indians of Canada had not yet been summoned, they desired they would appoint some of their young men hardy & swift of foot to carry Belts and deliver a Message of Invitation. Their Answer was that they were glad to see us, would call a Council and consider of it. Here I must remark that the Indians never enter into a Controversy upon these occasions, but after hearing what you have to say, answer as above that they will consider what you have said . . . The Behavior of the poor Savages at a public Meeting ought to put us civilized people to the Blush. The most profound silence is observed, no interruption of a speaker. When any one speaks all the rest are attentive.[15]

Tilghman's meeting with Molly Brant is described in a rather full entry for 15 August.

> . . . this morning we were honored with a visit from the favorite of the late S^r. William Johnson. I could not help being affected at the sight of this poor Creature when I reflected on the great Change of her situation in life. For nearly 20 years he lived in what may be

called a state of royalty for no prince was ever as much respected by his subjects as S^r. William was by the different tribes of Indians. They speak of him now with a kind of adoration, they say there never was such a man and never will be such another . . . When Molly, for so is this Squaw called, came to us, she saluted us with an air of ease and politeness, she was dressed after the Indian manner, but her linen and other Cloathes the finest of their kind. One of the Company that had known her before told her she looked thin and asked if she had been sick, she said sickness had not reduced her, but that it was the Remembrance of a Loss that could never be made up to her, meaning the death of S^r. William. Upon seeing Mr. Kirkland an Oneida Missionary, she taxed him with neglect in passing by her House without calling to see her. She said there was a time when she had friends enough, but remarked with sensible emotion that the unfortunate and the poor were always neglected. The Indians pay her great respect and I am afraid her influence will give us some trouble, for we are informed that she is working strongly to prevent the meeting at Albany, being intirely in the Interests of Guy Johnson, who is now in Canada, working upon the Cachnawagers, as it is supposed.

On this same day Colonel Francis addressed the Indians in Council assembled, giving assurances of the pacific intentions of the Twelve Colonies (Georgia had not yet sent representatives to the Continental Congress) toward the Six Nations, asking that "you shut your ears and fortify your minds against any such evil and false reports."[16] Abraham, a Mohawk sachem, acted as interpreter on this occasion.[17] A reply to Colonel Francis was made by Kirkland's old adversary, the Oneida sachem Kanaghquaesa, who spoke with a certain shrewdness and perhaps unconscious humor:

> Brother Solihonay and our Albany Brother, Commissioners from the Twelve United Colonies: You have now opened your minds. We have heard your voices. Your speeches are far from being contemptible. But as the day is far spent, we defer a reply till tomorrow. As we are weary from having sat long in council, we think it time for a little drink; and you must remember that Twelve Colonies are a great body.[18]

"A modest hint," said Tilghman, "that the drink should be in proportion. But we knew the Consequence too well to indulge."[19]

On Wednesday, 16 August, the Commission:

Met the Indians again in Council, who gave us a full answer to our speech of Yesterday, which they complied with every respect, Except that of sending some of their young Men to invite the Indians of Canada. They artfully evaded this by telling us the thing would be impracticable at this time because a Man one of our own Blood was already there endeavouring to draw (pulling strong was their expression) their Minds from us and to prevent their coming down. We asked them who this Man was, they answered they did not chuse to mention his Name, but they had pointed him out sufficiently. Colo Guy Johnson was the person pointed at. They delivered us what they call a Path Belt thereby desiring us to make their way clear to Albany & prevent any mischief happening on the way. This we assured them of and parted with wishes of meeting again in a few days in Albany. It is plain to me that the Indians understood their game, which is to play into both hands.[20]

Rather than press the point, the preliminary meeting ended, and the scene of negotiations was shifted to Albany on 19 August. The tribes were slow in gathering, and it was not until 25 August that actual treaty discussions commenced. Although all the tribes of the Confederacy would be present, including some Stockbridges,[21] it would be composed chiefly of Oneidas, Tuscaroras, and some of the Mohawks from the lower regions of their territory. General Schuyler estimated their number at seven hundred.[22] In spite of this poor representation, the congress opened at 11:00 A.M. on 25 August in the Dutch Church. The pipe of peace was smoked, and General Schuyler delivered the message from Congress. Seghagenrat, an Oneida chief, pledged the friendship of the Indians; the commissioners in turn assured the Indians of their attachment to the Six Nations and explained the unity of the Twelve Colonies. All questions of land dispute would have the attention of Congress. On 27 August, in the midst of the conference, General Schuyler was called away to participate in the campaign against Canada. The other commissioners carried on ably, however, promising that trading posts would be reestablished at Schenectady and Albany where the Indians could exchange furs and other goods for manufactured products which had become a necessity for them. A matter of singular importance to the Indians, which the commissioners also promised to facilitate, was the continued assignment of two blacksmiths to Indian territory so that their axes, hoes, and kettles could be repaired.[23] The conference concluded on 1 September with a round of the traditional "yoe-haas" from every nation present.[24]

In addition to including a wide range of pertinent observations on the Indians, Tilghman wrote revealingly about himself. His journal affords insights into his character totally lacking in the hundreds, if not thousands, of letters he wrote for his own or Washington's signature during the period 1776 to 1783. A case in point is his introduction to and subsequent friendship[25] with Betsy Schuyler, later to marry Alexander Hamilton. It is possible that Hamilton met Betsy through Tilghman, as Hamilton was already serving as an aide to Washington when Tilghman joined the headquarters staff. The two not only served together for years but became intimate friends as well.

On 22 August, still at Albany, Tilghman records his meeting with Betsy:

> I called at Genl Schuyler's seat to pay my compliments to the Genl his Lady & Daughter [Ann, whom Tilghman had met the day previous]. I found none of them at home but Miss Betsy Schuyler the Generals 2^d daughter to whom I was introduced by Mr. Commissary Livington who accompanied me. I was prepossessed in fav^r of this young Lady the moment I saw her. A Brunette with the most good natured lively dark eyes that I ever saw, which threw a beam of good temper and benevolence over her whole Countenance. Mr. Livington informed me that I was not mistaken in my Conjecture for that she was the finest tempered Girl in the World.

Two days later, on the evening prior to the formal opening of the conference, Tilghman dined with the General "who has a palace of a House and lives like a prince."[26]

> The ladies from Carolina,[27] the Commissioners and several Gentlemen from the neighbouring provinces were there. Having occasion to meet some of the Indian Chiefs in the evening, they asked if I had an Indian name being answered in the negative, Tiahogo & the Chief of the Onondagos did me the honor to adopt me into that Tribe and become my father.

That the Indians liked the auburn haired paleface was obvious, but they were not above having their own good-natured amusement at his expense.

He christened me Teahokalonde a name of very honourable signification among them, but much the contrary among us. It signifies having large horns. A Deer is the coat of arms, If I may so call it, of the Onondago Tribe, and they look upon horns as an emblem of strength, Virtue and Courage. This name might have made a suspicious man very unhappy, and made him feel his Temples every now and then for the sprouting honours. The christening cost a bowl of punch or two which I believe was the chief motive of the institution.[28] [Sprouting horns, of course, were the traditional symbols that a man's wife was unfaithful.]

The next day When Business was over I was admitted into the Onondago Tribe, in presence of all the six nations [sic], and received by them as an adopted son. They told me that in order to settle myself among them they must chuse me a wife, and promised that she should be one of the handsomest they could find. I accepted this proposal with many thanks. Miss Lynch and Miss Betsy Schuyler have promised to stand Brides maids—I expected when I came to Albany to have soon been heartily tired of it, and so I should, but for the arrival of the Carolina Ladies and the coming of Gen[l]. Schuyler's family to town. We now form a very agreeable society. I don't know a greater pleasure than for Acquaintances to meet in a strange place. It seems to be the interest of each to oblige the other and to make the time pass as agreeably as possible. I imagine that it is for this reason that the most lasting intimacies are made abroad.[29]

On Saturday, 26 August (which Tilghman erroneously designated as the 27th) he elaborates more on this sentiment, which has had universal application through the ages.

There is something in the behavior of the Gen[l]. his lady & daughters that makes you acquainted with them instantly. I feel myself as easy and free from restraint at his seat as I am at Cliffdon (the home of Benjamin Chew, a Chief Justice of Pennsylvania's Supreme Court), where I am always at a second home.

Tilghman was operating under restraint in one direction, however, as the following observation clearly shows. In his journal for Monday 28 August, he wrote:

I sat near an hour this evening hearing a parcel of Stockbridge Indian Girls sing Hymns. They far excell the Oneidas in this, and add to the account that they are pretty and extremely cleanly they speak tolerable English too, so that I believe I must make an

Aquaintance among them when my fair Country women are all gone, for I think they are superior to any of the Albanians, a Miss Ransolaer excepted who is the Belle of the Town and therefore a little of the Coquette. I will have a Tete a Tete with her before I go. And give her a place in my Journal.

Attracted to the young Indian girls, he was not about to make a move in their direction until "the Carolina ladies" and the Misses Schuyler had vanished from the scene.

On 1 September the conference was over and Tilghman and the commissioners prepared to return to New York. Betsy Schuyler, who had been in Saratoga for a short visit, returned to Albany. Tilghman wrote: "Who should bless my eye sight this evening but good natured agreeable Betsy Schuyler just returned from Saratogha [sic]. I declare I was as glad to see her if she had been ever so old an Acquaintance." The day following the group left Albany on board Captain Lansing's sloop. Aside from leaving his new found friends, Tilghman had had enough. The town was crowded with Indians[30] and soldiers.

> . . . it is hard to say which is the most irregular and Savage. The former are mutinous for want of liquor the latter for want of pay, without which they refuse to march. The Troops raised in and about New York are a sad pack. They are mostly old disbanded Regulars and low lived foreigners. The companies raised in the country are hale hearty young men and seem fit to undergo hardships. From the accounts Gen[l] Schuyler gave us of the state of his Army, I tremble for him in his Expedition ag[t] St Johns he wants almost everything necessary for the equipment of an army.[31]

A lover of good wine, Tilghman addressed his brother directly in an enthusiastic description of the Madeira provided by Mr. Douw at a dinner during the negotiations.

> Then Brother Richard we had Madeira and plenty of it. That cost our host £32 stirling and has been 8 years in his cellar. It was most excellent. They drink far better Madeira in this province than in ours. In their public Houses a great distance from N York their Madeira is unadulterated and as good if not better than you generally meet with in our best Taverns in Phila[d].[32]

On 6 September 1775, from the sloop returning the commissioners to New York and now anchored at Paulus Hook, opposite New York, Colonel Francis addressed a letter to John Hancock, President of the Continental Congress, informing him that it was his hope to be in Philadelphia five days later and to be able to give to the Congress on 14 September "an account of our proceedings."[33] In the report, prepared by Tilghman, a statement by the commissioners to the Six Nations included the following language:

> Brothers of The Six Nations - We yesterday heard with pleasure your answer to the speech of the Twelve United Colonies, and we return thanks to the Great Governour of the Universe, that he has inclined your hearts to approve and accept the brotherly love offered to you by them. It makes us happy to hear so wise and brave a people as our brothers of the Six Nations publickly declare their unalterable resolution to maintain and support peace and friendship with the Twelve United Colonies. This, brothers, you have said, and we most sincerely believe you.[34]

To which Captain Solomon, the Chief of the Stockbridge Indians, replied:

> Brothers, appointed by the Twelve Colonies - We thank you for taking care of us at Albany. Depend upon it, we are true to you, and mean to join you. Wherever you go, we will be by your sides. Our bones shall lie with yours. We are determined never to be at peace with the red coats, while they are at variance with you . . . If we are conquered, our lands go with yours; but if we are victorious, we hope you will help us to recover our just rights.[35]

The trip was over. The promises of peace—uneasy at best—would not last long.

PART TWO

THE WAR YEARS

1776-1783

CHAPTER 6

The Long Road Begins

Upon the breaking out of the troubles, I came
to a determination to share the fate of my country . . .
—Tench to Matthew Tilghman, 10 June 1782

Tench and Colonel Turbutt Francis had been back in Philadelphia for less than a week when the Second Continental Congress convened there on 13 September 1775. Fast moving events were bringing the colonies closer than ever to open conflict with Great Britain. Tench's paternal uncle, Matthew Tilghman—more than ever ready to breathe the fires of defiance at the British Crown—again headed the Maryland delegation. Other members included Samuel Chase, considered an outright incendiary, William Paca, and Thomas Johnson. In the assembly was a delegation from Georgia, thus giving representation for the first time to all thirteen colonies.

An extralegal form of government assembled by the disaffected Americans, the Continental Congress had first met in Philadelphia a year earlier, in an initial session of seven weeks. Its most significant business had been the adoption of a Declaration of Rights. Then as in this case the Maryland delegation had been chaired by Matthew Tilghman, who guided it with a steady hand. In little more than a century infant provincial assemblies had been transformed from weak advisory bodies into powerful legislative institutions. By this time provincial leaders from all thirteen colonies, schooled in the art of political opposition, were from a common podium resisting at all costs what were considered blatant British attempts to rob them of their rights to manage their own affairs.

Not a revolution in the accepted sense, the American Revolution was rather a colonial rebellion against external authority. It has been said to have been, "the work of an energetic minority, which succeeded in committing an undecided and fluctuating majority to courses for which it had little love, leading it step by step to a position from which it was impossible to recede."[1] Students of the stunning political creation accomplished by the Founding Fathers have wondered how a relatively small group of delegates from thirteen loosely affiliated colonies—having a total population of no more than three million free souls—could produce a form of government emulated by so many others. The best explanation seems to be that there was then a deference to excellence in public life with an underlying belief that uncommon men should rule. The truly singular fact is not that so many sage and decent men were then alive, but that they were brought together in Philadelphia by a common philosophy which transcended regional interests and a variety of social and economic backgrounds.

Well-meaning people in England found it difficult to understand the intensity of feeling in America where the tax on tea, looked upon in England as a mild expedient for raising needed revenue for the defense of the colonies, was considered an outrageous intrusion into local autonomy. Britain's internal debt, resulting from the Seven Years' War, was enormous. Landowners in England were taxed at a rate no less than twenty percent on the income from their holdings while the American colonists, now freed from hostile menace and secure to expand to the seemingly limitless west, were the principal beneficiaries of the defeat of France. Small wonder that many Englishmen thought the colonists should share the burden.

Maryland's revolutionary leaders, called the "popular party" by their contemporaries, had first assumed power in 1774. Basically they were conservatives, the mounting strain in Anglo-American relations having little to do with their ascendency. Tench's father James, writing from Philadelphia on the 2nd of October of that year to a friend in England, had this to say regarding his brother Matthew's political views:

One of my Brothers, the Speaker of the Maryland Assembly, is of this Congress and lodges with me, And yet I know nothing of what's going. He can neither divulge, nor I inquire, consistent with the principles of Honor, You'll give me the Liberty in this private Way, to say, he is a man of steadiness and Moderation, and of the strictist Virtue, and utterly averse from all violent Measures. And yet I can find that he is not without Apprehensions of Consequences fatal to the Repose of both Mother Country and the Colonies, should the parliament or the Ministry, which is the same thing persist in their present system. . . . My Brother seems exceedingly tired of the business and I believe thinks upon the whole there is too much heat amongst them [the members of the Continental Congress], His plan is to keep off all violent proceeding's and to make a firm and respectful remonstrance containing the reasons of non importation and other modes of opposition, He is a firm stickler for the Liberties of America under a proper subordination to and connexion with the Mother Country . . .[2]

James's appraisal of Matthew's intellect was faultless; he did less well in summing up his politics, however, as Matthew Tilghman was to go down in Maryland history as the leader who took the necessary steps toward the final break with Britain and was to be the acknowledged father of the new state's first constitution. The importance of the letter, nevertheless, is twofold; it shows not only the existence of close family ties between two powerful brothers despite widely divergent political views but demonstrates that ample opportunity existed for Tench to absorb his Uncle Matthew's political philosophy since they lived in the same household in a period critical to Tench's emergence as an American patriot.

By the middle of 1775 independence had become a burning issue. The battles of Lexington, Concord, and Bunker Hill had been fought and Congress had authorized a Continental Army with George Washington as its commander in chief. Before the year was out Congress would reorganize the army effective 1 January 1776, with an authorized strength of 20,372 officers and men to be enlisted for a period of one year. New England had made up its mind and Virginia was keen for separation—keener even than New England. New York and Pennsylvania were hesitant and conservative forces in Maryland and North Carolina were delaying the issue. By early 1776 Washington was advocating independence, and Nathanael Greene and other army leaders were of the same mind.

However, it was the Englishman Thomas Paine whose facile pen would fan the fire into unquenchable flame. In Philadelphia, where he had arrived in late November of 1774—bearing with him invaluable letters of introduction from Benjamin Franklin whom he had been fortunate enough to meet in London—he was earning a precarious living as a journalist, largely through contributions to Robert Aitken's *Pennsylvania Magazine*. Self-educated and an unmitigated abolitionist, this "ingenious, worthy young man," as Franklin described him in his letters of introduction, railed against slavery and wrote on the subject of women's rights. *Common Sense*, an anonymous, two-shilling pamphlet of forty-seven pages, was published in Philadelphia on 10 January 1776. In it Paine demolished the idea of kings everywhere, past, present, and future and called for an immediate declaration of independence. The colonies must fall away eventually, Paine said, why not break now while their society was still uncorrupt, natural, and democratic? *Common Sense* was an immediate success, not because it said anything new but because of its vigorous wording and timeliness. More than 100,000 copies were quickly sold and it brought decision to many wavering minds. Paine's authorship soon became known and shortly thereafter he enlisted in the Continental Army.

While the precise date is not known, Tench reached his decision to close out his business affairs and join the military almost immediately after his return from German Flats. As was the case with the Marquis de Lafayette, later to become his close friend, Tilghman had become the committed man—"l'homme engagé," in Lafayette's own words. In some way the outbreak of the Revolution energized Tilghman, giving him a concept of himself as a man with moral purpose. Service to his country and loyalty to the American cause became driving forces in his life. Aside from his father, many of his close relatives and friends, among them Joseph Galloway, John Dickinson, Andrew Allen, Tench Coxe, and Thomas McKean, failed to perceive that the middle ground is more often than not untenable in an era of revolutionary upheaval. Some, like McKean, finally reached a commitment to American independence. Others like his first cousin Tench Coxe were to join the same exodus from Philadelphia which took his father back to Maryland. Tilghman, however, marching to the beat of a different drum, was ready to make the ritual passage and to embark on the long road to Yorktown and beyond.

As Pennsylvania was without a militia or any organized military force whatever, the summer of 1775 had seen the formation of volunteer military units in and around Philadelphia.[3] Tilghman associated himself with the volunteer company of which Sharpe Dulaney was captain.[4] Called by its friends the "Ladies Light Infantry" and derisively by its detractors the "Silk Stockings," it was composed primarily of young men from Philadelphia's most prominent families. Tilghman was a Lieutenant in the 3rd Battalion.[5] Soon after the reorganization of the Continental Army, Congress mandated a levy of 4,300 men against Pennsylvania. Philadelphians were quick to act; a large public meeting was held in front of the State House to discuss ways of meeting that requirement.[6] As part of the forces to be contributed, Captain Dulaney's Light Infantry unit was incorporated into the Continental Army in what was called the "Flying Camp," a term used to denote a body of armed men available for quick movement.[7] This realignment took place in June or July of 1776 when Tilghman, by now a Captain, and his group joined other elements of the Continental Army in New Jersey. Composed primarily of Pennsylvania troops but including also units from Maryland and Delaware, the Flying Camp had as its mission the defense of Pennsylvania from invasion by the British, then encamped on Staten Island. Never intended as a permanent part of the Army, the Flying Camp was dissolved on 1 December 1776 after participation by some of its elements in the Battles of Long Island, Harlem Heights, White Plains, and Fort Washington. Many of the officers and men joined newly organized Continental regiments.

Tilghman told of his early decision to join the military in the letter he later wrote to his Uncle Matthew on 10 June 1782 (quoted in Chapter 5):

> Upon the breaking out of the troubles, I came to a determination to share the fate of my Country . . . It has ever been a maxim with me to depend upon myself and not build upon the emoluments of Office which are as precarious as the events of life. They are well enough as contingencies and as Suit I have a right and reason to expect some advantages from them - Indeed some of my public Friends have been kind enough to assure me that a due recom-

pense shall be made me for my adherence to the barren Military Line, where they flatter me with saying that I have been useful.[8]

The last statement no doubt refers to his steadfast refusal to accept pay, an aspect of Tilghman's long service which figured prominently in General Washington's communication to Congress when requesting his commission as a Lieut. Colonel (See Chapter 9).

On 8 August 1776[9] Tilghman joined Washington's staff as an aide-de-camp and secretary. Often referred to as Washington's "volunteer aide,"[10] he was probably first brought to Washington's attention by others. Oswald Tilghman, in his *History of Talbot County, Maryland, 1661-1861,* stated that

> From some intimations contained in his letters it would seem that it was the purpose of Captain Tilghman, originally, to serve one campaign, the most of the early troops having been mustered in for short terms; but his behavior in the service in which he was then engaged was such as to attract the attention of his superiors in rank. His own personal merits as shown in the field, his high social position, his liberal education *supported it is true by the recommendations of partial friends in Philadelphia,* caused him to be invited to take a place upon the staff of the commander-in-chief . . .[11]

Whether the assignment was initiated by Tilghman or by Washington is not known; the latter appears more likely, with Tilghman's reference to himself as a "volunteer" signifying primarily his service without pay—a totally voluntary action.

Whatever the circumstances were which led him into the inner circle of those that surrounded Washington, it is certain that when Tilghman joined the select group he did so within the framework of a well established family connection. Washington's ties to the Tilghmans were close and intimate, his diary recording numerous occasions in the years immediately preceding the Revolution when he was either visiting the Tilghmans in Philadelphia or they him at Mount Vernon. Beginning in April 1772 and extending over the next three years there are twenty-five such entries mentioning specifically James or Matthew Tilghman, including one entry for 25 December 1772 when "Mr. Tilghman" spent Christmas at Mount Vernon. There is ample reason to believe that this refers to Judge James Tilghman (1743-1809), often called "James Tilghman, The Patriot" to distinguish him from his much older uncle James Tilghman, Loyalist and father of Tench. The former, who lived and practiced law in Annapolis, was thus much closer to Mount Vernon than his Uncle James in Philadelphia. Judge James Tilghman enthusiastically supported the Revolution by signing the "Association of Freemen" on 26 July 1775 and was appointed to Maryland's Council of Safety on 18 January 1776.[12] After independence he became the state's first Attorney General. The divergent political views of the two Jameses support the contention that the Patriot visited Mount Vernon more frequently than the Loyalist, although a friendship between Washington and the Loyalist is a matter of record. Washington's diary for 27 August 1773 states that

> Govr. Eden, Captn. Ellis, Mr. Danl. Dulany and Mr. George Digges, as also Miss Nelly Calvert, Miss Tracy Digges and Mrs. Jenny Digges, came over with me to Dinr., also came Mr. Ben Dulany and Mr. Tilghman - all of whom stayd all Night.[13]

It seems likely that the reference to this "Mr. Tilghman" is to Tench's father, due to his earlier close association in Annapolis with Daniel Dulany and the compatability of his political views with those of Governor Eden. Later, on 5 September 1774, when the First Continental Congress assembled in Philadelphia at Carpenters' Hall, Washington was present although he did not note the fact in his diary. On 9 September, however, he records that he "dined at Mr. James Tilghman's,"[14] an obvious reference to Tench's father. On 25 May 1775 Washington, again in Philadelphia, dined at Mr. James Tilghman's and spent the evening at the City Tavern.[15] A week later, on 2 June, he dined at Mr. Joseph Shippen's and spent the evening at Mr. James Tilghman's.[16] In these same years Matthew Tilghman is mentioned four times as being an overnight guest at Mount Vernon. In the light of such a strong family relationship, Tench could have been no stranger to the commander in chief. Consequently, when Tilghman's availability was brought to his attention, Washington quickly accepted—readily understandable in view of Washinton's predilection for surrounding himself with qualified officers from respected families whose personal qualities could withstand the closest scrutiny.

Moreover, the offer was timely. At Washington's headquarters official correspondence lay unanswered, and essential staff work was at a standstill. Colonel Joseph Reed had departed in May—ostensibly on leave but never to return—with the consequence that Colonel Robert Hanson Harrison was the only aide left to assist the commander in chief in these often tiresome but vitally important duties. Harrison, who had practiced law in Alexandria, had been an occasional legal adviser to Washington and his frequent hunting companion.

When Tilghman began his duties as an aide, Washington's headquarters were in the Motier house, in New York City, at what afterwards became the intersection of Varick and Charlton streets.[17] British vessels carrying reinforcements were anchored off Sandy Hook and an attack was expected at any time.[18] In a letter dated 13 August 1776, one of the first written to his father since joining Washington, Tench wrote as follows:

> Since I wrote to you last, 96 Sail of Vessels have arrived at the watering place and within the Hook, part of them this day. We suppose they are the Transports with Foreign Troops - To our great amazement they still continue inactive, which is much in our fav^r for we are receiving Reinforcements every day. The Pennsylvania and Maryland Troops are a prodigious thing for us - Even the Eastern people acknowledge their Superiority - The General has brigaded them together and puts the utmost Confidence in them. Our Strength by Land is very great, besides our Musquetry and Rifles behind Lines, Col^o Knox [Henry Knox, later Major General Knox and Chief of Artillery throughout the war, and Secretary of War in Washington's first administration as President of the United States], the Commandant of Artillery, tells me he has a train of 40 Field pieces ready at a moments Warning. This is not merely Report of the Colonels, but I have seen the Guns with all the Artillery Stores ready for action. You can have no Idea of the Generals Merit and Abilities without being with him, few Words serve him, but they are to the purpose and an Order once given by him is implicitly obeyed thro' every Department. His civilities to me have been more than I had a right to expect, but I endeavor to make it up by my Assiduity in executing his Commands, in some of which I have given him very particular Satisfaction.[19]

Two days later Tilghman wrote to his father again, whom he invariably addressed as "Honored Sir," expressing his reluctance to leave the service, despite an earlier intention to stay for one campaign only. He also touched upon the subject of their political differences, later to be stated in much stronger language. (See Appendix I.)

Extraordinarily competent, honorable, modest, notably considerate of others Tilghman soon became, with Harrison, the mainstay of the staff, earning the respect of all with whom he had contact. In an amazingly short time Washington came to regard him as a man of nearly perfect discretion and talked with him freely on any subject, ignoring the fact that his father was a well-known Tory. For the next seven years Tilghman was to give the best of his strength and abilities to his commander in chief, not only having a hand in everything of a confidential nature but also relieving Washington of a thousand and one detailed matters.

In the late summer of 1776 the New York Provincial Convention appointed a Committee of Correspondence, composed of William Allison, Robert R. Livingston, Henry Wisner, and Henry Duer,[20] with Gouverneur Morris as its chief correspondent, to keep it advised of developments at Washington's headquarters. The Convention had become a roving body, compelled to meet at various places a dictated by the fluidity of the military situation. Intelligence from the revolutionary army's headquarters was vital to the New York Convention as the enemy's principal American base occupied its largest city, effectively dividing the northern and southern colonies. Through Colonel Duer, Tilghman was asked[21] to write a daily letter from headquarters to inform the Committee of Correspondence "of all such Public Incidents as you think interesting—".[22] Accepting the task with the approval of Washington, Tilghman carried on this correspondence from 22 September to 21 October 1776. It then stopped because of Tilghman's more pressing military obligations; his dispatches, however, written in the midst of the campaign, describe minutely the events of this short period.[23] After Alexander Hamilton joined Washington's staff as an aide in March 1777 Hamilton reopened this correspondence with the New York Convention.[24]

Active participation in combat was a normal function for Washington's staff and Tilghman was under fire as often as any. Three weeks after he became an aide, the three day battle for control of New York began. On Long Island Tilghman went into combat during the first day's fighting, when the British broke through a gap in the American lines. The British commander, Lieut. General William Howe, had landed about 15,000 troops at Flatbush on 22 August. After brief skirmishing the American outposts retreated and within the next three days Howe, supported by the British fleet under the command of his brother Vice Admiral Richard ("Black Dick") Howe, was able to bring his force up to 20,000 men. The Continental Army, ineptly led, suffered a disastrous defeat. General Howe's envelopment plan worked perfectly. Washington did not arrive from Manhattan until late in the day when the battle had been irretrievably lost. Taking command from General Putnam, Washington saw that it was only a matter of time before he would be under attack by the Royal Navy at his rear and by Howe before him. Unfavorable winds had providently kept British warships out of the East River. As a result, on the night of 29 August, under cover of rain and fog and ferried by John Glover's Marblehead regiment, including many former sailors from Salem, Washington was able to extricate the American force of 9,500 men with all its baggage and equipment. Tilghman stayed at Washington's side throughout the entire operation, escaping with him in the last boat. Howe captured only three stragglers who had lingered behind to plunder. "Our Retreat before an Enemy much superior in Numbers, over a wide River, and not very well furnished with boats certainly does credit to our Generals," Tilghman wrote to his father. "The thing was conducted with so much Secrecy that neither subalterns or privates knew that the whole Army was to cross back again to N York."[25] It was a brilliantly executed maneuver, admired even by the British, making them painfully aware for the first time that Washington was a military adversary to be reckoned with.

One bright spot in the Long Island disaster was the resistance of the American right wing. Smallwood's Maryland Macaronis, their brilliant uniforms of buff and scarlet hidden by brown smocks, and led that day by Major Mordecai Gist,[26] held at bay the entire British left, covering the American retreat with a loss of nearly half their own numbers, thus beginning a career which was to close splendidly five years later in the gallant bayonet charge at Eutaw Springs, earning them the soubriquet of "The Bayonets of The Revolution."[27]

Subsequent to the Battle of Long Island and prior to his first dispatch to Colonel Henry Duer for the Committee of Correspondence Tilghman had written a letter to his friend Colonel Smallwood, then at New York, with an urgent request for information—wanted no doubt for Duer and his Committee. Under date of 20 September 1776 he wrote;

> We are in the most painful suspence imaginable about you and our Maryland officers and if you can get as much leisure as will afford an opportunity to write, we beg to be favored with a line. I wrote you and requested an answer directed to me on the Eastern Shore; since then I have been called over to the Council (of Safety) and am now in Annapolis. But as our body are so very anxious to hear something from you, and as I have doubt of your scarcity of time I shall readily dispense with your not answering me upon your writing a letter to the Council. We feel ourselves deeply interested in your welfare. We lament your loss on Long Island but glory in the honor you have brought to our province and yourself.
>
> A letter would be well received. We have a report by the post that New York was taken by the English on Sunday evening, but have no letters. This makes us the more desirous of hearing from you - indeed every day must be important, and if you cannot, perhaps some of your officers may. Don't direct to our body generally, but to one of us individually.[28]

The British were not long in following up their advantage. On 15 September, before Washington could move all his army and stores north to Harlem Heights, Howe landed at Kip's Bay, on the eastern shore of Manhattan Island. Writing from Harlem Heights on 16 September Tilghman described what then happened:

> Our Army totally evacuated New York yesterday, the Enemy landed a party of about 3000 from Appearance four miles above the City where they encamped last Night. They kept up a very heavy fire from their Ships while their Men were landing, altho' no Body opposed them, I imagine they did it, thinking we might have men concealed behind some lines on the Water side. We removed everything that was valuable, some heavy Cannon excepted, before we left the Town. Our army is posted as advantageously as possible for Security, out of reach of the Fire of the Ships from either River and upon high Grounds of difficult Ac-

cess. I dont know whether the New Eng^d Troops will stand there, but I am sure they will not upon open Ground. I had a Specimen of that yesterday. Hear two Brigades ran away from a small advanced party of the Regulars, tho' the General did all in his power to convince them they were in no danger. He laid his Cane over many of the Officers who shewed their men the Example of running. These were militia, the New England continental Troops are much better.[29]

Howe had let opportunity slip through his hands again by dawdling at the beachhead. The British had the port they wanted and would hold it for the rest of the war, but the American Army was still intact.

Harlem Heights and the high ground toward the Hudson River still stretch, clifflike, southward to the present site of Columbia University and Barnard College. To the southeast McGowan's Pass stood in the vicinity of present 107th Street while still further south, down the center of the island lay the rolling, wooded tract which is now Central Park. By the afternoon of 15 September the bulk of Washington's army had encamped on this elevated plateau.

After the easy victory at Kip's Bay the British opened an attack on Harlem Heights, appearing "in open view and sounded their bugles in a most insulting manner, as is usual after a fox chase . . . it seemed to crown our disgrace." So wrote General Joseph Reed to his wife.[30] Washington, however, outwitted them, luring crack British and German outfits into a trap, and then sending additional troops around to their rear to cut off their retreat. He committed to the action the reorganized militiamen who fought gallantly to wipe out the disgrace of the day before, slugging it out eyeball-to-eyeball almost with the same British regulars who had chased them off Long Island and waded through them at Kip's Bay. Alexander Hamilton, later to be summoned to Washington's entourage to serve as an aide but now serving with a New York artillery outfit, kept his guns pouring round after round into the enemy's lines in a steady, morale-building bombardment. "General Putnam, General Greene, many of the General's family, Mr. Tilghman, etc., were in it, but it was really to animate the troops, who were quite dispirited, and would not go into danger unless their officers led the way."[31]

Suddenly the British began to retreat. The blue green kilts and feathered bonnets of the fabled Black Watch and the bright red coats of the elements of the First Regiment of Foot Guards, whose very names were the terror of the world, fell back before New England militiamen and Maryland and Virginia Continentals. The eighteenth century musket and cannon smoke was heavy and inert but through it all Hamilton, from the higher ground from which his artillery was firing, could see in the distance British and Hessian reserve units moving up to occupy McGowan's Pass—eight to ten thousand men, hidden by the hill to which the enemy was being driven. It was too much of a risk for Washington. Summoning Tilghman he ordered him to break off the pursuit. The sight of a flying enemy was so unusual that it was with difficulty that Tilghman got the men to obey. In a letter written three days later[32] Tilghman described the action:

> The Gen[l] finding they [Colonel Knowlton and Major Leitch, both of whom subsequently died of wounds sustained] wanted support ordered over part of Col[o] Griffith's and part of Col[o] Richardson's Maryland Regiments, these Troops tho' young charged with as much Bravery as I can conceive, they gave two fires and then rushed right forward which drove the Enemy from the Wood into a Buckwheat field, from whence they retreated. The General fearing (as we afterwards found) that a large Body was coming up to support them, sent me over to bring our men off. They gave a Hurra and left the Field in good Order . . . We find their force was much more considerable than we imagined when the General ordered the Attack. It consisted of the 2nd Batt[n] of the Light Infantry, a Batt[n] of the Royal Highlanders and 3 Comp[s] of Hessian Rifle Men. The prisoners we took, told us, they expected our Men would have run away as they did the day before, but that they were never more surprised than to see us advancing to attack them. The Virginia and Maryland Troops bear the Palm.

On Harlem Heights that day Washington's army had been transformed from a beaten mob to an effective fighting force, and every man knew it. The Americans did not follow the script. Ad-libbing outrageously, they had actually driven some of the enemy's best regiments for more than a mile, broken off, and retired in good order. Of the engagement Joseph Reed wrote,

> You can hardly conceive the change it has made in our army. The men have recovered their spirit and feel a confidence which before they had quite lost. I hope the effect will be lasting.[33]

Angry bewilderment beset Howe's forces; Von Donop went so far as to say that if his Jaegers had not come up when they did, the British and Scottish troops would have been captured.

Before Howe made his next move, an event took place which even today is a source of controversy. Shortly after midnight on Saturday, 21 September, a cry which every eighteenth century city dweller dreaded was heard in New York's streets: Fire! A young British officer, Lieutenant Frederick MacKenzie of the Royal Welsh Fusiliers, was aroused by the sentry at his billet to discover that the fire, which had started in a shed near Whitehall Slip, was completely out of control. A high wind was blowing from the south. As women and children rushed out of burning houses and as men tried to work the engines and to form bucket lines, the flames swept on. Dock, Bridge, Stone, Marketfield, and Beaver streets were soon engulfed. Dutch houses, from Peter Stuyvesant's day, soon became glowing ovens as great mansions and sleazy hovels alike were consumed by the roaring inferno. General Howe refused to commit his whole army to fighting the blaze, fearing it might be part of a plan to attack his forward positions. Nearly a quarter of the city, between six hundred and one thousand houses, was destroyed before soldiers and sailors could bring the fire under control, creating firebreaks by pulling down dozens of houses.

The fire was a major disaster for the British and for the Tories. "Our distresses were great before, but this calamity has increased them tenfold," wrote one New Yorker. "Thousands are hereby reduced to beggary."[34] The origins of the fire remain a matter of doubt. After the landing of Howe's army on Long Island the Americans had given serious consideration to destroying the city. General Greene had urged it strongly. "I would burn the city and suburbs," he said, and for the following reasons:

> If the enemy gets possession of the city, we can never recover the possession without a naval force superior to theirs; it will deprive the enemy of an opportunity of barracking their whole army together . . . It will deprive them of a general market . . . Two-thirds of the property of the city of New York and the suburbs belongs to the Tories. We have no very great reason to run any considerable risk for its defence.[35]

Washington put the decision squarely up to Congress, questioning the advisability of allowing the city to stand, in the event of its abandonment, as winter quarters for the enemy. Congress was quick to order that it be spared, expressing confidence that the Americans would "recover the same." Washington was not one to disobey orders but it is apparent from his reply that he thought it might be done surreptitiously despite his orders to the contrary.[36]

Tilghman's views on the matter were clear cut. On 25 September he addressed his father from Headquarters, Harlem Heights.

> I take the opportunity of letting you know by M^r. Bache, who has been here establishing the post office, that all Matters between the two armies have remained perfectly quiet since the 16th. Many and various will be the Reports concerning the setting fire to New York, if it was done designedly, it was without the knowledge or Approbation of any commanding officer in this Army, and indeed so much time had elapsed between our quitting the City and the fire, that it can never be fairly attributed to the Army. Indeed every man belonging to the Army who remained in or who were found near the City were made close prisoners. Many Acts of barbarous cruelty were committed upon poor creatures who were perhaps flying from the flames, the Soldiers and Sailors looked upon all who were not in the military line as guilty, and burnt and cut to pieces many. But this I am sure was not by Order. Some were executed next day upon good Grounds . . . I went down to the Enemy's lines yesterday with a Flag to settle the Exchange of prisoners, which I believe will generally take place. I met a very civil Gentleman with whom I had an Hours conversation while my dispatches were going up to General Howe. He told me that every vigorous Step was taken to keep the British Army under the strictest Discipline, but that the Hessians could not be restrained without breaking with them as they claimed a right of plunder, and that Genl Howe was obliged to pay for the Excesses they committed.[37]

As September ripened into October Washington, well aware that Howe would move to trap him on Manhattan Island, pondered his next move. Tilghman meanwhile was making himself extraordinarily useful, and his relationship with his chief was growing closer day by day—and fortified by each succeeding crisis. This was the season too when Tilghman's steadfastness brought forth a discerning comment from Joseph Reed, again in a letter to his wife:

When I look around, and see how few of the numbers who talked
so largely of death and honour are around me, and that those who
are here are those from whom it was least expected (as Tilghman),
I am lost in wonder and surprise. Some of our Philadelphia
gentlemen who came over on visits, upon the first cannon, went
off in a most violent hurry. Your noisy sons of liberty are, I find,
the quietest in the field . . . An engagement, or even the expectation of one, gives a wonderful insight into character. But we are
young soldiers.[38]

"I am detained here by no particular engagements entered
into with the General," wrote Tilghman to his father on 7
October,

so far from it, that tho' he has repeatedly told me I ought to have a
Compensation for my Services, I have refused, telling him, that as
I only intended to stay with him as long as the active part of the
Campaign lasted, I wished to serve as a Volunteer. If I had no
other Tie than that of Honour I could not leave the Army just
now, but there is another if possible more binding with me. The
General has treated (me) in a Manner the most confidential, he
has intrusted me and one other gentleman of his Family, his
Secretary, with his most private Opinions on more Occasions than
one, and I am sure they would have been given in a different
Manner than they would have been to some others that the World
imagines have great Influence over him. Was I to leave him now,
crowded as he is by Business, of good part of which I am able to
relieve him, would not my conduct appear suspicious to him,
would it not look as if I had ingratiated myself with him purposely
to make myself Master of his Secrets, and then to take an Advantage. The season will soon arrive when every Man not in any
particular Command may leave the Army with Credit, and till that
I cannot think of returning home.

By no means sure of surviving the war Tilghman continued by
saying,

We shall see this Winter how Matters are likely to settle, if I live, I
can then determine what is to be done in the Way of Business . . .
The two Armies are as quiet as if they were a Thousand miles
apart, it begins to look very like an inactive campaign.[39]

While the two armies sat facing each other from fortified
positions, speculation continued in the American camp as to

Howe's next move. With characteristic deliberation and equal sagacity Howe had decided to make a landing on Frog's Point (originally called Throckmorton's Point, soon shortened to Throck's or Throg's and thence to Frog's Point), a small peninsula sticking out into the sound from the mainland almost due east of the American lines. "All our attention is taken up in watching the Motions of the Enemy who moved a considerable part of their Army up the Sound yesterday and landed them at a place called Frog's point," wrote Tilghman on 13 October. "By their not moving from thence it looks as if they wanted to divert our Attention while some other Object is in view."[40] Washington, however, immediately saw the danger in Howe's flanking move and in a council of war assembled at headquarters, participated in by the controversial General Charles Lee who had just rejoined the main army after a successful defense of Charleston, South Carolina, decided to withdraw as far as White Plains. Lee had argued vigorously for a general retreat to safer positions, a course which—if followed—would have prevented another disaster. However, in deference to a resolve of Congress, made on 11 October, that "if it be practicable . . . to obstruct effectually the navigation of the North River," it was decided to leave some 2,000 men at Fort Washington, high in the present West 180s, to maintain the line of sunken hulks and chevaux-de-frise running to Fort Lee on the Jersey shore opposite. These submarine defenses had in fact been already breached by the British, and it is difficult to follow Washington's reasoning. A worse military decision has seldom been made.

Since writing from "Valentine's Hill, 4 Miles from Kingsbridge," on 22 October, when Tilghman had informed his father that "We are just setting off for the White Plains where the General intends to fix Head Quarters for the present," nine days were to elapse before another letter followed. There was, of course, no censorship of military mail in that era, and Tilghman's letters to his father and other members of his family are remarkably free with information—somewhat analogous to one of Eisenhower's aides writing home to say that within a few days headquarters would be established in Normandy. Distances, however, were comparatively great and communications difficult; moreover both armies were operating in clear view of hundreds if not thousands whose views were in direct conflict with the aims of one side or the other, thus affording each commander ample opportunity for intelligence. Consequently, Tilghman's forthrightness, which today would be considered not only indiscreet but downright dangerous, was matched in many instances by similar letters from his fellow officers.

On 28 and 29 October the pursuing Howe attacked again. The Battle of White Plains, measured by the numbers engaged, was a small affair, but the British were momentarily checked, thus giving another lift to the spirits of the hard-pressed Americans.[41] Tilghman's letter to his father of 31 October, written primarily to allay any fears the latter might have over Tench's safety, contain as well a brief but concise account of the engagement:

> As all Accounts of Actions are much exaggerated before they reach you, I always take the earliest Opportunity of informing you of the Truth and at the same time of letting you know that I am safe and well. On Monday morning we recd. Information that the Enemy were in Motion and in march towards our Lines, all our Men were immediately at their Alarm Posts and about 2000 detached to give the Enemy as much annoyance as possible on their Approach. There were likewise a few Regiments posted upon a Hill [Chatterton's Hill] on our Right, of which we had not had time to throw up Works, which Hill commanded our Lines which were but slight and temporary ones. About Noon the Enemy appeared full in our Front in vast Numbers, their Light Horse reconnoitered our Lines, and I suppose not chusing to attack them, filed off towards the Hill, on which they began a most furious Cannonade, followed by a heavy Column of Infantry, our Troops made as good a Stand as could be expected and did not quit the Ground, till they came to push their Bayonets. We lost about 100 killed and wounded. Smallwoods Regiment suffered most, he himself is wounded in the Hand and Hip but not badly. Capt. Braco and Scott killed. From all Accounts of Deserters and prisoners the English Army suffered more than we did, for as their Body was large, the Shot from our Field pieces and Musquets, could scarcely miss doing damage. Six of their Light Horse Men were killed and one of the Horses, a very fine one, taken by one of Miles's Officers and made a present to the General - Content with the possession of the Hill, they sat down about Six hundred yards from us and have never fired a Gun since. We have moved all our Tents and Baggage and Stores before their Faces, and have put them on the Heights just above the plain where they at first were.

This letter also reinforces Tilghman's earlier statements concerning the origin of New York's disastrous fire of 21 September.

> Much has been said of the Clemency of the British Army, at first landing they attempted to restrain the Soldiery, at least from hurting what were deemed Tories, but the Hessians would not be restrained, they made no Distinction and Gen¹. Howe dare not punish them. The British Troops seeing the Foreigners rioting in plenty and plundering all before them, grew restless and uneasy, and are now indulged in the same Excesses. The people who, tho' informed against as Tories, were protected by Gen¹. Washington and paid for what they would sell, have come in and informed us that they were stripped of their all whenever the Enemy advanced upon them. The Foreigners who have been taken, all agree that a Liberty of plunder without Distinction is what they expect and insist upon. *New York was set on fire by a Party of them who robbed a Rum Store and set the Fire agoing in their Liquor.* After this, which is strictly true, can they ask the Americans to lay down their Arms, before such a licentious Crew are removed? We are on Horseback or busy from Sun Rise to Sun Set, and all the time I find to write is at Night . . . I would write oftener, but as I said before I have not time.[42]

Following Howe's failure to finish him off at White Plains, Washington moved his army to a stronger position on the heights of North Castle. The garrison at Fort Washington remained in place, a mistake of gigantic proportions. On 15 November Howe sent 8, 000 troops against the fort. In a well-executed strike and after a courageous resistance by the defenders, it fell. The American defeat was one of the most expensive of the war—230 officers and 2,607 men fell into the hands of the British. In addition Howe took 146 cannon, 12,000 rounds of artillery ammunition, 2,800 muskets and 400,000 cartridges.[43] Unable to send assistance, Washington watched in rage and frustration from Fort Lee, on the Jersey shore. Four days later Fort Lee fell, leaving New York securely in possession of the British and nothing to keep them out of New Jersey.

With the fall of the Hudson River forts Washington had no choice but to retreat south across New Jersey with his army, now reduced to less than 3,000 men. Almost trapped at Newark, he cut off the pursuit by escaping to Pennsylvania across the Delaware, taking all available boats with him to effectively stop the enemy. Howe, never an aggressive commander, spread his forces along the north shore of the Delaware and retired to winter quarters in New York.

Washington, meanwhile, knowing that unless a victory was forthcoming to encourage reenlistments and thus prevent his pitiful forces from shrinking even further, in desperation plotted a counterstroke. In the gathering dusk of a frigid Christmas day, John Glover and his saltwater boatmen from Massachusetts began to ferry a strike force back across the treacherous, ice-clogged Delaware.

The crossing of the Delaware by Washington and his men on Christmas night to attack the Hessians at Trenton is one of the Revolution's most thoroughly documented events, immortalized as well by Emmanuel Leutze in his outsized painting, "Washington Crossing The Delaware," now hanging in the Metropolitan Museum in New York. Tilghman, who was with Washington throughout the action, described it to his father in a letter written two days later from headquarters at Newtown. Largely overlooked by historians, it describes in a few short paragraphs the drama of a great moment in the war. He wrote,

> I have the pleasure to inform you that I am safe and well after a most successful Enterprise against three Regiments of Hessians consisting of about 1500 Men lying in Trenton, which was planned and executed under his Excellency's immediate command. Our party amounted to 2400 Men, we crossed the River at McKonkey's Ferry 9 Miles above Trenton, the Night was excessively severe, both cold and snowey, which the Men bore without the least murmer. We were so much delayed in crossing the River, that we did not reach Trenton till eight o clock, when the division which the General headed in person, attacked the Enemy's out post. The other Division which marched the lower Road, attacked the advance post at Phil. Dickinson's,[44] within a few minutes after we began ours. Both parties pushed on with so much rapidity, that the Enemy had scarce time to form, our people advanced up to the Mouths of their Field pieces, shot down their horses and brought off the Cannon. About 600 run off the Bordentown Road the moment the Attack began, the remainder finding themselves surrounded laid down their Arms. We have taken 30 officers and 886 privates among the former Colo Rahls the Commandant who is wounded. The General left him and the other wounded Officers

Capture of the Hessians at Trenton. Painting by John Trumbull.
Courtesy: Yale University Art Gallery.

upon their parole, under their own Surgeons, and gave all the privates, their Baggage ... If the Ice had not prevented Gen[l] Ewing from crossing at Trenton Ferry, and Col[o] Cadwalader from doing the same at Bristol, we should have followed the Blow and drove every post below Trenton.[45]

Colonel Johann Gottlieb Rall, in command of the Hessians, seems to have been singularly unfitted for the command at Trenton, given to him reluctantly by Howe in recognition of his excellent performance at White Plains and elsewhere. Addicted to comfort and pleasure, his lack of knowledge of English was a serious handicap in matters of intelligence and security. While he took great pride in the appearance of his troops, he was utterly indifferent to their welfare, thinking nothing of keeping them waiting in formation for several hours—if perchance he had slept late—for the sole purpose of having them parade beneath the window of his billet for his inspection.[46] Moreover with a spit and polish soldier's mentality he viewed the Americans with scorn, lacking any conception of what they were fighting for. Saying, "Let them come - we'll go after them with the bayonet," he not only had failed to safeguard his position adequately but had totally ignored as well a warning given him the night before Washington attacked. Immersed in a card game and drinking heavily, he thrust into a pocket unread a note given him by an aide. Perhaps he intended to read it later but he never did; it was found in his pocket after his death two days later.

Washington and Tilghman were riding down King Street close to where the mortally wounded Rall was being carried to his quarters by an American officer when word reached them that the Knyphausen Regiment had surrendered. In less than an hour a thousand Hessians were killed or taken prisoner while casualties on the American side were astonishingly light—two officers and two privates wounded, one of the officers being Samuel Blatchley Webb, another of Washington's aides. Although Trenton had been captured, it was not safe to remain there. Therefore, almost immediately after the battle Washington took his exhausted forces back across the river.

Washington's success at Trenton surprised everyone; Howe was staggered by the news. He stopped Lord Charles Cornwallis, who was about to return to England, and dispatched him forthwith to New Jersey to take command. Washington, meanwhile, had rallied his forces, promising a bonus of ten dollars, hard money, to men who would extend their enlistments. From Newton on 29 December Tilghman informed his father that "We are just going over to Jersey again in pursuit of the Remainder of the Hessian Army who have left Bordentown—The General waits while I write this much."[47]

Enough men had agreed to stay so Washington, anxious to exploit his success and "keep up the Pannick,"[48] took his shabby little force of 1,600 men back across the Delaware on New Year's Day, 1777. But this time he was faced by the energetic and aggressive Lord Cornwallis, a different breed of cat entirely from the leisurely Howe—now Sir William by virtue of his triumph on Long Island. In enemy country, Washington knew that the British were in positions from which they could attack from several directions at once. Just before they closed in, Washington's men slipped out of their lines and around Cornwallis's flank to attack the rear at Princeton, twelve miles away. The engagement was short, but fought bitterly. Washington, standing in his stirrups, saw his men rout the British force. "It's a fine fox chase, my boys!" he shouted in exultation—no doubt mindful of the insulting fox hunting calls blown at him by British buglers at Harlem Heights in mid-September.

But Princeton was no place in which to linger. The Continentals, too exhausted for further action, hurried to reach the western highlands of New Jersey and the heights around Morristown to hole up for the winter; the British returned to the comforts of New York. The fox hunt was over, but the wily old American fox had escaped the British hounds.

Twice chosen by Washington as a winter quarters for the main American army, strategic Morristown lay on a steep-sided plateau, protected on the east by low-lying wooded ravines and on the west by Thimble Mountain—a two hundred and fifty foot vantage point commanding the flats of the Passaic River and approach roads over which any hostile force would have to move. It was 6 January 1777 when the army set itself to endure doggedly another winter in the field. Although some troops remained billeted in public buildings, stables, or barns, most were housed in huts built on the slopes of Thimble Mountain. A number of well-to-do families offered their houses to Washington as headquarters, but he chose Freeman's Tavern, sometimes called Colonel Jacob Arnold's, a sizable structure on the northwest edge of the Commons, big enough to house his aides and to offer as well a conference room for an unending stream of visitors.[49]

So ended Tilghman's first full season of campaigning with his general. Having clinched the victory at Trenton by the Battle of Princeton, Washington had now changed the entire military situation and brought fresh hope to what had seemed a lost cause. The volunteer aide whose original intention was to sign on for one campaign only was now totally committed to that cause and to the General who led it; to desert either was simply unthinkable. In addition to four more winter encampments with victory not even remotely in view, there lay ahead more hardship and privation, major battles, petty jealousies, political turmoil, treachery, and slanderous criticism which drove sensitive men to shoot it out on the dueling field with those whose remarks they found offensive. The long road seemed to have no turning.

CHAPTER 7

Enter Lafayette

Permit me to put you in mind of an old friend
by introducing to your particular notice
the Marquis de Lafayette . . .
—William Carmichael to Tench Tilghman
Paris, 17 March 1777

His Majesty intends to open this year's campaign with ninety thousand Hessians, Tories, Negroes, Japanese, Moors, Esquimaux, Persian archers, Laplanders, Feejee Islanders, and light horse. With this terrific and horrendous armament, in conjunction with a most tremendous and irresistible fleet, he is resolved to terminate this unnatural war the next summer, as it will be impossible for the rebels to bring an equal number in the field. His Majesty has also the strongest assurances that France will co-operate with him in humbling his seditious subjects; and as his admiral and general are still extending the arms of mercy for the gracious reception of those who will yet return to their duty and allegiance, for Heaven's sake, ye poor, deluded, misguided, bewildered, cajoled, and bamboozled Whigs! ye dumbfounded, infatuated, back-bestridden, nose-led-about, priest-ridden, demagogue-be-shackled, and Congress-becrafted independents, fly, fly, oh fly, for protection to the royal standard, or ye will be swept from the face of the earth with the besom of destruction, and cannonaded in a moment into nullities and nonentities, and no mortal can tell into what other kind of quiddities and quoddities.[1]

The Americans and the French, however, had other plans. Humiliated by the loss of Canada at the conclusion of the Seven Years War and the harsh terms of the Treaty of Paris in 1763, France was left with a strong desire for revenge. A clandestine French agent had been in the colonies in 1775, a year before Silas

Deane, a Connecticut lawyer and former delegate to the Continental Congress, arrived in Paris to secure French assistance for the American cause and recognition of independence for the embattled colonies.[2] Working with Charles Gravier, Comte de Vergennes, the French Foreign Minister and that most astounding and versatile character, Pierre Augustin Caron de Beaumarchais (watchmaker, author of the plays *The Barber of Seville* and *The Marriage of Figaro*, entrepreneur, and secret agent), Deane succeeded in setting up a clandestine operation which two hundred years later would have done credit to the Central Intelligence Agency. Trading under the name of Rodrique Hortalez et Cie, Beaumarchais, the pivotal figure, employed a fleet of forty vessels to funnel ammunition and other assistance to the Americans, most shipments being routed through the West Indies.[3]

While the disaster on Long Island delayed open intervention by the French into the war for at least two years, the American cause was immediately popular in France, and a number of French officers—many of whom were on half pay or none at all—volunteered for service in the rebel army. The most notable, of course, was the Marquis de Lafayette.[4] The single individual most responsible for the coming of Lafayette to America was William Carmichael,[5] a close friend of Tilghman's from Maryland's Eastern Shore. Years later, in 1824, Lafayette himself acknowledged this while on his last visit to Maryland in which he spoke of his wish to see "the honored widow of a dear brother in General Washington's family, Col. Tilghman . . . as well as a daughter of my friend, Carmichael, who first received the secret vows of my engagement in the American cause."[6]

Carmichael, born in Queen Anne's County, Maryland, had inherited a considerable fortune and as a young man mingled freely with the leading families of Maryland.[7] It was during this period of his life that he and Tilghman became friends. After attending the University of Edinburgh, Carmichael settled in London. Although an expatriate he had resolved to return to America to offer his services to the revolutionary forces, but an unfortunate illness detained him in Paris until the arrival of Silas Deane. Carmichael volunteered his help, remaining in France until 1778. Later he was sent by the Continental Congress to Spain where he served with distinction on a diplomatic mission, died, and was buried.[8]

Carmichael's wide acquaintance with prominent men and his familiarity with continental social usage gave him unique qualities which Deane and the other comissioners—Arthur Lee and Benjamin Franklin—lacked; consequently they relied on him extensively. His influence abroad and his contributions to the Continental Congress have been largely overlooked.

Immediately following the culmination of secret negotiations with Lafayette, deKalb, and other officers—French, German, and Dutch—and less than a week before the first of this small band, moving surreptitiously, boarded the *Victoire*, the ship which Lafayette had purchased and equipped from his own pocket to take them to America, Carmichael wrote a letter of introduction on their behalf to Tilghman. Aware of the latter's close relationship to Washington and ever anxious to ease the way for Lafayette and his companions in the strange new world where their dreams of military glory would end in either fame or oblivion, and where all but deKalb[9] would be faced with the difficulties of coping with a foreign language, Carmichael addressed his friend Tench from Paris on 17 March 1777 as follows:

> Permit me to put you in mind of an old friend by introducing to your particular notice the Marquis de Lafayette and the Baron deKalb, as well as the Colonels Lafler[10] and Valfeit.[11] The first of the first connections and fortune in France. The latter all officers of the first consideration here in their different ranks. I beg you to introduce them to the gallantest of our countrymen, who, I hope, want no example to inspirit them to act to deserve the continuance of the admiration of Europe which they now have. If such should be wanted, see in the Marquis an example too striking not to be followed, a young nobleman with a clear fortune of £15,000 sterling a year preferring every danger in search of glory to the tranquil pleasures such connections and such fortune gave him, with the example of almost all his predecessors who fell in battle to deter him.[12]

Thus were sown, even before Lafayette set foot on American soil, the seeds of his close friendship with Tilghman, to endure for Tilghman's lifetime and beyond.[13] By far the best extant portrait of Tilghman is one in which he stands beside Lafayette and Washington.[14] This portrait, a celebrated painting by Charles Willson Peale, has been widely reproduced and captures also the appearance of Lafayette as described by a contemporary:

> At this period of his life, the Marquis de La Fayette was a noble looking man, notwithstanding his deep red hair. His forehead, though receding, was fine, his eye clear hazel, and his mouth and chin delicately formed, exhibiting beauty rather than strength. The expression of his countenance was strongly indicative of a generous and gallant spirit, mingled with something of the pride of conscious manliness. His mien was noble - his manners, frank and amiable - his movements, light and graceful. Formed both by nature and education to be the ornament of a court and already distinguished by his polished manners and attractive qualities, in the circle of his noble acquaintance, his free principles were neither withered by the sunshine of royalty, nor weakened by flattery and temptation.[15]

The passage of *Victoire* from Bordeaux to South Carolina took fifty-seven days and was unusually rough. Despite these adverse conditions, Lafayette spent his days alone with deKalb, wrestling with the English language,[16] determined to let nothing block his commission as a major general in the American army, an appointment which Silas Deane had strongly recommended in a letter to the Continental Congress on 7 December 1776.[17]

On the night of 13 June 1777, ashore at last, Lafayette laid his weary head on the fresh clean linen of a bed at "Prospect Hill," the plantation of Major Benjamin Huger, near the mouth of the Great Pedee River, close to Georgetown, South Carolina.[18] Headed for Charleston the *Victoire* had made a landfall "twenty-five leagues higher up" to escape possible interdiction by the British. Six weeks later, after a grueling trip to Philadelphia over atrocious roads, Lafayette offered his services personally to the Continental Congress. On 31 July 1777, he received his cherished commission and joined Washington's forces on the eve of the battles of the Brandywine and Germantown. His English, passable but still imperfect, got sympathetic attention from both Tilghman and Hamilton. John Laurens of South Carolina, the third aide who spoke French, would not join Washington's official family until 6 September 1777.[19]

Before the first winter encampment at Morristown was over, newly appointed aides would include not only John Walker in

Washington, Lafayette, and Tilghman at Yorktown.
Painting by Charles Willson Peale.
Courtesy: Maryland Office of Tourist Development.

February and Hamilton in March but also Richard Kidder ("Dick") Meade, more often Washington's choice for riding assignments than for originating or transcribing important correspondence. Whether headquarters was in Freeman's Tavern or the Ford House, as it was to be in the winter of 1779-80, the single most important factor in its operational efficiency was for the aides to be sufficiently near Washington so that he could summon them easily—day or night. For the most part they slept in one room, adjacent to or across the hall from the commander in chief.

It must be remembered that Washington's headquarters was a focal point for political as well as military matters. All intelligence came to him there, and from headquarters flowed all major orders to subordinate commanders as well as correspondence with public officials. At the beginning of the war all letters emanating from headquarters were copied in books of blank pages, of varying size, minus all indexing, devoid of line spacing, and classified only as to personal or official correspondence. As the war continued the volume of headquarters correspondence increased to enormous proportions, making this letter book method hopelessly inadequate. Shortly after Tilghman joined the staff, this procedure was discarded; and letters written thereafter were preserved in their tentative or corrected drafts, or copies were folded and filed away in special chests entrusted to the commander in chief's guard.[20]

Washington's constant complaint was that he was inundated with paperwork. "At present my time is so taken up at my desk, that I am obliged to neglect many other essential parts of my duties; it is absolutely necessary . . . for me to have persons that can think for me, as well as execute orders." As an acknowledged leader of a nation that did not yet exist, he was forced to deal not only with the military aspects of the war but with an often quibbling and divided congress. Consequently, he had to rely on Tilghman and other trusted aides to produce the reams of essential, clearly written, not to say elegantly styled, material that brought to bear the authority of his signature and office on a myriad of matters ranging from grand military strategy and politics to the smaller but no less troublesome ones of officers' promotions, billets and supply, arrearage in troop pay, and expiring terms of enlistment.

Tilghman's service of seven years (the longest of all the aides) in closest association with Washington was to have a profound effect upon both men. Although eleven years younger than Washington, Tilghman brought to his office a heightened maturity which Washington found indispensable. With Washington in battle, bivouac, or camp—dispatching orders, preparing reports, and corresponding, under the general's direction, with Congressional leaders and all commanders—he became his alter ego. In a letter to his father written in this winter of 1776-77, Tilghman spoke of Washington's work load by saying, "Indeed the Weight of the whole War may justly be said to lay upon his Shoulders,"[21] and later,

> I have the satisfaction of feeling that I have contributed largely by my personal application to the Cause in which I am engaged and which I am certain will end in the Freedom of this Country which I hope to see a happy and settled one. If it pleases God to spare the life of the honestest Man that I believe ever adorned human Nature I have no doubt of it. I think I know the Sentiments of his [Washington's] heart and in property and Adversity I never knew him to utter a Wish or drop an expression that did not tend to the good of his Country regardless of his own Interest.[22]

In 1783, when all but the Last Hurrah was over, Washington would write to Tilghman,

> I receive with great sensibility and pleasure your assurance of affection. There are but few men in the world to whom I am more attached by inclination than I am to you.[23]

Three months later another letter from Washington expressed his sentiments no less strongly.

> It has been happy for me, always to have Gentlemen about me willing to share my trouble, and help me out of difficulties. To none of these can I ascribe a greater share of merit than to you.[24]

Washington, however, did not sit quietly at Morristown. Even though his army was weak and poorly clad, he sent out detachments to harass the British with such success that by 1 March not a British or Hessian soldier remained on Jersey soil, except at New Brunswick and Amboy. His whole force fit for duty at Morristown was now about eight thousand men, all from provinces south of the Hudson, forming five divisions of two brigades each, under Major Generals Greene, Stephen, Sullivan, Lincoln, and Stirling.[25] Colonel Henry Knox, the artillery commander, had been made a brigadier-general by Congress sitting at Baltimore. (Congress had fled to Baltimore on the rapid approach of the British to Philadelphia. By late February, heartened by the victories at Trenton and Princeton, it returned to Philadelphia.)

Meanwhile life in and about Morristown became smoother, and morale in the army improved tremendously. Old formations stayed on, and Washington's forces swelled rather than shrank, augmented largely by fresh troops from Maryland, which raised five full regiments of infantry in addition to the two which she already had in the field. There was room even for the amenities, and into the New Jersey hill town came Martha Washington. Her arrival was the signal for the wives of other ranking officers to join their husbands as she began entertaining quietly for visiting diplomats and other dignitaries. If a review or parade was held Tilghman, Hamilton, Laurens, and the other aides would turn out in their best dress uniforms of blue and buff with a double line of flat gilt buttons, nine to a side, gold epaulets, corded twill waistcoats, split-fall breeches, white gloves, hair powdered and combed, and boots with silver spurs.

"Colonel Tilghman [is] a modest, worthy man who from his attachment to the General voluntarily lives in his Family and acts in any capacity that is uppermost without fee or reward," wrote Mrs. Theodorick Bland, a sister-in-law of Mrs. Washington's, in a letter to Mrs. Fanny Randolph after a visit to Morristown in May 1777. She thought Alexander Hamilton "a sensible, genteel, polite young fellow, a West Indian," Colonel John Fitzgerald, "an agreeable, broad-shouldered Irishman," Colonel George Johnston "witty at everybody's expense," but not able to take a joke on himself, and Captain Caleb Gibbs, "a good-natured Yankee who makes a thousand blunders in the Yankee style and keeps the dinner table in constant laughter." They were all, despite Gibbs's blunders, "polite, social gentlemen who make the day pass with a great deal of satisfaction to the visitors."[26]

The commander in chief's guards, sometimes referred to as the Life Guards, were under Gibbs's command. In April 1777, as a result of a spying episode in Morristown, there was general concern that the guard had to be strengthened. Washington felt himself safe among Virginians, and so a levy was made against each Virginia regiment in winter quarters there for four men, all five feet ten or close to it. They were to be, "Sober, Young, Active and well made."[27] Then, oddly enough, this picked body of southerners was put under the command of a Yankee—Gibbs being from Massachusetts.

This was the season too when James Tilghman's diametrically opposed views on the propriety of the American cause brought forth his son's strongest criticism, although Tench never wavered in his loyalty and devotion to his father. After Tench had joined Washington's Official Family this filial tie to an acknowledged Loyalist on the part of his aide-de-camp often brought the open admonition to the commander in chief that he risked disaster. Washington, however, knowing his man well, remained resolute, and his trust in Tilghman finally put an end to such talk. This trust was not betrayed. From headquarters at Morristown on 21 April, 1777, Tench wrote frankly to his father regarding their divergent views:

> I late last night rec^d yours of the 21st. The Contents really make me exceedingly unhappy as I find myself unable to agree with you in Sentiment upon the present Measures . . . I will say nothing upon the score of Politics because it is a subject that ought not at this time be discussed upon Paper. I wish it might be dropped in all future letters between us, because they may probably fall into other hands than mine. I know that your sentiments proceed from a Conviction that present measures are wrong and therefore hurtful to the Country, to the welfare of which I am sure you are at heart a sincere good Wisher, but all will not make the same allowance . . .[28]

It was 28 May 1777 before Washington broke camp to move out of his strong position in the Short Hills of New Jersey and into the Middlebrook Valley. By skillful maneuvering he was able to evade efforts by British General Sir William Howe to bring on a major engagement before ready to commit his revitalized army. In the waning days of summer, however, it became evident that Sir William, who had sailed from New York on 23 July with 15,000 troops and who disembarked at Head of Elk, Maryland, on 25 August was advancing on Philadelphia, and a battle was inevitable. Washington immediately set forth through the city to bar the way. On 24 August, in fine weather, patriotic Philadelphians turned out en masse along Front and Chestnut streets to see the commander in chief lead his men to the south to confront Howe, Cornwallis, and Von Knyphausen. The sidewalks, still wet from a recent rain, were jammed. There was a small advance guard and then Washington, dressed in his finest blue and buff and mounted on his best horse. He ws flanked by his Chief of Artillery, General Knox, Tench Tilghman, the recently arrived young Marquis de Lafayette on his way to his first engagement in North America, and other aides.

The Philadelphia Light Horse came next, then George Baylor's and Theodorick Bland's Virginia dragoons. Nathanael Greene led his division twelve abreast, followed by William Alexander, the Earl of Stirling.[29] "Mad" Anthony Wayne, who once said to his chief, "If you'll plan it, I'll storm hell itself," was a familiar figure, coming as he did from nearby Chester County. Major General Benjamin Lincoln was there, as was that pastor-turned-soldier, Peter Muhlenberg, leading his brigade with massed fifes and drums, giving cadence to the steady tramp of the infantry, interrupted with overtones from the ceaseless creaking of wheeled artillery. For more than two hours the main American army passed through the cobbled streets. Philadelphia and other east coast cities would see these citizen soldiers, who were beginning to create the impression of a genuine fighting force, time and time again.

On the morning of 11 September, at Brandywine Creek, the battle was joined. The morning began in fog but ripened to a noon of blazing heat. The wily Howe, using his favorite flanking technique, encircled the Americans to the north and in a fierce and many-sized fight forced the day. Among the American wounded was Lafayette who took a bullet in the leg. It was a decisive victory for the British but unlike Long Island found the Americans ready and able to fight again. The way to Philadelphia had been laid open, however, and on 18 September the Continental Congress decamped, moving west to Lancaster and then on to York. On 26 September Cornwallis led British and Hessian Grenadiers into the city while the remainder of Howe's command remained encamped on the outskirts, at Germantown.

An uneasy conquest for the British, the loss of Philadelphia was much more easily sustained by the Americans than had been anticipated. Congress was still functioning, and the army was still intact. Within a matter of days Washington, reinforced and undeterred, boldly decided to attack the main British force massed around Germantown. On the morning of 4 October he launched his blow, a huge pincers movement and probably too complex. Because of the complicated plan and another fog much worse than that encountered at Brandywine, the Americans were again repulsed. The battle, however, was an American success pyschologically with Washington's boldness in defeat surprising the British and impressing the French.[30] Cliveden, the country home of Chief Justice Benjamin Chew became the strategic center of the battle and was badly damaged. Woodwork was splintered, plaster shattered, and stonework crumbled. Marble statues adorning the lawn and stone lions imported from Italy and presented to the second Mrs. Chew by a relative[31] were sadly battered by the balls of the American six-pounders. Headless, armless or legless they still remain in place, mute witnesses to the havoc of battle.

Two days after the encounter, in which his assigned role included reconnaissance with General Nathanael Greene,[32] Tilghman described the battle of Germantown to his father:

I have the pleasure to inform you that I am well after a pretty severe action at Germantown on the 4th. The attack was general, and had not the excessive fogginess of the morning hindered our Wings from knowing of the Success of each other it would have ended in a total defeat of Genl. Howe. When he came into the field he found matters so far against him that orders were given to make Chester the place of Rendezvous in a Retreat. The Attack was made upon two Quarters at day break. The right wing commanded by his Excellency in person entered Germantown by the way of Chestnut Hill, the first Guard was at Mount Airey, this was carried without much resistance, and the light Infantry and one or two Brigades being posted near, the action soon became severe, we pushed them by degrees from Mount Airey below the lane that leads by the Colledge. A party took post in Cliffdon House and did us considerable mischief from the Windows, the House must be much damaged by our Cannon shot of which a vast number was fired thro' it. Genl Green who commanded our left Wing attacked nearly at the same time that we did, he surprised a Camp near the Market House and drove the Enemy across the town some towards Shippens Common and others down as far as Logans Hill. Had the day been clear everything was in our Hands, but one of our Columns pressing down were mistaken in the fog by part of Gen[l] Greens for the Enemy, while ours mistook his Troops in the same Manner. This unluckily made both halt, and quickly occasioned both to retreat, without any real Cause. The Enemy, taking advantage of the cessation of the pursuit, rallied their men and got up a Reinforcement of the Hessian and British Grenadiers who had been in Philad[a]. We had brought no more ammunition than the men could carry in their Cartouches and that being nearly expended and the Men fatigued with marching all Night we returned to our Camp. Gen[l]. Nash of the North Carolinians was the only Officer of distinction killed. Col[o]. Stone is wounded in the leg and many other Officers, two of the Generals family are wounded. M[r]. Lawrens of Carolina slightly and M[r]. Smith of Virginia his leg broke. The Maryland Regulars bore the brunt of the day, they behaved amazingly well and suffered more in proportion than the others. We are informed the Enemy had one Gen[l]. Officer[32] killed and one wounded. Col[o]. Walcot and Col[o]. Bird it is said were also killed. They attribute their salvation to the Bravery of Lord Cornwallis, who rallied their Men and brought a Reinforcement. Gen[l]. Howe was much blamed by the Army, who said they had been amused by him with an account that the Rebel Army was dispersed. We shall be reinforced by near four thousand Men in two or three days from the Northern Army and from Virginia. We shall then try the fortune of another day.[33]

Following the fight at Germantown the British, dependent on supplies shipped up the Delaware River past American held forts, were virtually bottled up by Washington in Philadelphia. At a heavy cost—two ships and three badly mauled Hessian battalions—free passage of the river was obtained by the British by the middle of November when Fort Mifflin, the last of the American outposts, fell after a six-day bombardment.

But good news for the Americans was not long in coming. A British force under Lieut. General John ("Gentleman Johnny") Burgoyne which had invaded New York in June had been decisively defeated, surrendering to General Gates at Saratoga on 17 October 1777, a major turning point in the war. Not only did it assure French participation on the American side, but also in large measure gave birth to the Conway Cabal, considered at that time a conspiracy against Washington. It so enraged Tilghman, Lafayette, Brigadier General John Cadwalader, and other Washington supporters that Cadwalader called Conway out and shot him in the mouth in a resulting duel.

Meanwhile Howe, with characteristic lack of aggression, decided to enjoy the comforts of Philadelphia and await the coming of spring. While unclear instructions from Lord George Germain, Britain's Secretary of State for the American Department, may have been partly responsible for confusion in the field, Howe had to bear much of the blame for the collapse of the optimism felt by the British in early 1777. His obsession with the importance of Philadelphia and his misjudging of time factors led him to leave Burgoyne to his own resources—a fatal blow to Britain's grand scheme for crushing the rebellion. Devoted to pleasure, to gambling, and to his mistresses—one of them the beautiful Mrs. Joshua Loring, whose husband as British Commissary of Prisoners is said to have prospered by feeding the dead and starving the living[34]—Howe inspired one British wag to write:

> Awake, arouse, Sir Billy,
> There's forage in the plain.
> Leave your little filly,
> And open the campaign.[35]

Later the *Battle of The Kegs*, a broadside published sometime after 1800 by Nathaniel Coverly, Jr., lampooned him even further. Sung to the tune of "Yankee Doodle," one verse went as follows:

> Sir William he, snug as a flea,
> Lay all this time a-snoring
> Nor dreamt of harm, as he lay warm
> In bed with Mrs. L(orin)g.
> Now in affright, he starts upright,
> Awak'd by such a clatter;
> He rubs both eyes, and boldly cries,
> "For God's sake what the matter?"[36]

In Philadelphia the winter social season of 1777-78 was one of the liveliest in memory, so much so in fact that Benjamin Franklin was led to state that Howe had not so much taken Philadelphia as Philadelphia had taken Howe.[37]

In stark contrast to the gaiety enjoyed by the aristocrats of the British officer corps, snug in Philadelphia, that winter was to be the Gethsemane of the American Revolution for Washington and his men. It was a winter, as the late Christopher Ward wrote, "whose story has been told and told again, but not once too often."[38] As it closed in, Washington conferred with his generals concerning a proper site for a winter encampment. Two principal factors would govern their decision: a capacity to supply the army with the food and clothing it so desperately needed and an ability to observe enemy movements from a strong defensive position. Valley Forge, seven miles above Swede's Ford, the site of present Norristown, and on the opposite bank, was chosen. It was a natural defensive position which Howe dared not bypass, as to do so would expose his flank and put the Americans between him and Philadelphia. A light snow added to the discomfort of 19 December 1777, already a cold and windy day, as the Continental Army, ill clad, ill equipped, and hungry, staggered into winter quarters. With no protection against the cold except worn and tattered tents and with blankets practically nonexistent, almost incredible hardship lay ahead.

At this point food and shelter for the army were Washington's most vital concerns. Despite constant pleas to Congress for supplies, it seemed at times that starvation and an appalling lack of clothes of any sort might accomplish what crack British and Hessian had failed to do—destroy the main American fighting force. From sheer necessity Washington was reduced simply to seizing supplies and sending out foraging parties to find what they could. While some nine hundred log huts, each designed to accommodate twelve men, were being hewn out of groves of standing trees by details of axmen, Nathanael Greene was put in charge of all foraging operatons. From the staff, augmented temporarily by George Lewis,[39] Washington's nephew, Tilghman was pressed into service as a *de facto* quartermaster, along with "Light Horse Harry" Lee, captain of a company of Virginia dragoons. Lee was sent into Delaware and adjacent parts of Maryland and Tilghman into New Jersey. Within a few days the first of a series of recurring hunger crises was averted by the great exertions of these men. Greene instructed his crews to "search the country through and through" and to seize every animal fit for slaughter. Lee found large droves of cattle that had been fattening in the marsh meadows of the Delaware River for the British army and Tilghman was able to collect abundantly in

New Jersey.[40] If distance or a lack of wagons prevented the bringing in of hay, corn, or other provisions the provisions or crops were to be burned, for the object secondary to feeding the Americans was to starve the British. The motto was "Forage the country naked!"[41] In all instances receipts were given, with a promise to pay later.

By January the huts had been completed, and food, while still in short supply, was not the matter of life and death it had been a scant few weeks earlier. When the defensive lines were completed, laid out in accordance with Washington's precise instructions, it was apparent that the Valley Forge position was one of unusual strength, and Howe was probably wise not to assail it.

During the winter of 1777-78 some of the most notable events of the Revolution occurred. These included the Conway Cabal, which sought to oust Washington from the high command and replace him with the less competent Gates; the return to duty from British prisoner-of-war status of General Charles Lee; the appearance of the bogus-Baron von Steuben (a godsend to the American cause despite his fabricated background); the gradual rise of Washington to heroic proportions and the dawning recognition of his true worth by Congress, the people, and the army; and, finally—and most significant of all—the welcome news that France had recognized the independence of the colonies and would actively intervene with money, arms, and men.

The malcontents of the Cabal had begun their drumming earlier; by the beginning of the winter of Valley Forge uneasiness and tension raced through the ranks like the virus of an unknown disease. The contrast between the brilliant victory at Saratoga, credited to Gates but in fact belonging to Arnold and Morgan, and the stalemate achieved by Washington in the Pennsylvania campaign persuaded some citizens, both in and out of Congress, that the time for a change in the high command was at hand. A malignant campaign followed to detract from Washington. Gates, an Englishman and the godson of Horace Walpole, had, by successful intrigue, gained powerful support in Congress. Indeed, he considered himself independent of Washington and reported directly to Congress. Furthermore, Washington's popularity and his insistence upon a large army of regular troops was seen by the pro-Gates congressional coterie, largely composed of New Englanders, as containing the seeds of a military dictatorship; Gates on the other hand was seen by this faction as more amenable to acceptance of Congressional direction of the war and was known to place a higher value on militia troops than did Washington and influential members of his staff. As an example of this "headquarters" view Tilghman had written to Robert Morris on 29 March 1777, "I congratulate you on the late arrival of arms, a few thousand of which I hope soon to see upon the Shoulders of Men, not Shadows, for such are Militia and all temporary Troops."[42] Consequently, Gates felt reasonably sure of support from Congress.

Thomas Conway, an Irish soldier of fortune, was the *grand chef* who provided the principal ingredient for this unsavory brew and its most troublesome member. An Irish Catholic, he had been taken to France at the age of six and educated there. At sixteen he entered the French Army and after a somewhat checkered career became a major in the Anjou Regiment in 1775.[43] Having received permission to go to America he reached Morristown on 8 May 1777, carrying a letter of introduction from Silas Deane. Washington, favorably impressed, sent him to Congress with a strong letter of recommendation. Five days later, acting on Washington's unusually commendatory remarks, he was made a brigadier general and assigned to Sullivan's Division. Following Brandwine and Germantown he had created in Sullivan's mind "a respect that amounted almost to awe."[44] Blocked in his extravagant demands for further promotion Conway turned for redress to Gates, the star in the north. Although clearly guilty, Conway was not the chief conspirator, but it is after him that the plot became known—perhaps the result of alliteration. Beveridge, in his highly regarded *Life of John Marshall*, summed it up well.

> Washington was the Revolution. The wise and learned of every land agree on this . . . Yet intrigue and calumny sought his ruin. From Burgoyne's surrender on through the darkest days of Valley Forge, the Conway Cabal shot its filaments through Congress, society, and even fastened upon the army itself. Gates was its figurehead, Conway its brain, Wilkinson its tool, Rush its amanuensis, and certain members of Congress its accessories before the fact.[45]

Dr. Benjamin Rush, medical director of the Middle Department, was among Washington's severest critics. Angry with Washington over conditions in army hospitals, he wrote to John Adams, after learning of Gates's victory over Burgoyne,

> I am more convinced than ever of the necessity of discipline and system in the management of our affairs. I have heard several officers who have served under General Gates compare his army to a well-regulated family. The same gentlemen have compared General Washington's imitation of an army to a uniformed mob. Look at the character of both! The one at the pinnacle of military glory, exulting in the success of schemes planned with wisdom and executed with vigor and bravery . . . See the other outgeneraled and twice beaten . . . forced to give up a city the capital of a state, and after all outwitted by the same army in a retreat. If our Congress can witness these things with composure and suffer them to pass without an inquiry, I shall think we have not shook off monarchial prejudices.[46]

Those who were close to Washington, i.e., Tilghman, Lafayette, Hamilton, Knox, Wayne, Greene, Cadwalader, and other loyal subordinates rallied to his immediate support. In a remarkable display of perception Tilghman had written to his father, six months to the day before Burgoyne's surrender at Saratoga, to refute certain criticism of Washington but even then alluding to the existence of a faction against him. From headquarters at Morristown he wrote,

> I do not think it yet too late to over set this Cabal, for so it is properly called, but it can only be done by Men of Sense and Rank stepping forth determined to give opposition to the power at present hanging over with undoubted intent to first subjugate and then Rule with a Rod of Iron.[47]

After the storm broke, Tilghman was quick to make his feelings known, equating disloyalty to Washington with disloyalty to the Revolution. A legacy of correspondence on the subject, as well as an appraisal by Charles Carroll of Carrollton of Tilghman's acknowledged help in frustrating the goals of the Cabal show clearly that his role was a major one. (See Appendix I.)

Thomas Scharf, in his *History of Maryland*, states that the Conway Cabal was "resisted and ultimately defeated by Charles

Carroll of Carrollton, Morris and Duer."[48] On 7 November 1777 the Board of War had been reorganized with Gates as President and Conway, newly promoted to Major General, as Inspector General. Mifflin, who had resigned that very day as Quartermaster General, was added, giving a decided edge to the anti-Washington faction. Washington's friends in Congress were able to have loyal Richard Peters retained as Secretary, but Carroll, an earlier member, and known as a supporter of Washington, was pointedly left off.[49] Soon a Committee of Inquiry was appointed to look into a reformation of the army in general and conditions at Valley Forge in particular. It was a foregone conclusion that the inquiry would be biased, with the dismissal of Washington as commander in chief as its ultimate purpose. After some bitter infighting the pro-Washington group managed to get Gouverneur Morris and Carroll appointed to the Committee to offset the majority opposed to Washington.[50]

It was a real victory for the Washington party and the single most important factor in the ultimate collapse of the Conway Cabal.[51] The success of these minority members was due largely to Carroll's efforts who, with Duer and other members of the committee, went to Valley Forge shortly after he and Duer were appointed on 20 January 1778.[52] The committee held its sessions at Moore Hall, the house of William Moore, about two and a half miles north of Washington's headquarters.[53] Carroll worked closely with Tilghman during this period, saying later of his role:

> Don't forget Tilghman. Washington was so straightforward and earnest that he never suspected treachery. But Tilghman was alert, always watchful, and the most wise of them could not circumvent him.[54]

Francis Dana, the committee chairman, was a reasonable man and big enough to admit his earlier misjudgment of Washington. Carroll and Morris were able to swing a majority to their way of thinking by clearly demonstrating that Congress, lacking any semblance of foresight, had saddled Washington with short-enlistment troops and a policy of using militia which handicapped the army for years and that more recently, mismanagement by the Quartermaster General and in the Commissary Department had been responsible for the suffering at Valley Forge. The final report, endorsed by Dana and submitted on 28 January,[55] not only cleared Washington of any misconduct but also placed the blame for conditions at Valley Forge where they belonged— squarely on the shoulders of Thomas Mifflin, the former Quartermaster General, present member of the Board of War and linchpin of the Cabal.[56]

By March it was clear that Washington's position as commander in chief was assured. The general rush of the alleged conspirators to disavow any part in a Cabal against him was accompanied by genuine demonstrations of Congressional support, as expressed by Eliphalet Dyer in his letter to William Williams of 10 March 1778: "Be assured there is not the most distant thought of removing Genll. Washington, nor even an expression in Congress looking that way."[57] Soon after, the Cabal collapsed completely, due largely to Washington's ethical conduct as contrasted to Gates's poor showing in other plans handed him by the Board of War, and, of course, to the findings of the committee at Valley Forge.[58]

Conway resigned on 22 April 1778, bringing to an end his short and unhappy tenure in the American army. On the following Fourth of July he fought a duel with General Cadwalader in which Cadwalader wounded him painfully but not mortally.[59] After addressing an apology to Washington Conway returned to France and resumed his military career. The French Revolution, however, swept him into exile where he died about 1800.[60]

The Hottest Day . . . and the Sound of an Uncertain Trumpet

My God, General Lee, what are you about?
—Washington to General Charles Lee
at the Battle of Monmouth

Washington's army was as much invigorated by the stunning news that France had recognized the independence of the American colonies and would join them in their war against England as it was by the coming of the spring of 1778. On 6 May shortly after a messenger from King Louis XVI's court had reached Valley Forge, having arrived at Falmouth Harbor (now Portland, Maine) on board the French frigate *La Sensible* which successfully eluded British patrols in the North Atlantic, von Steuben marshalled the troops in a great review, displaying new uniforms and new precision in drill. Drums rolled under a gentle springtime sun, fifes piped, and the artillery roared out a salute such as had followed no victory on the battlefield. Washington ordered rum all around, and the rest of the day was given over to boisterous celebration.

On 20 May Major General Charles Lee had returned to the army from prisoner of war status. In New York, where he had been held, he had enjoyed all the amenities, including his hounds and his bottle, and apparently was on the point of resuming his allegiance to George III when he was exchanged for several British officers in American hands. The Battle of Monmouth, scarcely more than a month away, was the first in which he was to participate after Washington arranged his exchange. In retrospect it is a pity that Washington bothered. Few catastrophes could have been greater than Lee's return. Despite his knowledge that Lee had been one of the early conspirators against him,

Washington—with Congressional support behind him for the first time since the beginning of the war—felt that he was now in full control. Consequently, he accepted Lee for what he in fact was, second-in-command.

Charles Lee was British-born, his father being the colonel of an Irish regiment. Experienced, he had fought all over Europe and with the Russians against the Turks. "Ounewaterike," or "Boiling Water," the Mohawks called him because of his hot temper. He was obscene, profane, and at times impious in his conversation. Wherever he went he took with him a pack of hounds whose ears he liked to stroke. He had been retired from the British army on half pay and was living in western Virginia when the Revolution broke out. He volunteered his services, and Congress, impressed by his self-proclaimed record, had made him a major general, third in rank to Washington, after Artemus Ward. Ward's resignation due to ill health, after the evacuation of Boston, led to Lee's promotion to second-in-command, next in rank to the commander in chief.

Except for a bisecting road and a rail line, the battlefield at Monmouth Courthouse (Freehold, New Jersey) is just as it was on 28 June 1778 when Washington's troops, fresh out of Valley Forge and whipped into an effective fighting force by von Steuben's unrelenting uniform system of training, struck at Clinton's army as it withdrew from Philadelphia to New York. Lafayette was entrusted with the advance column, as Lee declined the command, having stated his opposition to the planned movement. The gradual reinforcement of the advance column to nearly 6,000 men, however, convinced Lee that if one-half of the army should move upon the enemy with the senior major general left behind, his honor would be compromised. Still the malcontent, Lee pressed Washington to return the command to him. After due consideration and with apologies to Lafayette, Washington decided in Lee's favor. After all, there was something to his argument. This decision was made despite the fact that the original plan of attack—to strike the British line obliquely while it was extended for nearly twelve miles with its baggage with the accumulating force of successive American divisions—was still to be carried out despite Lee's opposition to it.

Lee's preparations were at best sketchy; he had apparently made no provision whatsoever for retreat. Foreseeing only a limited action, Clinton's counterattack caught him totally by surprise. Moreover, although knowing that Washington with the main army was to his rear in a supporting position, he made no effort to inform Washington of the developing trouble. The retreat, which became confused through conflicting orders and rumors, was general but not a panic. Learning from a straggler that Lee was retreating, Washington—with Tilghman by his side—rode off in search of him.[1] Now the scene was becoming even more confused. Lee's men were marching to the rear through an area where Washington's men, close on their heels and knowing nothing of Lee's orders, were still advancing. Meanwhile a dumbfounded commander in chief, anger mounting, was still looking for Lee and reliable information. He soon had it from Colonel Israel Shreve, commanding the Second New Jersey Line. Far from being frightened by the British, Shreve showed some amusement when asked why he was retiring. Shreve smiled and "in a very significant manner"[2] answered that he did not know the reason but that he had been ordered to retreat and he was.

After ordering Shreve to remain where he was, Washington and Tilghman spurred their horses forward. Lee came back with the last retreating unit. Riding up to him, Washington angrily demanded "with some degree of astonishment"[3] the reason for the retreat. Lee, temporarily deserted by his boring capacity to talk endlessly, could only answer, "Sir? Sir?" After Washington repeated the question, Lee answered that due to confused intelligence and the fact that his own orders had not been properly obeyed, prudence required a withdrawal. Colonel Aaron Ogden of the New Jersey Line is reputed to have uttered a "strong expletive" and then said, "By God, they are flying from a shadow."[4]

There are many versions of this dramatic meeting on the field of battle between the two generals, but all who saw it agree that Washington was enraged and that Lee seemed confused and embarrassed. When General Charles Scott, an eyewitness, was later asked if he ever heard Washington swear, he answered,

> Yes, once, it was at Monmouth, on a day that would have made any man swear. Yes sir, he swore on that day till the leaves shook on the trees, charmingly, delightfully. Never did I enjoy such swearing, before or since. Sir, on that memorable day he swore like an angel from Heaven.[5]

Another soldier said that Washington shouted, "My God, General Lee, what are you about?"[6]

Fortunately, Washington was able to control his anger. Tilghman, who had been listening intently, spoke up to say that Lieut. Colonel David Rhea of the Fourth New Jersey had passed a few minutes previously and had said that he knew the terrain well and that if he could be of assistance he would be glad to help. Washington reacted immediately. "Get him!" were his orders to Tilghman.[7] When Tilghman returned with Colonel Rhea, certainly the most useful guide ever to stand on a field of battle, the latter told Washington that the ground where they stood was part of a long elevation, protected in the front by a swamp. In intense heat and depressing humidity there began a period of intense activity as Washington began to juggle his men in a new defense line, part of which ran behind a hedgerow. Livingston and Varnum formed their regiments here, where the principal action was to be, as Washington—after an urgent call for artillery—dispatched Tilghman and General Cadwalader to reconnoiter the left.[8]

And now the real Battle of Monmouth began—the longest and perhaps the most spectacular of the war. It lasted all day in ninety-two-degree heat—so intense that men fell dead from it alone. It was a duel between George Washington and Sir Henry Clinton, both excellent strategists and utterly fearless. Each side had about 12,000 troops in the field. The British commanders under Clinton were Cornwallis, Knyphausen, Monckton, and Simcoe while the Americans were led by Lafayette, Stirling, Greene, Wayne, Knox, Maxwell, Jackson, Morgan, Woodford, Dickinson, and Stewart, in addition to those already mentioned. Over the heads of those in the front lines an artillery duel, the heaviest ever known in America, was conducted on both sides with consummate skill. The Chevalier de Mauduit du Plessix, second-in-command to Major General Knox, laid down an enfilading fire that shattered every musket in the advancing British line.[9] "Mad Anthony" Wayne and his men covered themselves with glory, standing up to successive bayonet charges by the Black Watch and the Grenadiers, beating them off in hand-to-hand fighting. Lieut. Colonel Henry Monckton, brother of Lord Galway, twice repulsed by Wayne, met his death on a third charge after exhorting his men to follow him. He lies buried today in the churchyard at Monmouth, under a monument to his memory.[10]

By late afternoon Clinton, realizing that his men had fought to a state of total exhaustion, surrendered the field to Washington. The upshot of the matter was that Monmouth was a drawn battle instead of the decisive American victory it might otherwise have been. In the face of general criticism from his fellow officers Lee wrote Washington an impudent letter; Washington immediately called his bluff and had him put under arrest. On 4 July 1778 a court-martial was convened to try him for disrespect to Washington, for disobedience of orders, and for making an unnecessary and disorderly retreat. Among the witnesses who appeared against Lee were Tilghman, James McHenry, John Brooks, and John Francis Mercer. Hamilton and Laurens also testified. The late Douglas Southall Freeman in his monumental biography of Washington pays special tribute to Tilghman's testimony at the court-martial:

> In general, Tilghman has been accepted here as the witness most apt to be accurate where a conflict of testimony is found. He was a man of high character, as indeed were all of the witnesses; he had a sharp sense of justice; he must have been at Washington's elbow during the colloquy; and he knew both Washington and Charles Lee well enough to understand what they said and, probably, what they meant. As a young man of ability he was apt to remember clearly all that occurred.[11]

Tilghman's complete testimony is set forth below:

> Q. Did you see General Lee on the 28th of June?
> A. On the 28th of June, as General Washington was advancing with the main body of the army between English-Town and Freehold Meeting, he met with Colonel Hamilton, who told him he had come from our advance corps, and that he imagined from the situation he had left our van and the enemy's rear in, they would soon engage. He advised General Washington to throw the right wing of the army round by the right, and to follow with the left wing directly in General Lee's rear to support him. He gave reasons for this disposition, which were thought good. While order was giving to make the disposition, a countryman rode up,[12] on being asked where he came from, he said, from towards the Courthouse; he was asked what news? he said he heard our people were retreating, and that that man, pointing to a fifer, had told

him so. General Washington not believing the thing to be true, ordered the fifer under the care of a light-horseman, to prevent his spreading a report and damping the troops who were advancing; but that certain intelligence might be gained, Colonel Fitzgerald and Harrison were sent forward; General Washington then rode on himself, and between Freehold Meeting and the morass that parted the two armies during the day, he met regiments - Colonel Grayson's and Colonel Patton's; Captain Moore, I think, was at the head of Grayson's regiment; upon the General asking him where these troops were going, the officer at first said they had been very much fatigued, and had been ordered off to refresh themselves; he then said the particular duty they had been upon was to secure two pieces of cannon which had been left upon some part of the field in danger. The General then desired him to take his men into a wood near at hand, as they were exceedingly heated and fatigued, and to draw some rum for them, and to keep them from struggling. The General asked the officer who led, if the whole advanced corps were retreating? He said he believed they were.

He had scarcely said these words when we saw the heads of several columns of our advanced corps beginning to appear. The first officers the General met were Colonel Shreve and Lieutenant-Colonel Rhea, at the head of Colonel Shreve's regiment. The General was exceedingly alarmed, finding the advance corps falling back upon the main body, without the least notice given to him, and asked Colonel Shreve the meaning of the retreat; Colonel Shreve answered in a very significant manner, smiling, that he did not know, but that he had retreated by order, he did not say by whose order. Lieutenant-Colonel Rhea told me that he had been on that plantation, knew the ground exceedingly well, and that it was good ground, and that, should General Washington want him, he should be glad to serve him. General Washington desired Colonel Shreve to march his men over the morass, halt them on the hill, and refresh them. Major Howell was in the rear of the regiment; he expressed himself with great warmth at the troops coming off, and said he had never seen the like. At the head of the next column General Lee was himself, when General Washington rode up to him, with some degree of astonishment, and asked him what was the meaning of this? General Lee answered, as Dr. M'Henry has mentioned, Sir, Sir. I took it that General Lee did not hear the question distinctly. Upon General Washington's repeating the question, General Lee answered, that from a variety of contradictory intelligence, and that from his orders not being obeyed, matters were thrown into confusion, and that he did not chuse to beard the British army with troops in such a situation. He said that besides, the thing was against his own opinion. General Washington answered, whatever his opinion might have been, he expected his orders would have been obeyed, and then rode on towards the rear of the retreating troops. When General Lee mentioned that his orders had been disobeyed, he mentioned General Scott particularly; he said General Scott had quitted a very advantageous position without orders. General Washington had not rode many yards forwards from General Lee, when he met Lieutenant-Colonel Harrison, his secretary, who told him that the British army were within fifteen minutes march of that place, which was the first intelligence he received of their pushing on so briskly.

The General seemed at a loss, as he was on a piece of ground entirely strange to him; I told him what Lieutenant-Colonel Rhea had told me of his knowing the ground; he desired me to go and bring him as quick as possible to him; to desire Colonel Shreve to form his regiment on the hill, which was afterwards our main position, and, I think, to get the two small regiments of Grayson's and Patton's there also, that the line might be formed as quick as possible. I conducted Lieutenant-Colonel Rhea back to the General; when I got there, I saw Colonel Livingston beginning to form his regiment along the hedge-row, where the principal scene of action was that day. Our retreating columns took up a great piece of ground, and there was one upon our left so far that the General thought it was a column of British troops endeavoring to turn our left; he desired General Cadwallader and myself to ride over and see what troops they were. I then left the hill, and did not see General Lee afterwards.

Q. Were our troops that you saw retiring, retiring in order or disorder, and in what particular manner?

A. The two regiments we first met, were in some disorder, the men were exceedingly heated, and so distressed with fatigue they could scarcely stand; the others, so far as their keeping their ranks in battalion or brigade, I think were in tolerable good order; but as to columns respectively in great confusion, as I am convinced a line could not have been formed of them in that situation. They neither kept proper intervals, nor were the heads of columns ranged.

General Lee's question. Was there a defile in the rear?

A. There was.[13]

On 12 August the court found Lee guilty on all three counts. So far as the Americans were concerned, General Lee was through. Gathering up his hounds he went back to his Virginia farm. He died on a trip to Philadelphia on 2 October 1782.

Monmouth was the war's last major battle in the north. On 29 June, the day after, Tilghman—at Washington's direction and for his signature—wrote to the President of Congress to say

> We forced the Enemy from the Field and encamped on the Ground . . . I cannot at this time go into a detail of Matters. When opportunity will permit I shall take the liberty of transmitting Congress a more particular account of the proceedings of the day.[14]

General von Steuben's iron discipline, instilled into the once ragged Americans on the barren parade grounds of Valley Forge, had paid off handsomely. By July the British were back in New York, and Washington and his army were at White Plains to keep an eye on them.

In the remaining days of 1778 only minor conflicts occurred in the north, and by 11 December Washington and the main army took up winter quarters at Middlebrook, New Jersey, a position from which Washington could move quickly south to the Delaware in case the British attacked Philadelphia in a surprise move. Just before Christmas, at the invitation of Congress, the commander in chief took off for Philadelphia for a six-weeks' stay, accompanied by Tilghman, Laurens, Hamilton, and by General Nathanael Greene. Lord Stirling was left in command at Middlebrook. Mrs. Washington had joined the General as the guest of Henry Laurens, the President of Congress, and it was a season of gaiety for most. In a letter from Philadelphia on 25 January 1779 to his fellow aide, James McHenry, left behind at Middlebrook, Tilghman's reactions were different. (See Appendix I for text of entire letter.) He wrote:

> . . . I suppose you think we must be, by this time, so wedded to sweet Phila. that it will break our hearts to leave it. Far from it I assure you my Friend. I can speak for myself, and I am pretty certain I can answer for all, when I say that we anxiously wait for the moment that gives us liberty to return to humble Middle Brook. Philada. may answer very well for a man with his pockets well lined, whose pursuit is idleness and dissapation. But to us who are not in the first predicament, and who are not upon the latter errand, it is intolerable.[15]

Already thinking of himself as an American and speaking confidently of independence, Tilghman revealed again the qualities of his character and intellect that endeared him to his friends and made him such a valuable member of Washington's staff.

Following the conferences for which Washington had been summoned, Tench left Philadelphia for Chestertown, Maryland, to visit his family—his first leave since joining Washington two and a half years earlier.

The entrance of the French into the war came as no surprise to Tench. More than a year before the news of the Franco-American Alliance reached Washington's headquarters at Valley Forge Tench had expressed himself forcefully about the significance of this development in a letter to his father.

> A War with France, which you may depend upon is inevitable, must unhorse the present Ministry and all their Connections. France has been wisely weighing the Value of that Commerce which Eng^d. has madly lost. She has had the ablest Heads and hands at Work to find out the annual exports of European Commodities to America and the Value of the imports of America to Europe. She has been taking means to establish the Manufacture of such Goods as America usually took from Great Britain, and is determined to send out those Goods in their own Bottoms guarded by their own Ships of War. I dont expect to see a declaration of War by France, she will pursue the above Measures and if England can sit tamely by and bear the insult — She is lost indeed.[16]

A year later, after the alliance had been signed but before he knew of it, Tench again stated his belief that France would enter the war. "The uncommon preparations by France in the West Indies cannot be for nothing. She has at least 8,000 men in her Islands.[17] Finally, after the fact, he speculated that the British might be forced to move their entire force in North America in order to counter the French threat in the West Indies.

> We are busy preparing to march to the North River. The British Army goes first to New York, ours of course will be near them - Ten Regiments go to Jamaica - perhaps they may be too late - I shall not be surprised if all the Troops leave the Continent to save the Islands. France has ten thousand men there ready to strike. I speak not vaguely. I know it as certainly as I know the Returns of our own Army.[18]

108

Throughout the war there remained the nagging question of his father's politics, an ever present source of concern to Tench. Although relatively quiescent in Chestertown, remnants of rumors of an earlier era attaching James Tilghman to the Loyalist sentiments of Daniel Dulany[19] persisted, as well as recurring evidence of his close association with the Penn family. Nonetheless, Tench rarely missed an opportunity to attempt to alter the course of his father's political views or at least to try to persuade him to take the Oath of Allegiance, obviously aware that it might ameliorate his position as a suspect member of a society becoming more and more convinced of victory in the struggle for independence. In two letters from Valley Forge, written shortly after France had actively entered the war and after the British Commissioners had offered the colonies everything short of independence—an action characterized by Tench as "the last effort to divide"[20]—Tench importuned his father to come to terms with the future. (See Appendix I for these letters as well as a third in which, despite the heavy demands of life at headquarters, Tench discussed at length family problems— brothers, sisters, uncles, and his grandmother on the Francis side all share in his concern.)

Following Monmouth, and well into the spring of 1779, military operations in the north virtually ceased. Both armies lay in their winter quarters until the summer was almost at hand. With other personal considerations temporarily shelved, the marriage of Tench's first cousin Peggy Shippen to General Benedict Arnold, a widower, in that same spring, brought Tench not only a troublesome in-law who was to cause him considerable embarrassment but also one who, by his treasonable conduct, could have dealt the struggling colonies a serious if not fatal blow. Arnold, considered one of Washington's ablest generals prior to his attempt to deliver West Point to the British, arrived in Philadelphia on 19 June 1778, as Military Governor, taking over Howe's old quarters in the Richard Penn house on High (now Market) Street. After his marriage to Peggy Shippen, he and his new bride lived there. It later became the presidential residence for the new nation.

While General Arnold's marriage placed him on the outer fringes only of Tench's family—and a Tory-oriented fringe at that—it is nonetheless true that when attempting to persuade

Washington to give him the West Point command for treasonable purposes, Arnold sought to use Tilghman to his own advantage. Much has been written about Arnold's life and his
attempt to sell out the American cause. Born in Norwich, Connecticut, he came from a well known and prosperous family. He
was the great-grandson—the fourth in succession to bear the
name—of Benedict Arnold (1615-78), the first Governor of
Rhode Island under the Royal Charter of 1663. His father successfully engaged in commerce with the West Indies but took to
the bottle and was generally believed to be dishonest. He died in
poverty, bereft of any sort of reputation or means. Young Benedict had a greater ability but was more corrupt. Although brave,
resourceful, and sensitive, he was also amoral, tempestuous, and
vain. In his youth at Norwich he showed the same depravity he
afterward displayed as a man at West Point. There was a cruel
streak in him and he was a show-off who liked to astonish his
playmates by clinging to the arms of a mill wheel and passing
under the water with it. As an adult he liked to live well, far
beyond his income. This was conspicuously true during his service as commandant in Philadelphia. Arnold's pay and allow-
ances as a major general amounted to about $332 a month in
Continental currency—then worth no more than a third of its
face value - and he had no private fortune.[21]

Nevertheless Arnold was well received in Philadelphia,
bringing to his new command a reputation enhanced by per-
formances in Canada and at Saratoga.

> I understand that General Arnold, who bears a good character,
> has the command of the city, and the soldiers conducted with
> great decorum. Smallwood says that they had the strictest orders
> to behave well; and I dare say they obey'd the order. I now think of
> nothing but returning to Philadelphia.

So wrote Sally Wistar from North Wales, on its outskirts, on 20
June 1778.[22]

Whatever the circumstances of his official life, Arnold had
become infatuated by Peggy almost from the day of his arrival.
Their courtship was resplendent, ending in Arnold's conquest of
the much sought after daughter of Edward Shippen, Jr. From
the first she was as much taken with him as he with her. Peggy's
grandfather Shippen became extremely nervous over charges

and rumors of charges against Arnold, and her father, according to family tradition, was prevented from forbidding the match only by his fear that the hysteria with which she greeted any opposition might damage her health. Moreover her fashionable friends rallied to Peggy's support by castigating those who opposed Arnold as "ungrateful monsters." "Poor Peggy," wrote Betty Tilghman. "How I pity her! At any rate, her situation must be extremely disagreeable. She has great sensibility, and I think it must often be put to trial."[23]

Peggy's marriage to Arnold took place in the library of the Shippen mansion on 8 April 1779. In the face of mounting rumors over the source of his wealth Arnold bought Mount Pleasant, a mansion on the Schuylkill described by John Adams as "the most elegant seat in Pennsylvania," as a wedding present for his new bride. An empty gesture, the property was so heavily mortgaged that the Arnolds could never afford to live there, and it was soon sold. The match was a disaster for Peggy, as it was for Arnold. In trying to keep up with the social set of the city, he spent money faster than he could honestly make it. Reduced to selling army supplies for his private gain, he brought upon himself the justifiable wrath of perceiving Pennsylvanians, a court-martial in January 1780, and a reprimand from Washington—a mild enough penalty for misconduct which would today mean instant dismissal from the service and a probable prison sentence.

Had Arnold chosen differently, if his second wife had come from "a patriotic family whose friends were adherents of the patriotic cause, and who would have refused to follow him away from the patriotic camp, would his treason have been consummated? It is most unreasonable so to suppose."[24] A Tory at heart when Arnold married her, Peggy remained one throughout her life. Within a month following the marriage Arnold had decided to offer his services to the British; his new bride was in on the plot from its inception. For generations Peggy's innocence was freely conceded by Arnold's worst enemies but recent research—beginning with Carl Van Doren's *Secret History of The American Revolution*, based largely on official British documents now in the manuscript collection of the Clements Library at the University of Michigan—makes it abundantly clear that she not only knew of his treacherous negotiations but actively aided him with them.[25]

Her old admirer Major John André, at this point in New York with the British occupying forces, was the recipient of her letters written to him containing coded messages for Clinton, sent at the direction of her husband.

Within eighteen months Arnold's scheme to surrender West Point to the British had been discovered, forcing him to decamp. He left behind a seemingly distraught Peggy, an infant son, and, most tragically of all, incriminating evidence which served as a death warrant for the unfortunate André. Captured by the Americans with the evidence on him, he was hanged as a spy—a drastic action considered unwarranted by many. In October of 1779 Peggy—by edict of the Pennsylvania Council of Safety—was banished from the state for the duration of the war.[26]

Not a bright chapter in the annals of the Francis-Shippen-Tilghman families. No effort will be made here to add to the very able coverage given by Van Doren and other historians to the details of Arnold's plot, since it is beyond the scope of this volume. However, there is no doubt that Arnold sought to use Tilghman in his aborted efforts at betrayal and that part of Tilghman's story will be related in Chapter 10.

For Tench, a far happier note was sounded in the month following the Shippen-Arnold nuptials. "During one of the few short furloughs which were accepted by Col. Tilghman, whose attention to duty has been likened by Washington to the unceasing toil of the slave,"[27] and after visiting his father in Chestertown he extended his journey to Talbot County to visit his Uncle Matthew at Bay Side. Here he met his cousin Anna Maria Tilghman, "of whose amiable traits, both of person and character, he had already been apprised by his own sisters . . ."[28] Tench was immediately attracted to her. "Her many engaging qualities which [have] never been effaced did not fail, at that time, to make an impression upon me," he later wrote.[29] "Captivated by the intelligence, amiability and beauty of his cousin,"[30] he would marry her in the spring of 1783.

In the last days of November 1779, after another year without major military operations in the north and after d'Estaing had failed to appear in American waters with an expected powerful fleet, Washington informed General Nathanael Greene that the main army would go into winter quarters, again at Morristown. The weather had already turned cold when on 1 December—in a severe hail and snow storm—units started arriving. An area called Jockey Hollow, about three miles southwest of the town, became the main camp site. Washington and his staff took over the mansion built by Jacob Ford, an early industrialist who had assembled a fortune mining New Jersey's iron deposits. Mrs. Ford, now widowed, and her children stayed on to share the house with the general and Mrs. Washington, the latter arriving before Christmas to spend the winter with her husband.

The general and his staff occupied the main building, except two rooms east of the center hall reserved for the Fords. The lower front room, on the left of the front door, became Washington's dining room. Immediately over it was the bedroom which he occupied with Mrs. Washington. Woefully cramped, Washington had two log additions made to the house, one for a kitchen on the east and another to the west, to be used as an office for himself, Tilghman, and Hamilton, the principal aides in attendance at this time. Crowded as they might be, Washington and his retinue were better off than the troops during a winter that turned out to be the most severe of the century. The troops were in tents throughout most of December, but soon an extensive "city" of log houses—all conforming to a standard floor plan of about fourteen by fifteen feet and accommodating twelve men—sprang up. These log houses were in rows of eight, three or four rows to a regiment, and parade grounds and company streets were interspersed at regular intervals. Constructed of notched logs, with chinks of clay as a sealant, each had a fireplace at one end and a door at the other. Officers' cabins were slightly larger and somewhat more elaborate. Practically all of the men were so housed before the turn of the new year, but it was February before all of the officers were accommodated. Windows apparently were not cut until spring.[31]

Although popular history would have it otherwise, this second winter at Morristown was harder than that of the previous year at Valley Forge. The army was never closer to collapsing. Bread and beef, the staples of a soldier's diet, were generally adequate, but the weather sometimes caused long delays in re-provisioning. Twenty-eight blizzards blasted the hills with unremitting violence, blocking vital supply roads with six-foot snow-drifts.[32] Early on in that dreadful time Tilghman, with gentle

113

humor, wrote to Royall Flint of the Commissary Department, with a requisition for rum and flour, adding that if Flint could not send both "a supply of the former would make up wonderfully for want of the latter."[33]

It was a season of excesses. The depreciation in the value of Continental currency was devastating, caused by the excessive issuance of paper money. A pair of boots cost $600 and a horse $20,000. For a "bad supper and grog," the Baron deKalb paid $850. Inflation was rampant. The subscription to a "dancing assembly" held that winter in Morristown was set at $400. Washington's own name headed the list of those officers indicating a wish to attend, followed by the names of Generals Greene, Knox, and Stirling. Other subscribers were Tench Tilghman, Alexander Hamilton, James McHenry, Richard K. Meade, Clement Biddle, Caleb Gibbs, John Moylan, Benjamin Brown, and John "Lawrence," the latter name no doubt intended to signify the subscription of John Laurens.[34]

Militarily there was little activity during the winter of 1780. British and German troops were in winter quarters on Staten Island; Washington dispatched Brigadier General William Irvine (born in Ireland, Irvine, 1741-1804, served principally with the Pennsylvania Continental Line) and Colonel Tilghman to reconnoiter their position and report back to him. Irvine and Tilghman had left Morristown prior to 10 January, as indicated in two letters from Washington to Tilghman dated 10 and 11 January 1780 respectively.[35] In them Washington asks specifically about weather and road conditions as well as "the State of the Ice at Amboy; whether it is to be crossed there also with a body of Troops." In addition Washington wished to know

> where our guards are along the Sound, whether we have any at Woodbridge and Amboy, and in a particular manner let me know whether the Ice is to be crossed at or near a Mill by the house of a Mr. C. Dusasway (on the Island) one mile or there abouts from Amboy East of it.

Four days later Lord Stirling led a badly managed raid against Staten Island. Hampered by subzero weather the effort was in essence a failure.

The encampment at Morristown was one of the Continental Army's severest trials. Held together by Washington's leadership and ability, the army survived a time of discouragement and

despair. Following the raid on Staten Island, when 3,000 Continentals crossed the frozen sound on sleighs, the British retaliated
with raids on Newark and Elizabethtown. Except for such skirmishes, the days were a seemingly endless succession of cold,
snow, and hunger. But as at Valley Forge momentous news
arrived with the coming of spring. In May Lafayette galloped
into Morristown to announce that France had six warships and
6,000 French soldiers on the high seas, bound for Rhode Island,
to aid the American cause.

CHAPTER 9

The Aides-de-Camp

We few, we happy few, we band of brothers
—Shakespeare, King Henry V, IV, iii

Band of brothers they were; always happy they were not. Thomas Simes's *Military Guide for Young Officers*[1], widely used by American officers in the Revolution, includes a section on the duties of aides-de-camp. In it Simes quotes the Mareshal De Puyssegur who, in his *Art Of War*, said

> In the time of the great Prince of Conde and Mareshal Turenne, the employment of aids-de-camp was always filled with officers of character. The reason is, that in a battle, a moment may change the face of affairs . . . It is necessary that he who carries (the General's orders), has comprehended the spirit in which the General meant it, and takes care not to deliver it in such a positive manner, as to oblige him who receives it to act up to the letter of the order, and not to leave him liberty to change it.[2]

No better illustration of the necessity for the possession of this indefinable quality in an aide-de-camp can be made than in a retrospect of the part played by Tilghman and Washington's other aides in the Battle of Monmouth.

During the Revolutionary War, Washington's aides-de-camp (or his official family, as they were sometimes called) were "the most remarkable group of young men to be found in the history of the United States. Washington's well-nigh unerring judgment in appraising men was never better displayed than in the choice of his confidential military assistants, for, no matter how much of their later success in life is to be attributed to the training they received under the Commander-in-Chief of the

1 1 6

Continental Army, there can be no question of the quick recognition, by the First American, of the latent capacity of these men who were so much younger than himself."[3]

Throughout the war, however, Washington was hard pressed not only to find but to keep competent officers around him. Many of them quarreled with him or otherwise wounded him in an emotional sense, either during the war or afterwards. John Trumbull[4] was an aide for twenty days only; Thomas Mifflin, one month; Stephen Moylan, four months; Edmund Randolph, seven and Joseph Reed, ten. In 1775 Horatio Gates became his first adjutant general only later to become a most dangerous rival. His first aide, Mifflin, when promoted joined the cabal against him. Reed, an old and trusted friend from Pennsylvania, second aboard in terms of early service, was so restive that when he was given leave to go to Philadelphia to attend to some pending litigation, would not at first return for all of Washington's supplications. He consented, finally, to take Gates's place as adjutant general, but subsequently abused Washington in a critical letter written to General Charles Lee. Washington learned of this from Lee's reply which fell into his hands. Although magnanimous toward Reed, the latter was so ashamed of himself that a full reconciliation did not come about until Washington put Reed in command of the cavalry on 23 June 1777.[5] In later years Randolph published an attack on Washington that made Washington violently angry.

Of the "beardless boys" who served Washington, Tilghman and Robert Hanson Harrison, called "the Old Colonel" by his younger associates, at first enjoyed the greatest intimacy and bore the main burden of secretarial duties. In the course of time, however, Alexander Hamilton became a chief pillar of support for Washington and enjoyed a measure of affection from the commander in chief which, by Hamilton's own admission, he did not return. Nevertheless, Washington's feeling for Hamilton was strong enough to bridge the quarrel of February 1781 at which time Hamilton abruptly informed Washington that he would resign his commission and leave the staff. Tilghman, one of the few men with whom Washington seemed able to keep an unbroken friendship with generally warm and spontaneous expressions of affection, stayed with his chief for seven years. Harrison came next with six years to his credit; John Laurens and Richard

Kidder Meade each served four years, Hamilton and David Humphreys three. Two later appointees, George Johnston of Virginia and Benjamin Walker of New York, served seven and ten months respectively.

Joseph Reed was thirty-four, Thomas Mifflin thirty-one, and Tilghman thirty-two when they came to headquarters; John Laurens was twenty-three and Alexander Hamilton not yet twenty-one when they joined the general's "family." But youth was no barrier to Washington's full employment of their abilities nor did it lead to any lack of confidence in their judgment. Tilghman, unmarried until after Yorktown and thus not subject to the concerns and responsibilities of married life for the entire span of his service with his chief, was only eleven years younger than Washington, a fact which undoubtedly contributed to the closeness which developed between the two men.

Aaron Burr, strange to say, was also a member of Washington's staff for a short period, having been invited to join it after his display of bravery with Arnold in the attack on Quebec. He joined Washington in May, 1776, at New York, but soon departed under the cloud of a dispute with Washington which to this day remains a mystery. Moreover his name does not appear on the official list of aides prepared from general orders, a resolve of Congress, or a definite documentary statement by the commander in chief.[6] Some said Burr's departure arose from Washington's objections to his morals; others claimed Burr had little respect for Washington's military ability. Afterwards Washington always regarded Burr with suspicion, dismissing him as an "intriguer" whenever his name came up.[7]

There were, in all, thirty-two aides (See Appendix II) - usually from four to six present at headquarters at any one time, with as many as twelve present at one point. At other times there were so few that visiting generals and indeed Mrs. Washington herself were pressed into duty as copyists.[8] Demands made upon the aides varied in accordance with the action; nevertheless the amount of work accomplished at headquarters was enormous. Often as many as fifteen letters a day would be dispatched from headquarters at the height of a campaign. When one considers all the logistical and tactical activity which also had to take place, including the issuance of general orders to manage an army of ten to fifteen thousand men, perhaps a forced march, and a battle being fought, some idea of the magnitude of the effort can be had.[9]

Tilghman and his fellow aides had to perform the entire spectrum of duties encompassed by the many-tiered army staff organizations of today. Wherever headquarters might be they worked day and night at tiny desks drafting routine correspondence or keeping notes on staff conferences and discussions. Orders and dispatches to subordinate comanders had to be composed, clear, and legible, even in the heat of battle. Fitzpatrick, editor of the multi-volumed *Writings of Washington*, makes the point that with the arrival of each new aide the older and more seasoned aides shifted as big a burden as possible onto the new arival, at least as far as preliminary drafts were concerned, and in many instances the finished product.

During these critical years Washington had to rely on his aides to produce for him, in his name, useful and elegantly styled documents so that he could carry on in a hundred different ways not only the prosecution of the war but the business of state as well. Tilghman, Harrison, Hamilton, Laurens, Randolph, and McHenry demonstrated varying literary styles but all wrote with taste, animation, and when called for, humor. "Tilghman's style," said Hamilton, who wrote much like him, "partook of the character of his sprightly temper. His sentences were brief and simple, giving results rather than the processes by which they were reached." To Hamilton "they seemed to have been written on the drumhead, but still always breathing throughout a general air of elegance."[10]

As general and aide Washington and Tilghman worked together to conform to the requirements of the situation and the people with whom they were dealing. Tilghman wrote reports to Congress on the constant needs of the Army. He interrogated prisoners and advised Washington on the movements of the enemy. He drafted passports, informal but effective, and financial documents. His diplomacy in handling selected visitors from the swarms who called on Washington concerning matters of real or imagined importance was notable and an added factor in lightening Washington's work load. Sometimes Washington would dictate a memorandum for transcription by Tilghman and at other times state the general idea and let Tilghman compose the text for dispatch over the general's signature. Often

Washington would simply sign what Tilghman had written. As the affinity between the two men increased during the war years, incidences of this sort became more frequent. In the collected writings of the two men, Tilghman's drafts which received Washington's signature are identified as to date and subject but credited to Washington,[11] whereas only letters that Tilghman signed are credited to him. As a matter of principle it would seem accurate to say that some documents written entirely by Tilghman, and signed by him, reflected Washington's views and not his own.

Similarly it should be pointed out that while allowing his aides great latitude in exercising well-earned discretionary powers in drafting communications to be signed by him, Washington in fact maintained essential control over his correspondence, as attested to in those instances where a comparison of a first draft with the document signed is possible. A case in point is Washington's letter to General Gates, 26 May 1778. In command in the north, Gates had summarily countermanded Washington's order for a shipment of rifles to the main army, then at Valley Forge. Fully two thousand troops camped there lacked muskets, despite opposing British forces in Philadelphia capable of attack at any moment. Tilghman, burning with rage at Gates's impertinence not to say his dangerous action, and fully aware of Gates's part in the recent fiasco of the Conway Cabal, drafted for his chief's signature a stinging rebuke and peremptory order to Gates—still basking in questionable glory arising from the American victory at Saratoga. Washington, however, in a manifestation of those qualities which enabled him to maintain the stasis of American resistance by holding his struggling forces together in the face of the British lion, struck out all of the peremptory parts of the letter and shifted the rebuke from a personal plane—upon which Tilghman had placed it—to the more acceptable line of official duty. Tilghman had written: "This countermand has greatly disappointed and exceedingly distressed me." Washington took out the personal pronoun and changed the sentence to read: "This countermand has greatly disappointed and exceedingly distressed and injured the service."[12]

Several factors tended to form the aides-de-camp into a palace guard—a coterie from which outsiders would hear not the slightest criticism of Washington, despite his shortcomings. As a distinguishing mark and "to prevent mistakes" the aides wore a green "ribband" between coat and waistcoat.[13] Added to this superficial winnowing was Washington's predilection for choosing gentlemen born and bred as his immediate comrades-in-arms. .

Although he did his best to keep it under control, Washington had an awesome temper. Frequently under great strain, his irascibility would surface, and the courtesy and affection with which he normally treated his young military comrades would disappear, only to reappear at a more relaxed time, such as at meals where no distinguished guest was present, when he would lay aside his dignity and the worries of the current campaign and enter into lighthearted conversation with them like some kindly uncle. The fact of the matter was that, in many instances, the force of Washington's personality was such as to overwhelm his "beardless boys." Washington's heart was warm enough, but long exposure to ingratitude, chicanery, and perfidy caused him to present a cold and austere exterior in his role as commander in chief.

Presidents and ranking generals can have no close friends while in office or exercising command. Denied the presence of his real family (although Mrs. Washington and his stepson, Jackie Custis, were with him intermittently throughout the war) and faced with the loneliness and responsibilities of his rank, Washington needed someone to trust, to confide in, to relax with. Friendship implies a good measure of equality. The confidant must be one who will not take advantage of his position. Seldom are such arrangements successful. Not only did Tilghman's unbroken devotion to Washington demonstrate that it was not impossible to love him and endure his moods, but in the matter of his commission his reluctance to push himself forward stood in marked contrast to Hamilton's insatiable ambition. Hamilton was often cited as the aide closest to Washington, but his lack of family background would seem to have disqualified him from Washington's initial consideration. However, he did possess what sometimes serves as an effective substitute—an attractive manner, a lively intellect and the air of an aristocrat. Moreover the quality of the friends with whom he surrounded himself—and his later marriage to Betsy Schuyler, blueblooded and wealthy—certified him as a gentleman. While there can be no doubt of Washington's admiration of Hamilton's intellect and of his capacity to deal effectively with a multitude of problems, it is certain that Washington's private feelings toward Tilghman far superseded those which he had for the impetuous Hamilton. Indeed it is doubtful if Hamilton ever really liked Washington or did more than merely endure him other than to nurture his own ambitions. Hamilton himself is the best authority for this. After he had broken with Washington in February 1781 he wrote to General Schuyler as follows:

> I always disliked the office of an aid-de-camp as having in it a kind of personal dependence. I refused to serve in this capacity with two major-generals at an early period of the war. Infected, however, with the enthusiasm of the times, an idea of the General's character which experience taught me to be unfounded, overcame my scruples, and induced me to accept his invitation to enter into his family. It was not long before I discovered he was neither remarkable for delicacy nor good temper . . .
>
> For three years past I have felt no friendship for him and have professed none. The truth is, our dispositions are the opposites of each other, and the pride of my temper would not suffer me to profess what I did not feel. Indeed, when advances of this kind have been made to me on his part, they were received in a manner that showed at least that I had no desire to court them, and that I desired to stand rather upon a footing of military confidence than of private attachment. You are too good a judge of human nature not to be sensible how this conduct in me must have operated on a man to whom all the world is offering incense.[14]

Perhaps a clue to the closeness of the relationship between Tilghman and Washington had its origins in the shortcomings of some of Washington's other intimates, but it was cemented by Tilghman's unfailing loyalty and his sense of the fitness of things. In addition to the trust generated by Tilghman's conduct, there existed the long pre-war relationship with Washington engendered by Tench's father James—regardless of his wartime Loyalist sympathies—and by his Uncle Matthew Tilghman. Unlike Tench, Washington had no facility in any other language and except for a rather strong turn for mathematics no purely intellectual interest. Nevertheless, the tastes and habits of the two men, stemming from the same social strata, were very similar, extending even to a fondness for foxhunting. And, finally, the overriding consideration was Tench's capacity for utter reliability, his capacity for keeping a discreet silence regarding matters at headquarters, and his refusal, often tested, to use his position to his own advantage.

Washington said it eloquently in a letter to the Honorable John Sullivan on 11 May 1781, written from Headquarters, New Windsor, recommending a promotion for Tilghman.

> If there are men in the army deserving of the commission proposed for him, he is one of them. This gentleman came out a captain of one of the light infantry companies of Philadelphia, and served in the Flying Camp in 1776. In August of the same year he joined my family, and has been in every action in which the main army was concerned. He has been a zealous servant and slave to the public, and a faithful assistant to me for nearly five years, a great part of which time he refused to receive pay. Honor and gratitude interest me in his favor, and make me solicitous to obtain his commission. His modesty and love of concord placed the date of his expected commission at the first of April, 1777, because he would not take rank of Hamilton and Meade, who were declared aides in order (which he did not choose to be) before that period, although he had joined my family and done all the duties of one from the first of September preceding.[15]

Tilghman's performance at this time has been characterized as done with "an abnegation which is almost incredible, and a magnanimity almost beyond praise."[16] Accordingly Tilghman's Continental commission as a lieutenant colonel conformed to his own wishes, dating from 1 April 1777 but issued 30 May 1781. Family tradition, quoting from the same source, held that promotion was offered earlier and often but uniformly declined because of Tilghman's unwillingness to be separated from his chief.

Despite varying degrees of affection toward Washington, the aides were almost uniformly fond of each other. Some of the letters which passed between them, if read today in the bar of an officers' club, would either provoke a riot or bring down utter derision upon the writer and the recipient alike. Tilghman, Laurens, Hamilton, and James McHenry—an especially close group—prided themselves upon the cultivation of learning, a pervasive knowledge of the classics and a veneration of the code of the heroes of antiquity. Theirs was the high-flown literary language of the eighteenth century that did not hesitate to express devotion to each other, formed in the arena of armed struggle, in such metaphors. John Laurens, in writing to Richard Kidder Meade signs off by saying: "Adieu: I embrace you tenderly . . . My friendship for you will burn with that pure flame which has kindled you your virtues." Hamilton he calls "My Dear," continuing with sentimental expressions of enduring affection. Hamilton, no less aware of the exalted rules of conduct by which they lived and often died, could respond with equal lack of embarrassment, "I love you." In berating Laurens for not answering his letters, Hamilton likens himself "to a jealous lover, when I thought you slighted my caresses, my affection was alarmed and my vanity piqued."[17]

Tilghman, in a more restrained fashion, nevertheless lets Hamilton know that he misses him, signing himself "Yr most affectionate T. Tilghman." This short letter, written from New Windsor on 27 April 1781, is interesting for a number of reasons, not the least of which is the humor for which Tilghman was noted. Hamilton was at De Peyster's Point, now called Denning's Point, on the east bank of the Hudson, opposite New Windsor. Part of the text follows:

> My dear Hamilton
>
> Between me and thee there is a Gulph, or I should not have been thus long without seeing you. My faith is strong, but not strong enough to attempt walking upon the Waters. You must not suppose from my dealing so much in scripture phrases, that I am either drunk with Religion or with Wine, tho' Had I been inclined to the latter I might have found a jolly Companion in My Lord who came here yesterday.[18]

Horses and their consequent care were items of extreme importance to the aides. Tilghman to his father from White Plains, 31 October 1776:

> We are on Horseback . . . from Sun Rise to Sun Set . . . I met with an Accident at Harlem Heights which I took upon as irreparable, I mean the loss of my faithful saddle Horse, who died in a few hours, from every Appearance in high Order and Spirit. I had rode him gently most of the day and never observed him fail, but about two Miles from Head Quarters. I suppose it must have been

Bots. I have mounted myself upon a pretty Mare, that will make an excellent Breeder, if I get her safe home.[19]

Similarly, John Laurens to his father, the Honorable Henry Laurens, on 30 August 1777, the latter then being President of the Continental Congress in Philadelphia.

I have just a minute to beg the favor of you to send my watch by Col. Tilghman: Messers. Pinckney and Horry arriv'd here yesterday, but they could not inform me certainly whether you had employ'd Hunt to buy me a horse. I am exceedingly in want of a vigorous steed that can gallop and leap well, not younger than four, but I would rather have him of six or seven years of age. Your kindness will excuse my hurry and the trouble I give. The gentlemen above mentioned gave me pleasure in informing me that you are well. Col. Tilghman will answer any questions respecting the motions of the enemy and our own.[20]

While demanding, life at headquarters was an exciting one, and the aides were a hard-riding, hard-working group. Aware of their responsibilities and of the authority which attached to their position, they were unsparing of themselves, delivering the commander in chief's orders with energy and drive, then checking to see that those orders were successfully carried through. Not all, however, was gunpowder and ink. Some of the more pleasant aspects of life at Headquarters occurred during the times when the army was in winter quarters and Mrs. Washington joined the General. One of the aides would ride out to meet her, perhaps as far as a hundred miles from camp, to escort her in. In the spring, when she again left for Mount Vernon, an aide would see her safely back. Pleasant duty, indeed, and a coveted one.

Pleasant, too, were those occasions given over to visiting dignitaries. The flavor of such a meeting is given to us by the French general, Francois Jean de Chastellux, in his description of his first visit to Headquarters and his introduction to Washington and his staff.

At length, after riding two miles along the right flank of the army, and after passing thick woods on the right, I found myself in a small plain, where I saw a handsome farm; a small camp which seemed to cover it, a large tent extended in the court, and several waggons round it, convinced me that this was his *Excellency's* quarter; for it is thus Mr. Washington is called in the army, and throughout America. M. de la Fayette was in conversation with a tall man, five foot nine inches high, (about five foot ten inches and a half English) of a noble and mild countenance. It was the General himself. I was soon off horseback, and near him. The compliments were short; the sentiments with which I was animated, and the good wishes he testified for me were not equivocal. He conducted me to his house, where I found the company still at table, although the dinner had been long over. He presented me to the Generals Knox, Waine, Howe, &c. and to his *family*, then composed of Colonels Hamilton and Tilgman, his Secretaries and his Aides de Camp, and of Major Gibbs, commander of his guards; for in England and America, the Aides de Camp, Adjutants and other officers attached to the General, form what is called his *family*. A fresh dinner was prepared for me and mine; and the present was prolonged to keep me company. A few glasses of claret and madeira accelerated the acquaintances I had to make, and I soon felt myself at my ease near the greatest and the best of men.[21]

Of all the aides only four were singled out for honors by Congress. George Baylor was voted a horse, properly caparisoned, when he brought the news of the Trenton victory, and Laurens was voted a lieutenant colonel with no prompting whatsoever from Washington, who was also instructed to give him a proper command when available. This honor Laurens declined as he was then serving as a volunteer on the staff at headquarters. In due course he was regularly comissioned as a lieutenant colonel and aide-de-camp. Laurens, like Tilghman, received no pay, but after his death in action at Combahee Ferry in 1782 Congress, in 1784, settled on his daughter Frances Eleanor Laurens monies in compensation for his salary as a soldier and diplomat.[22] Congress voted Tilghman a horse, properly caparisoned, and "an elegant sword," in testimony of the high opinion in which it held his merit and ability; but the greatest honor had already been conferred upon him when Washington selected him to bear his official dispatches to Congress announcing the victory that was to end the war. David Humphreys was later sent to deliver to Congress the British flags captured at Yorktown, and Congress rewarded him with a sword.

In retrospect, and despite the personality conflicts which led some of the aides to be less than comfortable with their chief, it is

Tench Tilghman's uniform. Courtesy: Maryland Historical Society.

evident that Washington did in fact have a keen insight into the human character which enabled him to surround himself with men of the highest calibre. In the postwar years his military family furnished the nation with a diplomatic representative to Spain and Portugal, an Associate Justice of the United States Supreme Court, six cabinet officers (Secretaries of State, War, Treasury, and an Attorney General), three United States senators, four governors of states, one Speaker of the House of Representatives, one President of the Continental Congress, and one delegate to the convention which framed the Constitution of the United States. Those who did not attain distinguished political positions nevertheless became citizens of local worth and reputation, with honors as lawyers, judges, or men of affairs. Longevity, of course, brought more opportunities. Laurens was destined to die in his twenty-eighth year, not surviving the war. Tilghman lived into the postwar era but was in his grave scarcely five years after Yorktown. Hamilton was the only one of this trio of companions who was to reach the full splendor of his career before the end came.

Washington's military family disbanded at Annapolis on 23 December 1783. The Continental Congress, then in session in the Maryland State House, had assembled to hear Washington's Farewell Address and to receive the resignation of his commission. With him were Tilghman, Humphreys, Cobb, and Walker. In that address, the formality of which gave little indication of the depth of feeling beneath his carefully chosen words, Washington spoke of his love and devotion toward those who had served him so well:

> While I repeat my obligations to the army in general, I should do injustice to my own feelings not to acknowledge in this place the peculiar services and distinguished merits of the gentlemen who have been attached to my person during the war. It was impossible the choice of confidential officers to compose my family should have been more fortunate. Permit me, Sir, to recommend in particular those who have continued in the service to the present moment, as worthy of the favorable patronage of Congress.[23]

Tilghman, six months married, would return home to his bride while the other aides would accompany Washington to Mount Vernon for a Christmas visit. It seems most fitting that in the last official act of the Revolution four of his aides-de-camp, in faded Continental uniforms and standing shoulder to shoulder with Washington, should lay down their commissions concurrently with their chief to return to the ways of peace and the building of the new nation which lay beyond the doors of the Old State House.

CHAPTER 10

Rochambeau . . .
and the Beginning of the End

> There is little doubt that our not being able to crush
> this reinforcement immediately upon its arrival
> gave additional animation to the spirit of rebellion,
> whose almost expiring embers began to
> blaze up afresh upon its appearance.
> —Sir Henry Clinton[1]

With the arrival at Newport of Lieutenant General de Rochambeau and the French fleet under Admiral de Ternay[2] on 10 July
1780 the thin stream of French aid widened to relative flood
proportions. Just what the course of history would have been had
the thirteen colonies capitulated to Great Britain can never be
known, but it is a truism that the main course of human history is
often altered by obscure events. Such would have been the case
had de Ternay and the Rochambeau convoy not won—by three
days only—a race against the auxiliary fleet dispatched from
England for New York under Admiral Graves. Warned as early
as 7 July of the approach of the French, Admiral Marriot Arbuthnot, British naval commander in chief on the American
station and then at New York, made no attempt at interdiction.
Had Graves arrived a few days sooner, the combined forces of
the two could have easily prevented the French from ever reaching Newport. Even after Graves's arrival the British still would
have had a chance of success had they played their cards properly. As it was, they played them very badly. Their intelligence

was so lacking that neither Arbuthnot nor General Clinton knew of the landings until 17 July.

Firmly established in Newport and safe against attack, French line Regiments with such ringing names as the Bourbonnais, Soissonais, Saintonge, and the Royal Deux-Ponts were prepared to give to Washington the assistance he so desperately needed. The officer corps embraced a full measure of the aristocracy of France, and French volunteers in the American army could look forward to fighting alongside men known to many of them from earlier campaigns, or in fact from childhood. In Rochambeau's personal suite were his aides the Swedish Count de Fersen, the Marquis de Vauban, the Marquis de Damas, the Chevalier de Lameth, Baron de Closen, and MM Dumas and de Lauberdiere. Four major-generals, the Baron and the Vicomte de Viomenil, the Chevalier de Chastellux, and the Marquis de Saint-Simon were in the expeditionary force as well as Brigadier-General de Choisy. Line officers included the Marquis de Laval, the brothers Deux-Ponts, the Marquis de Custine, the Vicomtes de Noailles and de Pondeux (the former Lafayette's brother-in-law), the Marquis de Rostaing, and the Marquis d'Audechamp. The artillery was commanded by Comte d'Aboville, and the Duc de Lauzun brought his own legion. Among others were the Vicomte Dillon, Alexandre Berthier, later a marshal under Napoleon, the Vicomte de Rochambeau, Commissary-General Claude Blanchard, and the Barons d'Ezbeck, de Bressolles, d'Anselme, and d'Espeyron.[3]

The British now belatedly but effectively blockaded the port. Having no way of knowing the disposition of Rochambeau, who had been placed under Washington's command by Louis XVI, the American commander in chief played a conservative game. Instead of going immediately to Newport, or having Rochambeau come to him and thus exposing both camps to too hasty action, Washington elected instead to dispatch Lafayette to Newport for extensive conferences with the French command and to report back to him with viable plans for future action. Thus it was not until September that Washington's first meeting with Rochambeau and de Ternay took place.

At the suggestion of Lafayette a conference was arranged for the 20th of that month. Held at Hartford, it was to be the first of three such councils-of-war, each increasingly important, at which we find the French-speaking Tilghman in a principal supporting role. A week earlier Washington had written to Colonel Nehemiah Hubbard, Deputy Quartermaster of Connecticut, informing him of the meeting and instructing him "to provide the best quarters which the town affords, and make every necessary preparation of Forage and other matters."[4] Washington's headquarters were then at the Hopper House, in Bergen City, New Jersey, on the Morristown Road. Setting out with two of his most astute aides, Tilghman and Hamilton, Washington's route took him eastward via Peekskill, where he talked with Benedict Arnold, then to Ridgefield, Danbury, Newtown, Waterbury, Southington, Farmington, and on into Hartford. He arrived there on the morning of 20 September, to be met by Colonel Jeremiah Wadsworth; Rochambeau arrived shortly thereafter. The conference was successfully concluded by the evening of the 21st. For future reference Hamilton embodied the main points covered into a memorandum entitled "Conference at Hartford," which was endorsed by Tilghman "Substance of Conference . . ." and by Washington "Result of A Conference . . ."[5] Rochambeau wrote subsequently that "we agreed upon all our movements," subject to the arrival of further French forces under Lieutenant General Loic de Bouexic, Comte de Guichen.

Within days, however, of this first meeting between Washington and Rochambeau an event took place which Washington called "a scene of treason as shocking as it was unexpected,"[6] and almost six months would elapse before the next meeting between the two generals. The "scene of treason" was the culmination of Arnold's attempt to turn the West Point garrison over to the British. Washington had left Hartford on 23 September via Farmington, Bristol, Litchfield, Kent, and Fishkill and then went to Colonel Beverly Robinson's house, below and opposite West Point on the Hudson River, where, with his aides, he arrived two days later. Arnold, whose continued entreaties to have the West Point command bestowed upon him had finally been successful, was using the Robinson house as quarters for himself and Mrs. Arnold. Some weeks earlier, on 31 July 1780, an encounter between Arnold and Tilghman showed the manner in which Arnold had been exerting every pressure to persuade Washington to give him the West Point command. It is best told in

Washington's own words, as recalled in the diary of Tobias Lear, private secretary to Washington in the postwar years and with him as Washington lay on his deathbed. The entry is that of 23 October 1786:

> When the French troops arrived at Rhode Island, I had intelligence from New York that General Clinton intended to make an attack upon them before they could get themselves settled and fortified. In consequence of that, I was determined to attack New York, which would be left much exposed by his drawing off the British troops; and accordingly formed my line of battle, and moved down with the whole army to King's Ferry, which we passed. Arnold came to camp at that time, and having no command, and consequently no quarters (all the houses thereabouts being occupied by the army), he was obliged to seek lodgings at some distance from the camp. While the army was crossing at King's Ferry, I was going to see the last detachment over and met Arnold, who asked me if I had thought of anything for him. I told him that he was the command of the light troops, which was a post of honor, and which his rank indeed entitled him to. Upon this information his countenance changed, and he appeared to be quite fallen; and instead of thanking me, or expressing any pleasure at the appointment, never opened his mouth. I desired him to go on to my quarters and get something to refresh himself, and I would meet him there soon. He did so.
>
> Upon his arrival there, he found Colonel Tilghman, whom he took a-one side, and mentioning what I had told him, seemed to express great uneasiness at it - as his leg, he said, would not permit him to be long on horseback; and intimated a great desire to have the command at West Point. When I returned to my quarters, Colonel Tilghman informed me of what had passed. I made no reply to it - but his behavior struck me as strange and unaccountable. In the course of that night, however, I received information from New York that General Clinton had altered his plan and was debarking his troops. This information obliged me likewise to alter my disposition and return to my former station, where I could better cover the country. I then determined to comply with Arnold's desire, and accordingly gave him the command of the garrison at West Point.[7]

The encounter took place almost two months before Arnold's plot was discovered. Obviously attempting to influence Washington through Tilghman, whose close relationship to his wife was known to him, Arnold was already dealing secretly with the British through a Philadelphia Tory named Joseph Stansbury, with the active connivance of Mrs. Arnold. Coded messages were being passed to Stansbury, via Peggy Arnold, all destined for Peggy's old admirer, Major André, now adjutant to Sir Henry Clinton. Arnold was to receive £20,000 in return for the surrender of the West Point garrison with its 3,000 men, artillery, and stores.

On 23 September 1780, the same day that Washington and his party left Hartford, some Westchester militiamen picked up a stranger dressed in civilian clothes trying to get through to the British lines. Identifying himself as "John Anderson," the civilian-clad stranger was really Major John André. On him were found plans of the West Point defenses, summaries of confidential reports written by Washington, and a pass signed by General Arnold himself.[8] Unaccountably, news of André's capture reached neither Arnold nor Washington until the morning of 25 September. Washington, accompanied by Lafayette, Tilghman, and Hamilton, arrived that morning at the Robinson house an hour after Arnold, who had been told of André's capture while at breakfast, had decamped. Abandoning his wife and infant son, he immediately left the house and rushed to his barge, in which he had himself rowed down the river beyond Verplanck's Point, where he took refuge on the British ship *Vulture*. Washington, still in ignorance of the conspiracy, crossed to West Point where he inspected the works, returning to the Robinson house "about noon."[9] At that point a messenger, who had missed Washington and his suite on the road, arrived with the incriminating evidence in hand. Hamilton was sent off immediately in the hope of capturing Arnold, but Arnold's headstart was too great and the pursuit was fruitless.

The rest is dismal history. To his credit and as a measure of his level-headedness Tilghman obviously did nothing but report to Washington Arnold's plea for the West Point command as Arnold had presented it to him earlier. The unfortunate André was the loser, being hanged as a spy. Arnold, whom the British could never bring themselves to love, was made a brigadier in their forces. Subsequently he led a foray into Virginia which was largely ineffectual, although he did succeed in raiding Richmond, putting the legislature and Governor Thomas Jefferson to flight. Always one to use his family connections, Arnold turned up at "Westover," the ancestral home of the Byrd family on the James River, some twenty-five miles below Richmond. Here he was entertained by Mrs. Mary Willing Byrd, another first cousin of Peggy Shippen Arnold's. Mrs. Byrd, widow of Colonel William Byrd, who had fought as a British officer in the French and Indian War, was the daughter of Charles and Anne Shippen Willing, and thus had more than one connection with the royal cause. Several letters had passed between Mrs. Byrd and Arnold which at the time were thought to be inimical to the American cause, but never proved. In February 1781 all of Mrs. Byrd's papers were seized by the patriots. Arthur Lee was later to write that "Arnold, with a handful of bad troops, marched about the country, taking and destroying what he pleased, feasting with his Tory friends and settling a regular correspondence with them."[10]

Back at the Robinson house, following the abrupt departure of her husband and a day later, Mrs. Arnold put on a display of hysterics, subsequently discovered to be largely feigned,[11] designed to fortify the belief held by Washington and Hamilton, who were witnesses to this dramatic spectacle, that she was innocent of any complicity in Arnold's defection. She was permitted to return to her family in Philadelphia but was later banished, as previously noted, by the Council of Safety. Reunited with Arnold in London, she lived out her life there, and died in 1804.

One aspect of the André-Arnold episode, seldom if ever mentioned in American history, was not lost on the British. The *Gazetteer*, a London daily, published on 20 November 1780 an account of André's death, pointing out that "If Washington had the temerity to order Clinton's Adjutant to the gallows, the American cause was far from breathing its last. Washington, always a cautious man, would never have inflicted so severe a sentence had he the least reason to suspect that he, too, might presently find himself before a court-martial."[12] The answer to the implied question, "Who will win the war?" lay less than a year away, in a little town in Virginia, four hundred miles to the south.

From December of 1780 on, for a solid year Tench became not only Washington's principal aide but, for a time, his only one.[13] Hamilton was at Albany, being married to Betsy Schuyler, and McHenry had gone along; Harrison and Meade were on leave, Greene was in the south, and Lafayette and Laurens were in Philadelphia trying to improve the situation with respect to supplies and reinforcements due from the French but nowhere in sight. The New Windsor house of William Ellison (stone-built and overlooking the Hudson and the snow-clad eastern banks), no longer standing, had become Washington's Headquarters. It was a superb setting, but the house was small and inconvenient, in no way comparable to the relative spaciousness enjoyed the winter before in the Ford mansion at Morristown.

Even after the return of the other aides, the period was to become one of the busiest of Tilghman's long service with Washington. Overworked and for a time ill,[14] nevertheless he alone composed almost the entire correspondence passing that winter from Washington to Rochambeau,[15] as well as several other lengthy and significant documents for Congress. Principal among these was a detailed reply by Washington to a *Report Of A Committee Of Congress* to Washington's earlier recommendations, made on 20 December 1780, on the composition of the army[16] as well as a rough memorandum, dated 15 July 1781, giving the rank and file strength of the Continental Army on that date by brigades, regiments, and detachments for a total of 5,835 men.[17] The first-mentioned document is interesting for a number of reasons, among them the abolition—from 1781 onward, but not yet retroactively—of the rank of colonel in the American army "to put us upon a footing with the enemy in point of exchange (they having few or none of that rank in service in this country)."

While his mood was to change perceptibly in the months to come, Tilghman struck a gloomy note in a letter to Robert Morris on 22 December 1780. Inflation was still rampant and the several states seemed little inclined to give Washington what was considered essential in the way of permanent troops.

> To be candid with you, I do not think the Contest ever stood upon more critical ground than at present. The people grow tired of a War, which has been of longer continuance than they were led to expect, and are alarmed and amazed to find that the enemy are, at this time of day, making strides which they could not effect at the beginning. The Reasons are simple, and would be as obvious as daylight, if there were not yet among us those who are determined never to see. Instead of securing an Army when our Money was good and the people were willing, we have lavished immense sums

upon Men of an Hour, whose terms of service have been spent in marching to and from the Army, and in their way devouring like Locusts all before them . . . The Enemy will undoubtedly reinforce their Army in this Country, and should they do it, as they threaten, between this and May next, I dread the consequences. Two things will save us, and that speedily - a sufficient permanent Army, and a foreign loan in aid of our own Resources . . . until the Army can be regularly cloathed - paid and fed by the means of a substantial Medium, we are only lingering out the time of our own dissolution. Can Men be expected to serve without provision - without Cloathing, without pay? Of the last, we have had none since March and no prospect of any . . . Perhaps there is no Man less apt to despond and I am sure there is none who will oppose longer than I will. But when I see the glorious prize for which we have been contending, within our reach, if we would but embrace the means of acquiring it, I am sick to death of our folly. May God of his infinite Mercy enlighten our understanding . . .[18]

Tilghman, however, could not foretell the future; these conditions would soon change, although worsening considerably before becoming better. The conflict between Britain and her rebellious colonies had now turned global, and Britain stood alone, fighting to maintain naval control in such widely separated areas as the Western Atlantic, the English Channel, the West Indies, and the Indian Ocean. Arrayed against her were not only the Americans but France, Spain, and Holland. On the American side, largely resulting from the conditions spelled out by Tilghman in his letter to Morris above, mutinies of the Pennsylvania and New Jersey lines had shaken the Revolution to its foundations. Furthermore, Washington was badly worried by Cornwallis's successes in Virginia. In this atmosphere, and oppressed by these cares, on the morning of 16 February 1781 Washington met Hamilton on the stairway of the Ellison house. The ensuing incident sparked the quarrel which would lead to Hamilton's separation from Washington's staff. In a letter written two days later to General Schuyler, Hamilton related the circumstances as follows:

Two days ago, the General and I passed each other on the stairs. He told me he wanted to speak to me. I answered that I would wait upon him immediately. I went below and delivered to Mr. Tilghman a letter to be sent to the commissary, containing an order of a pressing and interesting nature.

Returning to the General I was stopped on the way by the Marquis de La Fayette and we conversed together about a minute on a matter of business. He can testify how impatient I was to get back, and that I left him in a manner which, but for our intimacy, would have been more than abrupt. Instead of finding the General, as is usual, in his room, I met him at the head of the stairs, where, acosting me in an angry tone: "Colonel Hamilton," he said, "you have kept me waiting at the head of the stairs these ten minutes. I must tell you, sir, you treat me with disrespect." I replied, without petulancy, but with decision: "I am not conscious of it, sir, but since you have thought it necessary to tell me so, we part." "Very well, sir," said he, "if it be your choice."[19]

Within the hour Washington sent Tilghman to Hamilton with an outright apology, accompanied by an expression of the General's admiration for Hamilton's talents. For anyone but the hot-headed Hamilton this would have been sufficient. Instead, with magnificent condescension, Hamilton agreed to talk over the matter with Washington if the latter insisted, while making it plain that he hoped to avoid such an interview, as nothing could alter his decision. Washington, with a measure of contriteness that so often succeeded his flashes of temper—a characteristic that men like Hamilton could never understand—consented.

While Hamilton's departure from Washington's family was "unalterable," he did have the good grace to stay on until a replacement could be found, not leaving for another ten weeks. In a letter to James McHenry he states:

> The Great man and I have come to an open rupture. Proposals of accommodation have been made on his part, but rejected. I pledge my honor to you that he will find me inflexible. He shall for once at least repent his ill-humour . . . I wait till more help arrives, at present there is beside my self only Tilghman, who is just recovering from a fit of illness, the consequence of too close application to business.[20]

To all outward appearances the break between the two men hardly caused a ripple at headquarters, and in March Hamilton and Tilghman again accompanied Washington to Newport for the second conference with Rochambeau. Tilghman had been convinced "that by then it would all have simmered down. Everybody was tired remarked the even-tempered Marylander, in cheerful understatement. It would never have happened if things were going better."[21]

The second meeting between Washington and Rochambeau at Newport, in the early days of March 1781, was cordial but in the end accomplished little. The second French division had not yet sailed, being blockaded in home waters by the British. Tilghman's presence in the Washington suite on this occasion is attested to by the fact that Washington's letter to Lafayette, by now in Virginia, written from Newport on 8 March regarding the departure of the French fleet from Rhode Island waters is in Tilghman's hand.[22] While the commander in chief captivated all Newport at the balls and receptions in his honor, he returned to New Windsor weary and unhappy.

Following these largely social events, a remarkable exchange of correspondence took place between Mr. George Olney, a civilian appraiser attached to the army, and Tilghman. The letters, according to one authority on Revolutionary documents, offer "the first real documentation of the lighter side of Washington's nature."[23] They have their genesis in an incident at a dinner party at the quarters of Colonel Clement Biddle at Morristown sometime in the winter of 1779-80. At this party Colonel Biddle was host to General and Mrs. Washington, General Nathanael Greene and the beautiful Mrs. Greene, known as a charming flirt, and George Olney and his equally beautiful wife. In this company, it appears, Washington grew playful—and the ensuing gossip set the teacups rattling in Boston, Wethersfield, Providence, and Philadelphia. A year later Mrs. Olney, much agitated by the spread of what she considered malicious rumors concerning her conduct at the party, asked her husband to seek out Colonel Tilghman at the ball at Newport to try to set the matter straight. Missing Tilghman at the Newport ball, Olney wrote Tilghman the following letter:

> My not seeing you after the Ball at Newport obliges me to take this method of requesting a favour of you, which I flatter myself your good-nature will induce you to comply with, and which I shall ever most gratefully acknowledge as an obligation. It is to ask His Excellency, and acquaint me with his answer, whether at Col^o. Biddle's Quarters in Morris Town, or elsewhere, "M^{rs}. Olney, in a violent rage, told him, *if he did not let go her hand, she would tear out his eyes, or the hair from his head; and that tho' he was a General, he was but a*

Man"; or whether she *ever* said a word to him that border'd upon disrespect. You will doubtless be surpris'd at this extraordinary request, unless you have heard that such a report has been industriously spread thro' the Country by some ilnatur'd, malicious person, which has greatly injured M^{rs}. Olney's reputation, but as I know it to be absolutely false, I cannot but hope you will kindly grant me a ready compliance, to enable me to justify her by producing an indubitable *written* proof of its untruth.[24]

Colonel Tilghman, gallant as ever, responded three days later on 14 March 1781 from Providence with a letter laced with affability and humor.

I am sorry to find that M^{rs}. Olney should have experienced a moments pain from the circulation of a story, which, if rightly represented, would have shewn, that instead of an affront being given or taken at the time alluded to, the highest good humour and gaiety prevailed. For the information of those who may think you would give a partial account of the matter, and for the confusion of those who have propagated so malevolent a report, I will, upon honor, briefly relate the circumstances, which I am authorised to do by his Excellency to whom I have shewn your letter.

The Winter before the last, when the Army was cantonned near Morristown, a large Company, of which the General and M^{rs}. Washington - General and M^{rs}. Greene - M^r. and M^{rs}. Olney were part, dined with Col^o. and M^{rs}. Biddle. Some little time after the Ladies had retired from Table, M^r. Olney followed them into the next room. It was proposed that a party should be sent to demand him, and if the Ladies refused to give him up, that he should be brought by force. This party His Excellency offered to head. They proceeded with great formality to the adjoining room and sent in a summons, which the Ladies refused - such a scuffle then ensued as any good natured person must suppose. The Ladies, as they always ought to be, were victorious. But M^{rs}. Olney, in the course of the contest, made use of no expressions unbecoming a Lady of her good breeding, or such as were taken in the least amiss by the General.

If the foregoing, which I have dressed in the stile of jest (for the whole matter was a jest) will answer your purposes, it will afford the highest pleasure . . .[25]

The facts of the matter remain hazy. Armed with Tilghman's explanation, Mrs. Olney fired off a letter to her erstwhile friend Katie Greene, saying:

On General Greene's account I am extremely sorry that in my own
justification I am obliged to send copies of the enclosed letters
(from Olney to Tilghman and from Tilghman to Olney) to Boston, Wethersfield and the Jerseys in order to convince those to
whom you told it, and those who may have heard it from others,
that it is utterly false.[26]

For all purposes that ended the matter, although Mrs.
Greene replied to Mrs. Olney, "you *did* say that you would tear his
hair out, and I can bring sworn evidence to the truth of it."[27]
Whether this was literally a tempest in a teapot, or in reality an
affair of honor between two respected women of the Revolutionary era will never be known, but it does cast even more light on
Tilghman's close relationship with Washington and on his ability
to ameliorate a set of circumstances which may have disgraced
his chief.

Whatever other attributes Tilghman may have had, he was
not infallible. In this same month of March 1781—overworked
and intermittently ill—he allowed to slip by a private letter written on the 28th by General Washington to his kinsman, Lund
Washington, then managing the plantation at Mount Vernon.[28]
In it the commander in chief, who had seen the French fleet sail
from Newport three weeks earlier,[29] deplored the fact that the
fleet had not seen fit to follow his suggestion regarding its current operation.

It was unfortunate, but this I mention in confidence, that the
French fleet and detachment did not undertake the enterprize
they are now upon, when I first proposed it to them; the destruction of Arnold's Corps would then have been inevitable before the
British fleet could have put to Sea. Instead the small squadron . . . was sent, and could not, as I foretold, do anything without
a land force at Portsmouth.

This letter with others from Headquarters was intercepted the
next day at Smith's Cove and promptly published in *Rivington's
Gazette*.[30] The dispatch of the original letter was an embarrassing
gaffe on Washington's part—one which Tilghman should have
stopped. Its publication brought forth expressions of pain from
both Lafayette and Rochambeau, the latter pointing out that the
French order to sail could have been countermanded by Washington if he had been so inclined.

In this fateful spring and summer of 1781—the effective threshold of the long march to Yorktown and the time-forge on which was fashioned the combined army-navy assault by the Franco-American alliance on the British main force under Cornwallis—events began to materialize, at first slowly and indecisively but then inexorably and with a momentum which was to provide an irresistible force. Most significant was the third and last conference between Washington and Rochambeau which took place at Wethersfield, Connecticut, between the 19th and 23rd of May. Remarkable for a number of reasons, it was in fact the genesis of the allied victory which was to follow. By far the most important conference of the war, plan after plan was conceived, only to be laid aside. For months the American army and its French allies had been reduced to inactivity, waiting for a long-promised second division of the French army, considered essential to success.

On 8 May, however, the French frigate *Concorde* arrived safely in Boston harbor, bringing the Comte de Barras to command the French fleet at Newport which, since the death of de Ternay, had been commanded by the Chevalier Destouches. It also brought General Rochambeau's son, the Vicomte de Rochambeau, with the latest instructions from the French court. Losing no time, General Rochambeau immediately requested the meeting, and Wethersfield was chosen as its site. Hartford was ruled out since the state legislature was in session and might occasion some inconvenience. Washington, accompanied by Generals Knox and Duportail and Colonels Tilghman and Wadsworth left New Windsor on 18 May via Kent, New Milford, and Litchfield, arriving at Wethersfield the day following and put up at the house of Joseph Webb, Jr., where the conference took place. About noon on the 21st the Count de Rochambeau arrived with Major General de Chastellux. Although expected, the Count de Barras did not attend—the appearance of the British fleet off Block Island having preempted his appearance. On 17 May Tench had written to Robert Morris, striking an optimistic note. (Morris had been appointed Superintendent of Finance on 20 February 1781.) John Laurens was in France seeking more aid and there seemed every reason to believe that it would be forthcoming.

Mr. Laurens is in France and has been favorably heard (from) which is a favorable circumstance. I set out tomorrow with His Excellency for Wethersfield where he is to have an interview with the Count de Rochambeau in consequence of the dispatches lately arrived from France. I conjecture that the Contents of them are agreeable. Our Affairs are certainly well in every quarter but our own, and I flatter myself that with a little foreign assistance and your good Management they will mend here. We are full of supplies and the present prospect of a Harvest is glorious.[31]

The Webb house is not only still standing but, thanks to the Colonial Dames of Connecticut, has been carefully preserved. The taverns where the conferees took their meals have disappeared, but the Silas Deane house, immediately to the north, is still there, also in a state of outstanding preservation and again due to the efforts of the Connecticut Dames. Wethersfield itself, then as now, contained a number of structures of architectural worth. In these ideal surroundings the two generals hammered out their plans for the next campaign. The brief entries in Washington's diaries give no details of the proposals and counterproposals discussed and rejected, although the substance of the conference, in the form of a series of questions asked by Rochambeau with Washington's answers, were carefully recorded by Tilghman.[32]

As an initial move Washington and Rochambeau agreed to put their armies in motion at once, making their junction on the banks of the Hudson and to come to a final decision as to their point of attack when dispatches were received from de Grasse. Washington, while favoring New York, was nevertheless painfully aware that the heavy French fleet would have a difficult time forcing the bar at Sandy Hook. Rochambeau, although expressly ordered by his king to subjugate himself and his army to the decisions of Washington—and thus be prepared to join in an attack on New York—was known to favor a campaign in Virginia, where Lafayette's forces were deployed against Cornwallis. On 24 May, both generals having departed Wethersfield to return to their respective headquarters, Tilghman drafted a circular letter to be sent to the governors of Rhode Island, New Hampshire, Connecticut, and Massachusetts calling for them to complete their Continental battalions by 1 July and "to hold a body of Militia (according to the Proportion given them) ready to March in one Week after being called for."[33]

Meanwhile there was a mountain of paper work to be attended to. While the New England troop levies were not met, much to Washington's disappointment, correspondence flowed in and out of headquarters in a veritable tide. It was a time too when other cares, some of a personal nature, vied for attention in Tilghman's crowded days. His brother William, whose Loyalist sentiments paralleled those of their father James, had sought Tench's help in safe passage to England in order to study law at the Inns of the Court. In two letters from New Windsor, written on the 10th and 12th of June, 1781, Tench informed him that

> it gives me pain to tell you that I cannot, Without subjecting myself to censure, interfere in the least in procuring your recommendations to go to England by way of France or Holland. I am placed in as delicate a situation as it is possible for a Man to be. I am, from my station, Master of the most valuable Secrets of the Cabinet and the Field, and it might give cause of umbrage and suspicion were I, at this critical moment, to interest myself in procuring the passage of a Brother to England. Tho' I may know his intentions are perfectly innocent, others may not or will not. You cannot conceive how many attempts have been made, some time ago, to alarm the General's suspicions, as to my being near his person - Thank God - He has been too generous to listen to them - and the many proofs I have given of my attachment have silenced every malignant whisper of the kind.[34]

And in the second letter:

> If you have not engaged passage to Europe from Philad[a] and will take my advice you will defer the matter 'till next Spring - There is the strongest probability that you will be able to put your resolution in execution then in a manner which can bring no reflexion upon your Connections or be of any future disadvantage to you - For you know very well that all are looked upon with Suspicion and jealousy who leave America to go to England and you also know that severe penal laws have been passed which affect the Estates of such persons. If then by waiting a few months you have a chance of avoiding both inconveniences I think you will do well to make the trial - the foundation of a peace is laid, and as Great Britain must by this time see that she cannot affect the conquest of this County and that all the maritime powers of Europe are determined that she shall not, I imagine the mediating princes will

not find much difficulty in bringing the contending parties to terms.[35]

Tench's advice prevailed and the trip was never made.

Of more immediate concern was the paltry state of Tench's own pocketbook. To Robert Morris, who was intent on raising capital for his newly chartered Bank of North America and who had requested Tilghman to act as his agent in this matter among the officers of the army, he had this to say on the 24th of June:

> I am afraid I shall be a very unprofitable Agent for I believe it may with truth be said that there is not an Officer in the Army from the Comm[r] in Chief downwards who is at this time able to pay in a single Subscription. You know they have received no real money from the public for the long time past and consequently have . . . to spend all they could possibly raise for their own support . . . Paper money of all kinds has so far become useless that I must beg the favor of you to send me twenty or thirty dollars in Specie by Doctor Craik who accompanies Mrs. Washington as far as Philada.[36]

We know of no acknowledgement of the receipt of this small but vital loan but due to the close association in the postwar years between Tench and Morris it's a fair assumption that it was not only made but repaid.

By early June the French were on the move, leaving Newport on the 10th for Providence and the march to the New York palisades. The long period of inaction had been particularly trying for Rochambeau, but now at last the Commander of His Most Christian Majesty's forces in America could again look forward to leading the flower of the French infantry in battle. Two of the regiments were especially dear to him, as he had fought side by side with them in the Seven Years' War, with the Soissonnais in Minorca and with the Bourbonnais, *les petit vieux*, as they were known in the French army, at Clostercamp. Together with the Royal Deux-Ponts and the Saintonge, no less distinguished units, their departure from Newport was not only a military spectacle of some proportions but a sad occasion for many of the townspeople as well, as the deportment of the troops during the year they were there had been exemplary and "many stories have been handed down from generation to generation, all in the same vein, telling of the pleasant and friendly relationships that existed between town and army."[37]

Within a matter of days Washington moved southward from the highlands, secure in the knowledge that de Grasse had at least arrived in the West Indies. Tilghman wrote

> We have a very agreeable intelligence from Guadeloupe if true in its extent. Captain Ledyard a man of intelligence and credit has arrived at New London. He reports that the Fleet from France under Mon^s Le Grasse [sic] had fallen in with the British Fleet cruizing off Martinico [sic] on the 29th of April, that a warm action ensued in which the British were beaten and lost two Ships of the line. I have little doubt but the French have arrived in the West Indies, but I don't place full confidence in the other part.[38]

It should be remembered that so far as the French were concerned, the war in the American arena was a comparatively minor part of the larger European struggle in which they were engaged, and it was to the European and West Indian areas that France was giving her main attention. In the eighteenth century, when the sea lanes were the world's highways, the West Indies were of enormous strategic importance, being at the center of ocean commerce. They bristled with forts, to watch the coming and going of ships. The attention that de Grasse focused on his presence there is readily understandable.

The situation was fluid, and Washington's fertile mind had to direct itself to alternate plans other than an attack on New York, to be decided upon once de Grasse's intentions were apparent. Accordingly, the American commander in chief appeared to have taken direct action to insure himself of adequate intelligence and—to some extent—to hedge his bets. Without openly acknowledging to Rochambeau that he was doing so, he dispatched a courier to de Grasse for a midsummer conference with the French admiral. The incident deserves attention, if for no other reason than because it is so little known. For this important role he chose Allan McLane, not a member of his official family but an officer in whom he had obvious confidence. For McLane it was his most important, most secret, and most forgotten mission. A hard riding cavalry officer, he had been reconnoitering the lines in front of Cornwallis in Virginia when chosen by Washington to acquaint de Grasse with the full details of the military situation in the colonies and to point out to him the advantages of sailing for the Chesapeake instead of against New York. While Washington still favored the all out blow against New York, he was flexible enough to envisage the possibilities presented by the brilliant alternative in the south.

Enrolled as a captain of Marines on the twenty-four gun privateer *Congress*, McLane sailed from Philadelphia in early June for a rendezvous with de Grasse. En route the *Congress* encountered a French frigate, learned the location of de Grasse's fleet and made a speedy contact. Alexander Garden, who talked personally with McLane, gives this account in his *Anecdotes of The American Revolution*, published in Charleston in 1822, of McLane's reception by de Grasse. Upon arrival

> he found the Count holding a Council of War, the object of which was to fix on proper measures for an immediate attack on the Island of Jamaica. But, before any definite arrangements could be made, the presence of M'Lean [sic] was called for, that he might be examined relative to the preparations made in America, for a combined attack by the Allies and American army, on the British force in the Chesapeake. To the interrogatories proposed, he gave such satisfactory answers, and developed such cheering prospects of success, that he was informed by the Count, soon as the Council broke up, that he would immediately proceed to America, and act as circumstances might require, until the hurricane months should have passed over.[39]

The precise weight of McLane's influence on de Grasse's decision to sail for the Chesapeake instead of New York may never be known, but there's little reason to doubt the word of this able man. If de Grasse had any doubts about his choice they were probably dispelled by the arrival of dispatches from Rochambeau, who forwarded his version of the Wethersfield Conference by the French frigate *Concorde*, which sailed from Newport just about the same time the *Congress* left Philadelphia. Almost immediately de Grasse began to choose his invasion fleet. He sent the *Concorde* back to Rochambeau with word that he would sail directly for the Chesapeake on 13 August from Santo Domingo in twenty-five to twenty-nine ships of the line, bringing with him the Gatinois, Agenois, and Touraine regiments—3,000 men in all —together with 100 dragoons, 100 artillerists, 10 field pieces, and a number of siege cannon and mortars. This dispatch was received on 14 August. It was in "clear, definite and concise terms, it resolved all doubts and determined the course of the war."[40] So assured, Washington and Rochambeau could lay aside any speculation and plan their assault on Cornwallis with confidence.

On 5 July Rochambeau's 4,800 French infantrymen had joined Washington's forces above New York, giving Washington a contingent of 10,600 men. For the next five weeks British positions around New York were thoroughly scouted. The situation proved too plain for argument; an attack upon them could not succeed, a circumstance which Rochambeau seems to have grasped somewhat sooner than Washington. Nevertheless, on 15 August, the day after de Grasse's message had been received, Washington sent an express rider to Lafayette in Virginia with instructions to so dispose his troops as to prevent Cornwallis from retreating into North Carolina. Two days later General Duportail was dispatched—posthaste—to de Grasse to inform him that "Rochambeau's French army and as large a part of the American army as could be spared would meet him in the Chesapeake."[41]

By 21 August the allied armies had started southward from New York. Cornwallis, meanwhile, had occupied Yorktown and Gloucester Point on Virginia's York River, a defensible position with a deep water harbor permitting communication with Sir Henry Clinton in New York. His reasoning appeared sound; he could either be reinforced to renew an offensive in the south or could be plucked off if threatened by a land offensive against him. In New York Clinton remained obsessed with the idea that Washington intended to attack him there—and small wonder, for the British had captured the mailpouch containing Washington's, Rochambeau's, and de Barras's letters regarding the Wethersfield Conference and the decision to abandon the southern move in favor of an attack on New York. Not until 1 September, when Washington's army and the French were well across the Delaware did Clinton wake up to the fact that the enemy had pulled off a giant coup and that it was too late for him to stop them. Had the captured dispatch been written for the sole purpose of having them fall into the hands of the British, they could not have accomplished their purpose better.[42]

Passing over the old battlefield at Princeton, the army pursued its route towards Philadelphia with increasing rapidity, Washington and Rochambeau reaching there on 30 August in

advance of their troops. At midday when they reached the suburbs, they were met by a large number of people and escorted to
the City Tavern, where there was an impromptu reception.
Robert Morris then took the command party, including Tilghman, to his house where these eminent officers plus a number of
Philadelphia's leading citizens were entertained at dinner. Toasts
were drunk to the United States, the Kings of France and Spain,
and to the speedy arrival of de Grasse in North American waters.

On 2 September Washington's ragged host—men from
New York and New Jersey, battle-hardened veterans who had
fought at Trenton, Princeton, Germantown, and Monmouth—
swung through Philadelphia in a cloud of dust "like a smothering
snowstorm," impelled by its commander's sense of urgency. A
day later came the French. Outside of town they stopped while
the soldiers powdered their hair and put on their white dress
gaiters. As they passed through in review before Congress and an
enthusiastic population they were dazzling in their resplendent
uniforms - the Soissonnais in white coats with rose-colored facings, the Bourbonnais in white and black; the Santonge in white
and green, and the Royal Deux-Ponts in blue coats with yellow
facings and cuffs.

With some difficulty Washington and Rochambeau escaped
the attention which the people of Philadelphia showered on
them and pressed on for Head of Elk where the troops were to
board transports to be provided by the French for the last leg of
the long march to Virginia. On the afternoon of 5 September
Washington had just passed through Chester, Pennsylvania,
when a courier from de Grasse brought word that the Admiral
held the Chesapeake with twenty-eight ships of the line. De
Grasse also reported that he had made contact with Lafayette
and was sending the Marquis de Saint-Simon ashore with 3,000
men to help contain Cornwallis in Yorktown. Rochambeau, momentarily separated from Washington, could see his usually
reserved commander in chief waving his hat at him with gestures
of excitement and joy as he approached. "I never saw a man so
thoroughly and openly delighted," wrote the Duc de Lauzun.

But Yorktown was still over 200 miles away. Spurred by the
golden hope of an opportunity which might slip away, the allies
reached Head of Elk only to find that the transports which had
been counted on were so few in number that only 2,000 men

could be accommodated. But Washington was cheered by the news that 1,800 Marylanders, the heroes of the Battle of Long Island, were on their way to Virginia. "Some are riding, some are sailing, some are walking," he was told, "but they will be there, General, before you are."[43] The rest of the army struck out for Baltimore, where it was hoped that more boats would be available. Washington and aide David Humphreys had by now far outstripped the vanguard, and not even Rochambeau could keep up with them. On 9 September they covered sixty miles to arrive at Mount Vernon—Washington's first visit in six years.

Meanwhile at Head of Elk Tilghman had broken off from the main body of troops and headed for the Eastern Shore where he hoped to pick up fresh horses, his being lame from the forced march. On 11 September, at Queenstown, he was able to requisition two through Lieut. William Hemsley, a kinsman, who procured the horses from Mr. John Chaires, whom Hemsley addressed as follows:

> Colo Tench Tilghman Aide De Camp to Genl Washington is now here with his Horses lamed & unfit to travell, he therefore wants two of Your Horses belonging to the State to proceed on to Virginia.
>
> The enclosed rect will be sufficient Authority for you to deliver him the Horses, & he will be accountable to the Council, or the Quarter master General. You will please send the white Horse you had from Mr Hollyday & the Sorrell Horse from Mr Browne, or instead of him one of the easyest going Horses you have. If you shou'd have any doubts abt the delivery of the Horses, I will answer the Consequences.
>
> P.S. Pray dispatch the Messenger as Colo Tilghman must be at Anns to-night.[44]

Riding one horse and leading the other Tilghman caught up to Washington and his suite at Mount Vernon late on the night of 12 September. Early the next morning the entire headquarters group, which now included Generals Rochambeau and de Chastellux as well as Washington, were on the road again.

The long haul from New Windsor to Virginia marked for Tilghman not only the culmination of a rigorous march but brought to an end as well a period in his long service with the commander in chief which had been at once the busiest, the most difficult, and the most productive of the seven years when he was at Washington's side. With Hamilton gone from headquarters Tilghman had become the unquestioned rod upon which Washington leaned most heavily—on a day-to-day basis, at strategic conferences such as Wethersfield and in meetings yet to come, afloat or onshore, with de Grasse. Beginning with Arnold's defection in late September 1780 and extending to and beyond the surrender of Cornwallis, it was also a time when Tilghman was doing double duty for the French. Lafayette, whose written English had become grammatically correct by the spring of 1781 but who still spoke the language with a French accent characterized as "quaint" by his associates, was in the habit of passing to Tilghman dispatches written in French, wanting them translated for Washington's benefit only by someone in whom he had implicit trust. From Holt's Forge on 1 September 1781 he wrote to Washington to say:

> From the bottom of my heart I congratulate you upon the arrival of the French Fleet—Some rumours have been spread and spy accounts sent out—but no certainty untill the Admiral's dispatches came to hand—Inclosed I send you his letter and that of Mis de St. Simon both of whom I request you will have translated by Tilmangh [Tilghman] or Gouvion alone as there are parts of them personal which I do not choose to show to others—[45]

On 13 September, a day's march out of Mount Vernon and just as an autumn dusk was about to settle on Washington's command party, about to go into an overnight bivouac on the banks of the South Anna River above Richmond, an express rider galloped into camp with a second dispatch from de Grasse. In addition to aides Tilghman and Humphreys the headquarters group now included Jackie Custis, Washington's stepson who had come along to help in any way he could. The news was momentous, equal in importance to de Grasse's first message announcing his arrival in Virginia waters. On 5 September, while de Grasse had been busy unloading, a large number of sail appeared beyond the bay—the combined flotillas of Graves and Hood, coming to relieve Cornwallis. Hastily ordering cables to be cut, de Grasse took twenty-four French ships of the line out to meet them. The Battle of The Virginia Capes, fought that same day, was not a particularly bloody one, but the strategic importance of the French victory cannot be overestimated. The British, tance of the French victory cannot be overestimated. The British, badly battered after several days of maneuvering and after the two fleets lost sight of each other, decided to return to New York. Once again de Grasse occupied the Chesapeake, Cornwallis was doomed, and the stage was set for the last and greatest spectacle of the American Revolution.

CHAPTER 11

Yorktown . . . and The World Turned Upside Down

> The play, Sir, Is Over!
> —Lafayette

> Colo Tilghman, one of my Aides de Camp,
> will have the Honor to deliver
> these Dispatches to your Excellency;
> he will be able to inform you
> of every minute Circumstance which is not
> particularly mentioned in my Letter . . .
> —Washington to the President
> of Congress,
> 19 October 1781[1]

Tilghman's Yorktown journal is tantalizingly brief. It begins and ends as follows:

22^d Sept 1781. Part of the Advanced Fleet with the French Grenadiers and Chasseurs and American light troops came up to College Creek.

23^d Remainder of the Fleet came up—American Troops debarked as fast as they arrived and ordered to encamp near the landing. Genl Lincoln is of the opinion that the large transports with the French line and the remainder of the American are in the James River—French Grenadiers and Chasseurs encamped below the Capitol, Olney and Hazen's Reg^t and some Companies of the 15th Infantry an Jersey Line not yet expected . . .

17th (Oct) In the morning Ld Cornwallis put out a letter requesting that 24 Hours might be granted to Commissioners to settle terms of Capitulation for the surrender of the posts of

York and Gloster. The General answered that two Hours only would be allowed to him to send out his terms in writing. He accordingly sent them out, generally as follow, that the Garrisons should be prisoners of War, the German and British Soldiers to be sent to England and Germany. The Customary terms of it and preservation of private property—&c. The General answered on the 18th, that the terms of sending the Troops to England and Germany were inadmissable. That the honors should be the same as those granted at Charlestown—private property preserved—&c. His Lordship closed with all the terms except those of acceding to the same honors as those granted at Chs Town. However the Commrs met—on our part Lt Colo Laurens and Viscount Noiailles—on the part of the British Colo Dundas, Majr Ross.[2]

In the interval between Washington's encampment on the banks of the South Anna River on the night of 13 September, en route to Williamsburg, and the first entry in Tilghman's journal nine days later, Washington and Tilghman had completed their forced march, made their rendezvous with Lafayette's troops, and Tilghman had accompanied his chief to the all-important council of war with Admiral de Grasse on board his flagship, the *Ville de Paris*, on 18 September. The shape of things to come was now even more apparent. During these crowded days Tilghman had time enough only to record, in fewest words, a description of the developing siege and of the action which followed. The journal's twenty-one entries cover a period of twenty-six days. All are short and some are of a multiple nature, such as "1st, 2d, 3d, 4th October throwing up Redoubts to cover our approaches and bringing Cannon and Stores from Trebetts landing upon (the) James River." While brief, the journal is nevertheless accurate, capsulizing on a day-to-day basis the unfolding of the last great battle in the American struggle for independence. In a small red book in its own slip-case, the journal has the appearance of being a gift from a relative or family friend. Tilghman apparently carried it with him throughout the war, as it contains entries, often fragmentary, about other battles as well as expense accounts for himself and General Washington.

Regiment by regiment, the French continued to pour into the peninsula between the York and James rivers, some marching by land but the greater number coming down the Chesapeake from Annapolis, Baltimore, and Head of Elk in small vessels furnished by de Grasse. By 25 September the last French and American troops from the north reached Williamsburg. Each time General Lincoln or Baron Viomenil touched a navigable waterway, they had sought boats.[3] Those officers unable to find vessels for their regiments had walked with them all the way from the north. The entire force—the French from Newport, Washington's Continentals from the Hudson, Lafayette's troops from Virginia, and additional French troops from Haiti—numbered about 16,000 men. Against them Cornwallis, holed up in Yorktown, had eleven British regiments, four Hessian, and one Provincial, as well as artillery and the cavalry of Simcoe's Rangers and Tarleton's Legion.

As soon as his army was assembled and its order of battle determined, Washington moved forward from Williamsburg and surrounded Yorktown, the Americans on the right and the French on the left. Cornwallis had established his main line of defense close to the town, which was situated on a thirty-five-foot bluff overlooking the York River and separated from Gloucester Point by about a half mile of deep water. From the beginning Cornwallis had recognized Yorktown as the death-trap it proved to be—impaled there not by the exercise of his own judgment but rather by orders from Sir Henry Clinton, a distant chief whom he could not disobey.

The siege was formally opened on 28 September and prosecuted in a thoroughly military fashion. Except for the storming of the redoubts (heavily fortified points in a strategic assault or defense line), Yorktown was not an infantry or bayonet battle but rather an action for the gunners, who gradually blew the British ramparts to bits. On 30 September Cornwallis abandoned his outer line of fortifications, thereby permitting the Allies immediately to occupy them and to bring up the siege guns landed from de Barras's fleet, capable of hammering all parts of the British inner line. There was much night firing. "The night of the 11th the 2d parallel was opened within 300 yards of the enemy's Works with scarce any annoyance only one man killed and only three or four wounded," noted Tilghman .

Following a most gallant night assault, two redoubts were carried near the river on the British left. Since Cornwallis now had some 6,000 men packed into a space scarcely 500 by 1,200 yards,[4] the allied bombardment was all the more effective, and on each succeeding morning the British viewed the seemingly inexorable French and American approach with fresh consternation. From behind the bluff leading down to the York River where he had taken refuge,[5] Cornwallis looked anxiously down the eleven miles to the Chesapeake Bay, waiting in vain for the relief promised by Clinton. It was too late. After a frustrating attempt to save his army by escaping across the York River to Gloucester Point— an attempt broken up by a violent storm which arose during the night to scatter and swamp his boats—on the morning of 17 October a red coated British drummer boy, accompanied by an officer showing the white, appeared on the parapets to beat out the signal for a parley. Lord Cornwallis had something to say to General Washington.

The allies, heeding the signal, gave orders for a temporary cease fire. Soon the incessant, devastating artillery bombardment stopped, and a hushed stillness fell over the field. The officer, blindfolded, was led to Washington's command tent. "Sir," Cornwallis had written, "I propose a cessation of hostilities for twenty-four hours, and that two officers may be appointed by each side, to meet at Mr. Moore's house, to settle terms for the surrender of the posts of York and Gloucester."[6]

Washington, negotiating from strength, granted a truce of two hours only in which Cornwallis had to submit, in writing, whatever he wished to say. By the afternoon of 18 October Colonel Thomas Dundas and Major Alexander Ross, the two commissioners appointed by the British, met in the house of Augustine Moore with the Allied commissioners, Lieut. Colonel John Laurens for the Americans and the Vicomte de Noailles, Lafayette's brother-in-law, representing the French. Negotiations continued until late in the evening. Tempers flared and heated discussions characterized the meeting. The British representatives hesitated about certain terms contained in Article III, which required the British to march out "with shouldered arms, colors cased and drums beating a British or German march." This was in retaliation for the humiliation visited upon General Lincoln, who had surrendered at Charleston and been refused desired honors. Before midnight the issue was settled on the allies' terms, and the truce extended until 9:00 A.M. on 19 October.

Back at headquarters Washington made some minor adjustments and immediately turned over the approved draft to Tilghman to transcribe the final copies. Two ceremonial copies were required. Throughout the early morning hours of 19 October the work went on, the scratching of quill pens on parchment paper continued until daybreak. The completed documents consisted of ten quarto pages, each thirteen by eight inches, including the last page, given over largely to signatures. Fully aware of the historic significance of the documents being produced, both Tilghman and Jonathan Trumbull, Jr., who penned the second copy, took extra pains to see that mistakes and interlineations were kept to a minimum. (See Appendix V.)

As dawn was breaking the work was finished and the completed articles dispatched to Cornwallis. Under threat of a renewal of battle, by 11:00 A.M. Cornwallis had reluctantly agreed to sign, as did Thomas Symonds, the senior British naval commander. The documents were then delivered to the now American-occupied Redoubt 10, where Washington and his officers waited. There the commander in chief added another line, in his own hand: *"Done in the trenches before York Town October 19th 1781."* Then he signed, as did Rochambeau and de Barras, the latter for Comte de Grasse of the blockading French Navy with the words, *"en mon nom et celui de Comte de Grasse."*[7] At 2:00 P.M., the defeated British army marched out from Yorktown, their band playing an old British tune, "The World Turned Upside Down." The French and American armies were drawn up, left and right respectively, on the surrender field to form a long allee. Washington, his generals, and his aides, were in mounted formation in the center of the right. The French command, resplendent in dress uniforms and decorations, were on the left, immediately opposite.

"Light-Horse Harry" Lee, an eye-witness, described the prevailing spirit of the hour.

> Certainly no spectacle could be more impressive . . . The captive army approached, moving slowly in column with grace and precision. Universal silence was observed midst the vast concourse, and the utmost decency prevailed . . .[8]

When the British Guards lay down their arms, Comte Guillaume-Mathieu Dumas, Rochambeau's Adjutant General, saw

Lieut. Colonel Robert Abercrombie, commander of the Light Infantry, pull his hat down over his eyes as he bit the hilt of his sword in frustration. Colonel von Seybothen, commander of one of the two Anspach battalions, shouted his command, "Ground muskets!" with tears running down his cheeks. Up and down the line of surrendering British and German forces other officers and men were similarly affected. So ended, in the clear autumn sunshine of a Virginia afternoon, the campaign that brought America her independence. Fifteen months after its arrival the French *Expedition Particuliere* had accomplished its purpose.[9] The war, except for minor skirmishes in the south, was over.

On the morning of Saturday 20 October 1781 a thin sun rose over Tidewater Virginia, bathing the ruins of Yorktown in soft shades of green, gold, and brown, filtered by the upward drifting smoke from a hundred camp fires. An early morning dew drenched every leaf, and spider webs closed the most unlikely apertures. In accordance with eighteenth century custom—anachronistic by today's standards—Washington, the French command, and their respective staffs had entertained Cornwallis and his senior officers at dinner the evening before. Now, shortly after daybreak, the American and French headquarters staffs were in full operation. Some officers had been up all night, intent upon getting official word of the victory to Philadelphia and Paris, the most important business of the day. Washington, all too well aware of the instability of the decentralized government under the administration of the Continental Congress, fully realized the danger of uncertainty. Consequently he held it vital that news of the triumph *be officially and promptly dispatched to Philadelphia.*

For the splendor of riding to Congress with the news the commander in chief turned once again to Tilghman, his most devoted aide. Familiarity with both water and terrain between Yorktown and Philadelphia and personal knowledge of Congressional leaders made Tilghman an obvious choice, but quite aside from such mundane considerations nothing could have been more appropriate, no other officer more deserving of the honor. This event, more than any other, thrust the consciousness of historians upon him, but the real value of his contributions to the American cause can only be measured in terms of his seven years of totally selfless service to Washington, the long period of privation and danger to which he was exposed, and the qualities of loyalty and self-effacement with which he performed his daily duties.

Despite a recent recurrence of the fever (probably malaria) which periodically beset him, Tilghman was determined to drive himself to the limits of his strength to cover as quickly as possible the distance between Yorktown and Philadelphia. He was weak and flushed as he left camp, having had little sleep for two nights running. In his dispatch case he had, in addition to Washington's letter to the president of Congress and the Articles of Capitulation signed by both sides, a letter from General Arthur St. Clair to James Wilson, a member of Congress.[10] With him as he rode off to the waterfront below Yorktown's bluff were David Humphreys from Headquarters, the Marquis de Damas, an aide to General Viomenil, the Duc de Lauzun, chosen by Rochambeau to carry the news to France, and the Marquis de Lafayette, who had come along to wish Godspeed to the two messengers.

As they passed through the now abandoned lines, the heavy siege guns brought from the French fleet were still in place, their naval heritage indicated by little iron dolphins, along with the Bourbon crest. In Yorktown ruin and desolation were on every side. Governor Nelson's house was little more than an arrangement of shell-riddled walls. Close by were the graves of the men killed at Redoubts 9 and 10, two look-alike low ridges of raw dirt—one for the French, one for the Americans. Tents and camps were everywhere as were soldiers - Gist's Brigade of Marylanders in their fringed leather jackets, others in frank makeshift, stirring in the early morning air. Wasting no time, Tilghman and de Lauzun and their companions rode past Grace Church and down to the river's edge where the rising tide lapped in irregular spasms at the bloated bodies of dead horses. Out in the stream lay the ruins of the British frigate *Caron*, only her charred masts and a portion of her stern showing. On the night of 10 October de Grasse had thrown red-hot shot into her, engulfing her sails and her hull in a spectacular conflagration[11] that lit up the river, the towns of Yorktown and Gloucester, and the camps of the two armies locked in their deadly struggle.

Tilghman's boat had been arranged for; the Duc de Lauzun was to be rowed downstream to the *Ville de Paris* for a last conference with Admiral de Grasse and then on to the French frigate *Surveillante*, being readied to carry him to the French coast as swiftly as possible. (For an account of Lauzun's voyage to France and of his reception at the French court, see Appendix IV.) Turning over their horses to an orderly who had accompanied them from headquarters, and after a last farewell embrace from Lafayette, the couriers were on their way.

Tilghman's course lay due north, out of the York River and up the Chesapeake to Annapolis, where he could board the packet which plied regularly between Annapolis and Rock Hall. From Rock Hall to Philadelphia was roughly a hundred and thirty miles, which he planned on covering with a relay of horses.

In a matter of hours the small boat cleared the York River, making—according to present-day estimates—about six knots per hour. At Goodwin Island, at the river's mouth the wind freshened, carrying the tiny boat and its passengers past New Point Comfort, at the entrance to Mobjack Bay, and out into the wide reaches of the bay itself. The day passed without incident; Tilghman, needing sleep, no doubt made himself as comfortable as possible and dozed off.[12]

He was awakened by a jolting movement that he recognized instantly as disaster. They had reached Tangier Shoal, the vast shallows that surround Tangier Island. Tilghman could see nothing, for it was by then dark, but he grasped what had occurred—the boat was aground. The wind had changed, swinging counter-clockwise from southwest to east. To put to best use this unfavorable circumstance, the skipper had reached too far on his starboard tack and had put his craft firmly on a sand bar. It was a common enough sailing accident, but it could not have happened under more trying circumstances. While Tilghman fumed impatiently, there was nothing to be done except to await the turn of the tide, and precious hours were lost.

It was now Sunday morning, 21 October. Once again in deep water, the way to Annapolis seemed clear. Throughout that morning and into the afternoon they sailed with a fair wind astern, but off the mouth of the Little Choptank River, thirty miles short of their goal, the wind left them entirely, and it was Monday morning before Tilghman reached Annapolis.

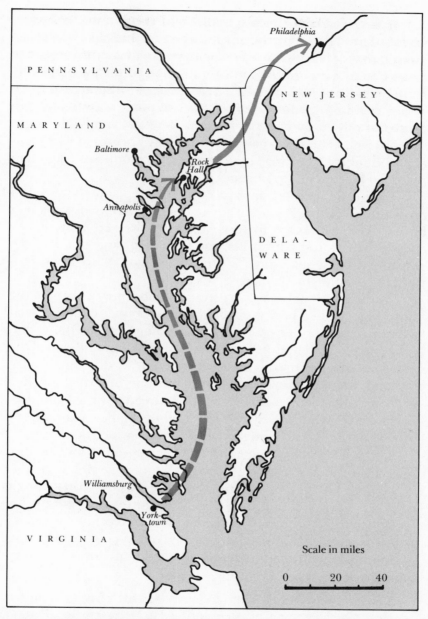

Route of Tilghman's ride from Yorktown, Virginia, to Philadelphia.

It is clear from the proceedings of the Council of Safety itself[13] that Tilghman, having reached Annapolis, presented himself to that body to give it the glittering news of the surrender as well as to arrange for the continuation of his journey. The Annapolis-Rock Hall packet, a sizable vessel running on a more or less regular schedule between the two ports, was designed to carry not only passengers but horses, wagons, and light freight loads as well. The state, having a number of horses at its disposal,[14] undoubtedly provided the first of such mounts as Tilghman resumed his journey to Philadelphia.

Again the weather, or lack of it, was to plague him. A fast crossing by the packet could take no more than two and a half hours. The whims of fortune, however, denied him such a speedy trip as the packet became becalmed, and the crossing consumed the entire day. Tilghman did not reach Rock Hall until the evening of Monday, 22 October.

Adding to Tilghman's frustration and impatience was the knowledge, gained in Annapolis from the Council of Safety, that "a letter from Count de Grasse to Governor Lee, dated the 18th had gone forward to Congress, in which the Count informed the Governor that Cornwallis had surrendered."[15] Although unofficial, and written and dispatched a full day before the actual surrender, this news, possibly received already by the Congress, Tilghman realized, added even greater importance to the speedy delivery of the *official* word from Washington which he carried.[16]

At Rock Hall he was first off the packet, headed for Chestertown, a second horse, and the possibility of several hours rest. Losing not a moment he spurred down the old post road through Forktown (now Edesville) and into Chestertown, shouting his message to those he passed along the way. On receipt of the news the townspeople of Chestertown turned out in noisy celebration. A contemporary account described the event in the flowery language of the day:

Newtown-on-Chester-River, October 23, 1781 - Last evening the Hon. Col. Tilghman, aid-de-camp [sic] to his Excellency General Washington, arrived here on his way to Philadelphia, with dispatches for Congress, containing an account of the happy reduction of the British Army in Virginia, under command of Lieut-General Earl Cornwallis. This great event was no sooner announced to the public than a large number of worthy citizens assembled, to celebrate this signal victory (in a high degree auspicious to the cause of Virtue and Freedom) which was done with a Decency and Dignity becoming firm Patriots, liberal Citizens and prudent Members of the Community. Admidst [sic] the roaring of Cannon, and the Exhibition of Bonfires, Illuminations, etc., the gentlemen (having repaired to a Hall suitable for the Purpose) drank the following toasts, viz: 1. General Washington and the Allied Army—2. Count de Grasse and the Navy of France—3. Congress—4. Louis XVI, a Friend to the Rights of Mankind—5. The United States—6. General Greene and the Southern Army— 7. Count de Rochambeau—8. The Memory of the illustrious Heroes who have fallen in defense of American Liberty—9. The King of Spain—10. The United Provinces—11. The Marquis de Lafayette—12. The Northern Army—13. The State of Maryland, the last in order but not the last in love.

One wonders, after so many toasts, if the celebration did not have more hilarity than dignity. We read further:

The next Evening an Elegant Ball was given by the Gentlemen of the Town, that the ladies might participate in the general Joy of their Country. A brilliant Company of Freedom's fairest Offspring assembled on this happy Occasion, and while they manifested the sincerest Attachment to the American Cause, they likewise shewed that "Grace was in all their steps."[17]

Tilghman, sick and sleepless for two nights and possibly longer, undoubtedly went to his father's house utterly exhausted for a much needed rest. It was daybreak on the morning of 23 October before he resumed his ride.

Beyond Chestertown the post road swerved toward present-day Kennedyville, then through Locust Grove and Georgetown, bound for Head of Elk. The road—one of the main thoroughfares of colonial America—was little more than a soft dirt track, foot-deep in mud after a rain. Travelers had to ford the Sassafras and Bohemia rivers. But Tilghman had ridden the road many times before and knew it well. All that day and through the empty darkness that followed—no one traveled at night—he drove forward, stopping only for a fresh horse wherever he could find one. In the early morning hours of 24 October, shaking with chills and fever, he cantered into the outskirts of Philadelphia. It was just past 3:00 A.M. when he entered the city. His old friend Thomas McKean was the President of the Continental Congress and resided in High Street, near Second. Tilgh-man knocked at his door so vehemently that a watchman was disposed to arrest him as a disturber of the peace. McKean, anxious to receive the news which he knew to be on the way, was out of bed in a flash. In no time the word had spread throughout the city. Watchmen, proclaiming the hour, shouted the word: "All is well and Cornwallis is taken!"

"In a minute," according to one account,

> the whole city was wild. Lights flashed in every window; men, women and children poured into the streets. The State House bell rang out its peal "Liberty throughout all the land to all the inhabi-tants thereof," and the American nation was born into the world.[18]

The unofficial word of the surrender, originating with de Grasse, had reached Philadelphia in the early morning hours of 22 October and had been read in Congress that same day. By order of the Executive Council, however, the public celebration of the victory was delayed until the arrival of official confirma-tion. "We impatiently await the arrival of His Excellency General Washington's official dispatches," said the *Pennsylvania Gazette*. With Tilghman's arrival on the 24th the news spread like wild-fire, and soon the entire city was rejoicing in public celebration.

The news did not please everyone, however. Miss Anna Rawle, daughter of Francis Rawle, a lately deceased but well-known Loyalist, and who was then living with her grandmother, Mrs. Edward Warner, in Arch Street, between Front and Sec-ond, recorded her reactions—doubtless shared by others of simi-lar political persuasion—in her diary:

> October 22, 1781—The first thing I heard this morning was that Lord Cornwallis had surrendered to the French and Americans - intelligence as surprizing as vexatious. People who are so stupidly regardless of their own interests are undeserving of compassion, but one cannot help but lamenting that the fate of so many worthy persons should be connected with the failure or success of the British army . . . However, as there is no letter from Washington, we flatter ourselves that it is not true. October 24—I feel in a most unsettled humour. I can neither read, work or give my attention one moment to anything. Tilghman is just arrived with dispatches from Washington that confirm it . . . [19]

CORNWALLIS IS TAKEN !

Lieut. Col. Tighlman of Washington's staff, announcing the surrender of Cornwallis, from
the steps of the State House, (Independence Hall) at midnight, October 23rd 1781.

"Cornwallis Is Taken." A Currier and Ives print showing Tighlman
[sic] reading a proclamation from the steps of Independence Hall,
Philadelphia, 24 October 1781. Published in 1876 as part of the Centennial Year of American Independence.

Meanwhile members of Congress, President McKean, the French Minister de Luzerne, and other dignitaries went in procession to the Dutch Lutheran Church where a service of thanksgiving was conducted by the Reverend Mr. Duffield, one of the Chaplains to Congress.[20] Flags were flown and salutes fired by the artillery on the grounds of the State House and by vessels in the harbor, which also displayed their colors. Just what part Tilghman took in the public jubilation is not recorded. In the forenoon hours of 24 October, the day of his arrival, he appeared before Congress for a lengthy interrogation[21] regarding the conduct of the siege at Yorktown, the Articles of Capitulation, and the intended disposition of prisoners taken. Following this he probably took to bed right away, exhausted—as he admitted—from exposure and fatigue after his arduous journey.

On Saturday, 27 October, Tilghman had recovered sufficiently to dispatch a report to Washington in which he wrote in part: (for the complete text of the letter, see Appendix I)

A Committee, consisting of Mr. Randolph, Mr. Carroll and Mr. Boudinot, were appointed to inquire of me the several matters of a particular kind, which were not included in your dispatches. They not only went into these, but into the motives which led to the several articles of the capitulation. And I have the pleasure to inform you that they were perfectly satisfied with the propriety and expediency of every step which was taken; and so, indeed, were the whole body of Congress, except the South Carolinians, whose animosities carry them to that length, that they think no treatment could have been too severe for the garrison, the officers, and Lord Cornwallis in particular.

. . . Upon the whole, Sir, you may be assured that the capitulation is considered by every unbiased person, both in and out of Congress, as highly honorable to the arms, and beneficial to the interests, of both nations.[22] . . . Whenever I am acquainted with your determination, I shall, without delay, join you. I am too much attached, by duty and affection, to remain a moment behind, when I think my presence can render any service or assistance to your Excellency.[23]

On Monday, 29 October, a resolution of Congress directed

the Board of War . . . to present to Lieutenant Colonel Tilghman, in the name of the United States in Congress assembled, a horse properly caparisoned, and an elegant sword, in testimony of their high opinion of his merit and ability.[24]

Illumination.

COLONEL TILGHMAN, Aid de Camp to his Excellency General WASHINGTON, having brought official acounts of the SURRENDER of Lord Cornwallis, and the Garrisons of York and Gloucester, those Citizens who chuse to ILLUMINATE on the GLORIOUS OCCASION, will do it this evening at Six, and extinguish their lights at Nine o'clock.

Decorum and harmony are earnestly recommended to every Citizen, and a general discountenance to the least appearance of riot.

October 24, 1781.

A flyer announcing the surrender of Cornwallis.
Courtesy: Historical Society of Pennsylvania.

Honored, rested, and enjoying himself in a city where he obviously felt at home, Tilghman was to partake in one more additional ceremony before departing for Chestertown and a visit to his immediate family, from whom he had been so long separated. Robert Morris, in a diary entry for 3 November 1781, describes the arrival of the colors captured at Yorktown:

> This day on the invitation of his Excellency the Minister of France I attended at the Romish Church a *te deum* sung on the account of the capture of Lord Cornwallis and his army. Soon after I arrived the colors taken by his Excellency General Washington with that army which were brought by Colonel Humphreys to Chester, there met by Colonel Tilghman and thence conducted hither by these two aide-de-camps [sic] of the general. The city troop of light horse went out to meet them and became the standard bearers as twenty-four gentlemen privates in that corps carried each of them one of the colors displayed, the American and French flags preceding the captured trophies which were conducted down Market Street to the Coffee House, thence down Front to Chesnut Street and up that to the State House where they were laid at the feet of Congress who were sitting, and many of the members tell me that instead of viewing the transaction as a meer matter of joyful ceremony which they expected to do, they instantly felt themselves impressed with ideas of the most solemn and awful nature.[25]

Almost immediately after Yorktown the French presence in America, so vital to American success, began to evaporate. Admiral de Grasse sailed with his fleet back to the West Indies, and Rochambeau's army went into winter quarters in Virginia. Many of the French officers fighting with the Americans (in contradistinction to those in Rochambeau's *Expedition Particuliere*) left to return to France individually. Lafayette sailed for home in December 1781, ending his active participation in the American struggle. Meanwhile, Washington moved his army to the Hudson, establishing headquarters at Newburgh. He would remain there for more than a year, directing the blockade of New York.

Although Tilghman would return to active duty, he took a long furlough to visit his family, regain his health, and press his suit for the hand in marriage of his first cousin, Anna Maria Tilghman, daughter of his Uncle Matthew, whom he had met earlier and with whom he was now deeply enamored.

PART THREE

PEACE —
AND A NEW ENVIRONMENT

1783-1786

CHAPTER 12

Marriage . . . and a Partnership
with Robert Morris

Tilghman, by this time, is I presume,
one of those domestic things called a Husband . . .
—Washington to Lafayette, 10 May 1783[1]

Why have you been so niggardly in communicating
your change of condition to us? or to the World?
By dint of inquiries we have heard of your Marriage;
but have scarcely got a confirmation of it yet.
—Washington to Tilghman,
2 October 1783[2]

In the general euphoria which swept the colonies following the surrender of Cornwallis at Yorktown, it was considered by most that the war was over. One thing was clear; public opinion in England would no longer support further efforts to subdue the American rebellion, a fact which was not lost on Congressional leaders, Washington, or the population at large. The difficulties, however, attendant to the demobilization of the Continental Army were immense. In the first place, no one knew for sure that the war was really at an end. Some wished that the troops be kept under arms, others that they be sent home on furlough, and still others that they finally be dismissed. Robert Morris, with an eye cocked on the national treasury, was one who advocated the latter course while emphasizing that the troops should not be returned to civil life "with murmers and complaints in their mouths." In the end a compromise was effected, with a general furlough agreed upon, so that if the fighting were resumed, the army might easily be assembled again. Through the efforts of the efforts of Morris, who pledged his own credit while negotiating a loan from the Netherlands, $750,000 was raised in order to give each furloughed soldier three months' pay. Consequently, large segments of the army were dispersed and leaves of absence granted many officers. Members of Washington's official family, realizing that the end was in sight, began to think of the postwar years and establishing their private careers.

Mindful of his promise to Washington to rejoin him when "I hear the route which your Excellency intends to take," Tilghman was back at headquarters by 21 November 1781, after a leave of absence in Chestertown of three weeks.[3] Washington by then had reached Annapolis on his march to the north and ultimate winter quarters at Newburgh. In this period of essential demobilization it is a simple matter to track Tilghman's presence at headquarters by observing Washington's correspondence, as much of it was drafted by Tilghman for the general's signature. Following his return to duty Tilghman stayed with Washington until 22 March 1782, when he took a protracted leave, bidding farewell to the commander in chief at Philadelphia.[4] He was gone for five months, returning to Newburgh on 11 August 1782.[5]

By the end of March in that same year Washington had been in Philadelphia for fifteen weeks, in headquarters established in Benjamin Chew's new house on South Third Street.[6] He had selected General Knox and Gouverneur Morris as commissioners for the exchange of prisoners, and a principal duty for Tilghman at this time was the drafting of instructions (dated 11 March 1782) to guide the commissioners in dealings with their British counterparts, General William Dalrymple and Mr. Andrew Elliott, named by Sir Henry Clinton. The negotiations between the commissioners are largely remembered by virtue of circumstances which gave rise to the "Asgill Affair," an unfortunate business stemming from the hanging by the British of Captain Joshua Huddy, of the New Jersey militia—a prisoner at the time—and the threatened hanging by the Americans of a certain Captain Asgill, a British officer captured at Yorktown, in reprisal. The matter dragged on until July, when Lady Asgill appealed to Marie Antoinette on her son's behalf. The latter appealed to Vergennes, who appealed to Washington, and Congress released Asgill. The incident assumed such international importance that Washington—following the death of Colonel

Tilghman—saw fit to expound on it at length in a letter of condolence written to James Tilghman to refute any aspersions, expressed or implied, on the character of his late aide-de-camp.

When Tilghman left Headquarters for his long leave of absence his mind was very much on his private affairs, and particularly on his consuming love for Anna Maria Tilghman, his first cousin, the second daughter and fifth (and youngest) child of his Uncle Matthew. Tench had first met her in 1779[7] and was captivated by the intelligence, amiability, and beauty of his cousin.

> Without pretensions to high culture, either in the lighter accomplishments, or the more solid acquirements, for which her residence in the country afforded small opportunity, she was nevertheless intelligent, as well as naturally endowed with a most excellent judgment. The habit of her father conversing with her freely and constantly upon public business, and his custom of having her with him at Annapolis when attending to colonial or state affairs, and at Philadelphia when serving in congress, made her familiar with the political movements and stirring events of the time. When thrown upon her own resources after his and her husband's death, she manifested a most excellent capacity for the conduct of her private affairs. Nor was she devoid of literary skill, as is shown by an unedited memoir of her father,[8] which she left behind her, and her numerous letters. In religion she was of the Church of England and its successor in America; and while holding to its doctrines with the tenacity of conviction, she was most liberal and tolerant of the opinions of those who differed from her in belief.[9]

A truly remarkable woman, the principal tragedy of her life was the premature death of her husband and the fifty-two years she spent as a widow, a circumstance which she seemed to have borne most admirably.

> She lived to a great age, retaining her faculties to the end unimpaired, honored and revered by all, beloved by her children and her children's children to the third generation. She cherished to the last memories of her early lost husband.[10]

By 1782, matters between himself and Anna Maria had progressed to the point of near spontaneous combustion. In the certain belief that the end of the war was in sight if not in hand, Tench wrote to his Uncle Matthew to inform him of his serious intentions and to ask for permission to press his suit on a course contemplated to lead to the altar. Uncle Matthew's permission was readily granted, and the marriage was scheduled for the winter of 1782. However, the illness of Charles Carroll, Barrister, who had married Anna Maria's elder sister Margaret, caused a postponement until 9 June 1783, when it took place in Saint Michaels Parish, Talbot County, Maryland.[11] A rare and most intimate letter from Tench to Anna Maria has survived the years. Tench, who could write with clarity and force when drafting documents for Washington, proved himself no less skillful when cast in the role of an ardent lover. Now in the hands of a descendant, the letter is full of the extravagant language and the graceful, romantic conceits characteristic of the late eighteenth century. It is remarkable, too, for the frankness with which Tench speaks of an earlier love, "a pursuit of a similar nature," the object of which remains shrouded in mystery. The letter, written from Philadelphia, is dated 6 August 1782 and is in Appendix I.

The marriage, albeit short, was a happy one, resulting in two children—both daughters—one born posthumously. The latter, Elizabeth Tench Tilghman, married Colonel Nicholas Goldsborough, of Otwell, Talbot County, Maryland, where Anna Maria was to die, aged eighty-eight, on 17 January 1843. The older daughter, Anna Margaretta, married—to the confusion of generations of genealogists and historians—*her* cousin, Tench Tilghman of Hope, another Talbot County plantation, producing a son. From this son came a grandson and also a great grandson, all named Tench.

In the five months that Tilghman was away from Headquarters in 1782, not only was he avidly courting Anna Maria but was also beginning his preparations for a return to his earlier occupation as a merchant. It was a period when his correspondence with Washington was shamefully neglected, leading the latter to scold Tilghman in an offhand, jovial fashion over lack of news from him, although rumors of the impending marriage of Tilghman had reached headquarters. From Newburgh on 10 July 1782 Washington wrote:

'Til your Letter of 28th. Ulto. (which is the first from you, and the only direct acct. of you, since we parted at Philadelphia) arrived, we have had various conjectures about you. Some thought you

Anna Maria (Tilghman) Tilghman, Tench Tilghman's widow.
Portrait by Thomas Beale Bordley. Courtesy: Mrs. Arthur L. Shreve, Jr.

were dead, others that you were *Married*, and all that you had *forgot* us. Your letter is not a more evident contradiction of the first and last of these suppositions, than it is a tacit confirmation of the Second; and as none can wish you greater success in the prosecution of this, if it is the plan you are upon than I do; so believe me sincere, when I request you take your own time to accomplish it, or any other business you may have on hand. At the same time permit me to assure you, that you have no friend that wishes more to see you than I do.

Perhaps it was the latter sentiment that cajoled Tilghman to return to duty; for whatever reason he was back at Newburgh by 11 August 1782,[12] to stay with Washington until just before Christmas of the same year,[13] his absence—along with that of Colonels Cobb and Trumbull—being noted by Washington in a letter to Major Hodijah Baylies written on 8 January 1783. He was not to see Washington until a year later, when he stood by his Chief's side in the Old State House in Annapolis as both resigned their commissions, entering without reservation into the ways of peace.

Throughout history one of the stock results of warfare has been the bestowal—particularly by the winning side—of high political and social influence on the military men who actively participated on the battlefields. So it was with the Revolutionary War, especially so since the nation's history began with the successful conclusion of that war. Ex-officers of the army had a genuine advantage. Those of relatively senior rank,[14] such as Tilghman, and those who shared a personal attachment to Washington, as Tilghman did, were not ony drawn to each other by common experience, but were also clothed with a special gratitude. Washington had urged Tilghman to stay in the army, but since Tilghman's natural disposition and early training inclined him more to the ways of peace, and in the light of a perceived reluctance on the part of Congress to establish and maintain a standing army commensurate with the national dignity, he declined.[15]

In June 1783, however, another avenue for national service presented itself when Tilghman was nominated to become Secretary For Foreign Affairs (Secretary of State) of the infant republic. Other nominees included Arthur Lee, Jonathan Trumbull, Jr., George Clymer, General Schuyler, and Thomas Jefferson. Clymer, Schuyler, and Jefferson all withdrew, causing Congress to throw out all the nominations while seeking more information from Europe on the diplomatic situation.[16] While the exercise was fruitless, it nevertheless demonstrated the extent of Tilghman's influence and the pervasiveness of his reputation.

Tilghman, meanwhile, was intent upon his plans to return to the mercantile business. In concert with Robert Morris, whose financial "art magick"[17] had brought the colonies through the worst of their financial woes during the war, Tilghman decided that the port of Baltimore provided the most promising base for the business which they proposed to establish. Morris, whose land speculations were later to ruin him, agreed to provide half of the anticipated working capital in return for half of the profits. Accordingly Tilghman and Morris each put up £2500, "current money of Maryland, in specie, at the rate of seven shillings to the Mexican dollar," with Colonel Tilghman entitled to an additional £400 annually "in consideration of his residence in Baltimore."[18] The articles of incorporation were dated 1 January 1784, and were to be in force for seven years. Mr. Morris signed in Philadelphia, where he was to continue to reside, in the presence of his partner there, Mr. John Swanwick, and Gouverneur Morris. Colonel Tilghman signed in Baltimore, his signature being witnessed by John Richardson and Jacob Sampson. It has been estimated that each partner's share was worth $12,000 in today's currency.[19] Tilghman was not a partner in, and consequently did not share in, the responsibility for Morris's Philadelphia mercantile banking enterprises.

The partners chose their base of operations well. A mere sixty acres when founded in 1729, Baltimore Town remained in obscurity for several decades, one port in many in Maryland's tobacco economy. A drawing by John Moale in 1752 shows only about two dozen buildings, including a brewery and Saint Paul's Church. In these days of its early development Baltimore was cut into two unequal parts by Jones Falls, a meandering stream which assumed a considerable width just before emptying into the Patapsco River. To the west was Baltimore Town proper, with its harbor, ships, ship chandlers, and warehouses, and to the east lay Jones Town, named for David Jones, one of the first to settle on the other, more distant side of the waterway. Still farther to the east lay Fells Point, later to flourish as a shipbuilding center.

But by the 1760s the fledgling town was bustling with goods and workers from all parts of the globe. Wheat, without question, was the basis of the prosperity which literally engulfed the new settlement within thirty years of its founding. Its whole economy was geared to process, store, transport, and sell the grain.

As the population on the frontier grew and wheat production increased, so grew Baltimore's port-related commerce. Its merchants, quick to see opportunity knocking, met the challenge by building more flour mills, more wharves, more warehouses, and more ships. An insatiable demand for manpower arose, with sailors, carpenters, iron workers, millers, and clerks in short supply.[20] The population, a mere five thousand before the war, nearly tripled by 1790, including more than 1,200 negro slaves. The English formed the majority, but the Irish and Germans were strong minorities. There were a few French as well. Baltimore's public buildings—particularly the courthouse, which incorporated a vault-like passageway to accommodate carriages—rivaled those in New York and Philadelphia. It was a vital and exciting place, on the verge of a great future.[21]

As a first order of business the new partnership, styled Tench Tilghman & Co., wrote at once to every European mercantile house with which Robert Morris had done business, informing them of the new business connection and of the firm's capabilities. It was immediately rewarded with a vast network of correspondents, owing to Morris's far-reaching influence in the prewar and war periods. From Cadiz, Bordeaux, London, Genoa, Barcelona, Hamburg, Leghorn, Lisbon, Falmouth, Bristol, Gibraltar, and Marseilles the letters poured in, offering or requesting services.[22] Reflecting the nature of the times the demand for flour was immediate, with the firm of Livingston and Turnbull, of Gibraltar, informing Tilghman that it would accept that commodity in unlimited quantities, suggesting that the ships carrying it return to Maryland with mules picked up in the West Indies.[23] Seldom did any mercantile firm enjoy such an auspicious beginning.

The house which Tench and his family occupied in Baltimore, always said to have been across Lombard Street from the Friends Meeting House, can now be placed with certainty on the

Robert Morris, "the Financier of the Revolution" and Tilghman's
postwar business partner. Portrait by Charles Willson Peale.
Courtesy: New Orleans Museum of Art.

north side of Lombard, between present Howard and Eutaw Streets, on a tract of land called "Lunn's Addition,"[24] then recently developed by Tilghman's friend and fellow Revolutionary soldier, Colonel John Eager Howard. Almost certainly not a row house, an idea of its appearance if not its size can be gained from the recently restored house at 9 Front Street (in Jones Town), the home of Baltimore's second mayor, Thorowgood Smith, who lived there from 1802 to 1804. Typical of the period, Smith's house was built of brick about 1790, two and a half stories high, with two dormer windows facing the street from an angled roof. Its facade is simple Georgian—three shuttered windows across the front of the second floor, directly over two more shuttered windows of similar size and shape (nine over nine panes) and a matching front entrance. Flat arches of gauged brick support the tops of the windows and the front door, opening beneath a leaded glass transom. The window sills are of fluted limestone; the trim traditionally white. Between the first and second stories an attractive architectural feature called a "belt"—four or five courses of brick—protrudes horizontally by several inches from the otherwise flat surface. Three marble steps lead to the front door, bordered on either side by a simple iron railing, painted black.

A massive chimney to acommodate a multiple number of flues arises from the north wall of the main structure. Behind the Smith house, as with most houses of the era, an L-shaped flat-roofed, two-story brick dependency containing the kitchen, pantry, and servants quarters connects with the main house. While not elaborate the overall appearance is most pleasing.

In such a house Tilghman lived while guiding the destinies of Tench Tilghman & Co. We can only speculate on its size but we do know it was big enough to accommodate his growing family and guests as well. For one in Tilghman's position—one of impeccable family background reinforced by war service of equal distinction—life in Baltimore must have been very pleasant in those days. From his house on Lombard Street it was but a short carriage ride to Mount Clare, where Anna Maria's older sister Margaret—recently widowed by the death of her husband Charles Carroll, Barrister—presided over one of the city's noteworthy homes. Friends and other relatives were on every side, and while travel was arduous and would remain so for the next three-quarters of a century, Tench and Anna Maria had parents, uncles, aunts, brothers, sisters, and cousins stretched in a semicircle resting on Philadelphia at one end and Annapolis at the other, with an overly generous number of them coming and going through Baltimore at all seasons of the year. The business was going well, a daughter was born to them, and the future looked bright.

On 14 January 1784 the Continental Congress ratified the Treaty of Paris, and the War of The Revolution was formally over. The closely-knit group which had once surrounded Washington was scattered; some were dead—Lord Stirling and John Laurens recently, Mercer since Princeton, and Charles Lee also, the once highly respected general who fell from favor after assuming the role of Washington's adversary in the days of the Conway Cabal. Baylor was an invalid from wounds received at Tappan. Harrison, the "Old Colonel," was a Chief Justice on the Maryland Bench and Elias Boudinot, a friend from the Morristown winters was President of the Continental Congress where McHenry—always "Mac" to Tench—was now a member. General Knox was Secretary of War under the Articles of Confederation and Alexander Hamilton, "Hammy," had returned to the private practice of law in New York. Lafayette, after a two year absence in France, was on the threshold of a return to America and a visit to Tench and Anna Maria in Baltimore. He would come to the United States again on a second postwar visit in 1824, with a stop in Plimhimmon to pay his respects to Anna Maria, for by that time Tench would be to his devoted widow only a hallowed memory.

CHAPTER 13

The Shadows Lengthen . . .
and an End Too Soon

Thus some of the pillars of the Revolution fall.
—Washington to Jefferson, 1 August 1786

The severe winter of 1784-85 left the port of Baltimore iced in until March, adding other difficulties to a local economy confused at best.[1] But despite war-born inflation which had bred a distrust of all but specie money, Baltimore continued to prosper. By 1782 its population had grown to 8,000. "Trade flourishes and the spirit of building exceeds belief. Not less than three hundred houses are put up in a year. Ground rents is [sic] little short of what they are in London."[2] By 1784 the city had grown so large that Calvert Street had to be extended northward, and in the same year three new markets were constructed: Marsh Market (now called Market Place and the site of Baltimore's Wholesale Fish Market), the Hanover Market at Hanover and Camden Streets, the last vestiges of which disappeared as late as 1973, and the original Broadway Market, for the convenience of the people of Fell's Point. The latter, in rebuilt fashion, still stands. Schools, libraries, and theaters sprang up[3]—even horse racing—and while the cultural expansion was not in any way systematic, the trend persisted.

For Tilghman, immersed in his mercantile life and now the father of his first-born, Anna Margaretta, who appeared on the scene on 24 May 1784,[4] a further treat was in store. Lafayette, his old comrade-in-arms, would visit Baltimore and stay with him and Anna Maria in their home on Lombard Street. In June 1784

Lafayette had embarked in the packet *Courier de l'Europe* for the United States, arriving in New York on 4 August.[5] After stops in Philadelphia and New York, he was met by General Washington in Richmond and conducted to Mount Vernon. Documentation of that visit is notably thin, but it is known that he stayed at Mount Vernon for a fortnight before journeying to Baltimore, Philadelphia, upper New York State, and Massachusetts. Leaving Mount Vernon on 28 August, Lafayette arrived in Baltimore on 1 September to be met with a thunderous welcome. "All classes vied in their attentions, and even the recent Irish emigrants joined in the general tribute of welcome and praise."[6] A great banquet of three hundred covers was given in his honor at Grant's Tavern, arranged by a committee consisting of Tilghman, John Smith, Nicholas Rogers, Samuel Purviance, and James Calhoun.[7] Smith and Rogers, like Tilghman, were former officers in the Continental Army.

The following congratulatory address was delivered by the committee consisting of John Smith, Samuel Purviance, James Calhoun, Tench Tilghman, and Nicholas Rogers, on behalf of all of the citizens of Baltimore. Tilghman himself may have read it, although there is no hard evidence to substantiate that fact:

Sir: — While the citizens of Baltimore embrace the present occasion of expressing their pleasure in again seeing you among them, they feel the liveliest emotions of gratitude for the many services you have rendered their country. They can never forget the early period in which you engaged in our cause, when our distressed and precarious situation would have deterred a less noble and resolute mind from so hazardous an enterprise: nor the perseverance and fortitude with which you shared the fatigues and sufferings of a patriotic army. They especially shall never cease to remember that the safety of their town is owing to those superior military virtues which you so conspicuously displayed against a formidable enemy during your important command in Virginia. But your love for this country has not terminated with the war. You have laid us under fresh obligations by your successful representations, to free trade from those shackles that abridge mutual intercourse. To that profound veneration and gratitude which we entertain for the singular interposition of your nation and its illustrious monarch, we have only to add our sincere wishes that you may long enjoy that glory which you, in particular, have so justly merited.

General Lafayette's answer:

Gentlemen: — Your affectionate welcome makes me feel doubly happy in this visit, and I heartily enjoy the flourishing situation in which I find the town of Baltimore. Amidst the trying times which you so kindly mention, permit me with a grateful heart to remember, not only your personal exertions as a volunteer troop, your spirited preparations against a threatening attack, but also a former period when, by your generous support, an important part of the army under my command was forwarded - that army to whose perseverance and bravery, not to any merit of mine, you are surely indebted. Attending to American concerns, gentlemen, it is to me a piece of duty as well as a gratification to my feelings. In the enfranchisement of four ports and their peculiar situation, it was pleasing to France to think a new convenience is thereby offered to a commercial intercourse, which every recollection must render pleasing, and which from its own nature and a mutual good will, cannot fail to prove highly advantageous and extensive. Your friendly wishes to me, gentlemen, are sincerely returned, and I shall ever rejoice in every public and private advantage that may attend the citizens of Baltimore.[8]

It was during this visit to Maryland by Lafayette that the Maryland Legislature passed an act declaring Lafayette "and his male heirs forever citizens of Maryland." As an official act of the State of Maryland it became a part of the Federal Law, when Maryland accepted the Constitution. While this question has not come before the Supreme Court, it is a reasonable presumption that the descendants of Lafayette may be considered citizens of the United States.[9]

The Society of The Cincinnati, composed of officers of the Continental Line, was founded 13 May 1783 at the Verplanck house, near the village of Peekskill, New York. Named in honor of "that illustrious Roman, Lucius Quintus Cincinnatus, and being resolved to follow his example, by returning to their citizenship, (the officers) think they may with propriety denominate themselves The Society of the Cincinnati."[10] The society may have been the brainchild of General Knox, who first advanced proposals for its organization three days earlier, in the cantonments along the Hudson River, near Newburgh. With the acceptance of the proposals, George Washington was asked to be its first President General. He accepted, serving in that capacity until his death.

Almost from its inception the charge was made against the Society that it created an aristocracy in the country, with emphatic opposition to the clause in the Institution which provided for hereditary succession.

> So much animosity developed that General Washington proposed that the hereditary feature be abolished. At the first triennial meeting of the Society, held at Philadelphia on 15 May 1784, the amended Institution was referred to the several State Societies for ratification. Some of them refused to accept these changes in the original Institution, and as unanimous assent was required to make the resolution binding, it failed to pass and the Institution has remained to this day as originally proposed and adopted . . . In France the Reign of Terror, with its attending massacres, did away with any further meetings there, though one of the last actions taken by Louis XVI, patron of the Order in France, was to approve a list of officers who had been proposed for membership.[11]

In America opposition to the Society eventually subsided, and at the present time all dormant branches—including that in France—have been revived and are now active and increasing in membership. It remains a military, benevolent, social, and non-political order, essentially in keeping with the concepts of its founders.

On 20 November 1783, at Mann's Tavern in Annapolis, officers of the Maryland Line, at the request of Major General Smallwood, met to organize the Maryland Society.[12] The Institution was read and adopted, and officers elected, General Smallwood becoming the first president of the Maryland Society. Tilghman was among the original members, each officer contributing a month's pay, ranging from $20 for an ensign to $166 for a major general. Others who became original members included Generals Williams and Gist, Lieut. Colonels John Eccleston and Nathaniel Ramsey, Majors John Swan and John Lynch, Captains James McFadon and Paul Bentalou—the latter of Pulaski's Polish Legion—and Lieutenants John Stricker, Clement Skerrett and John Brevitt. In addition to the above, all of whom served in the Maryland Line, Lieut. Colonel Robert Ballard of the 4th Regiment of the Virginia Line and Captain John Bankson of the Pennsylvania Line, officers who had taken up residence in Baltimore, joined the Maryland Society.[13] It is interesting to note that William Paca, the Signer and incumbent

Governor of Maryland, was made an honorary member in the absence of military qualifications. Sharp-eyed readers familiar with Baltimore and its history will recognize at once the names of men who either played a prominent part in the development of postwar Baltimore or who gave their names to streets in the rapidly growing town, or both.

On 30 October 1783 General Washington wrote to Major L'Enfant, commissioning him to purchase eight badges (referred to as "Eagles") of the Cincinnati in Paris. This L'Enfant did, and the President General presented one to each of his principal aides-de-camp. The "Tilghman Eagle," as it known in the society, is one of the best preserved copies known, and is the Eagle from which official replicas were made upon the Society's order in 1935.[14] On 7 June 1784, from Baltimore, Tilghman wrote to Washington to thank him:

> . . . I beg leave to take this opportunity of acknowledging the rect. of your Excellency's letter of the 18th of May from Philada. accompanied by a Badge of the Order of the Cincinnati, of which Society I have the honor of being a Member. I pray your Excellency to accept my warmest and most grateful thanks for this distinguishing mark of your attention and regard. I had before received many proofs of your Esteem, but I must confess you have by this last instance of your goodness, made the most flattering addition — I shall now wear my Badge with a full conviction of having deserved it, or it would never have been presented by the illustrious hands of him, whose modest Nature — unsullied honor — and true Glory it was the object of the Institution to commemorate —[15]

The short respite of Tilghman at Mount Vernon in September 1781 while accompanying Washington and Rochambeau on the forced march from New York to Yorktown was to be his first and last visit to Washington's plantation although he was asked, indeed entreated, on a number of occasions to come for a visit and to bring Anna Maria with him. From 1784 on, however, Tilghman was to play an important part in helping the commander in chief step down from center stage as America's idolized military hero and resume his life as a successful Virginia planter. Even while actively engaged in establishing the foundations of his mercantile business Tilghman found time to become Washington's agent for every sort of business transaction, from purchasing articles for domestic or plantation use to selling the products of Washington's farm. The relationship was in fact simply the continuation of the long standing bond between the two men, with the substitution of one set of responsibilities for another, since Tilghman became a civilian (in reality, if not officially) before Washington, and had taken up these new duties while Washington was still at Newburgh. Typical of their correspondence of this period is Washington's letter to Tilghman written from his headquarters there on 10 January 1783. It is a long letter, too lengthy to be quoted in full, and deals with matters of state as well as those of domesticity. (For appropriate extracts pertaining to the Washington and Tilghman relationship during this period, see Appendix I.)

The range of Tilghman's activities for his former chief knew no bounds. He contracted for carpenters and masons,[16] he hired servants from the lists of newly arrived immigrants at the port of Baltimore and tried to find a combination of tutor and secretary for Washington and the children of his household. When Washington wanted to complete the greenhouse (orangery) at Mount Vernon he asked Tilghman

> to give me a short description of the Green-house at Mrs. Carroll's . . . the information I wish to obtain is, the dimensions of Mrs. Carroll's Green-house, what kind of a floor is to it, how high from that floor to the bottom of the window frame, what height the windows are from bottom to top, how high from the top to the ceiling of the house, whether the ceiling is flat, or of what kind, whether the heat is conveyed by flues, and a grate, whether those flues run all round the House, the size of them without, and in the clear. Whether they join the wall, or are separate and distinct from it, if the latter, how far they are apart, with any suggestions you may conceive necessary.[17]

Washington's interest was understandable enough, since the greenhouse at Mount Clare, supervised by the barrister's wife, Margaret Tilghman Carroll, was famous for its exotic produce, including pineapples, oranges, lemons, and broccoli.

Within a week Tilghman had dispatched a letter to Washington with answers to all his questions, plus a detailed sketch of the greenhouse at Mount Clare. (See illustration, page 189 and Appendix I.) The letter is interesting for a number of reasons, not the least of which is the light shed upon indoor horticulture as practiced in the eighteenth century.

There can be no doubt that the magic name of Morris had a great bearing on the prosperity, albeit short, of Tilghman's mercantile life. Morris's business acumen, which at this point had not deserted him, also led Morris to make available to Tilghman—in the early days of the Tilghman-Morris business relationship—the advisory services of John Swanwick, a partner in the Philadelphia firm of Willing, Morris and Swanwick. In the first six months of the existence of Tench Tilghman & Company Swanwick wrote a series of letters to Tilghman setting forth in detail certain procedures, all eminently proper, to be followed in the operation of the new firm.[18] Meanwhile Morris, versatile as ever, was following other pursuits. In October 1785 he was elected to the General Assembly of Pennsylvania for the special purpose of defending the formation and operations of the Bank of North America, being re-elected the following year. In 1787, the year following Tilghman's untimely death, he was a delegate to the convention meeting in Philadelphia which gave the United States its Constitution. The position of Secretary of the Treasury was offered to him and declined, but he was one of Pennsylvania's first two representatives in the United States Senate under the organization of the new government, serving from 1789 to 1795. Not until three years later did his disastrous speculations in vast tracts of western lands catch up with him, leading to financial ruin and in February 1798, to imprisonment—a full twelve years after the death of his limited partner Tench Tilghman.

In 1785 Morris had completed arrangements with the French Farmers General, the French tobacco monopoly, to supply it with 60,000 hogsheads of tobacco over the next three years, a quarter of which was to come from Maryland. While Morris was Tilghman's only partner at the beginning of their commercial enterprise, James Carey soon joined Tench Tilghman & Company, an association which was to last until Tilghman's death and beyond.[19] The first cargo shipped by Tilghman for Morris's account left Maryland in December 1784, before the contract with the French had been signed. In 1785 Tench Tilghman & Company shipped 1,891 hogsheads to France under the terms of the contract, far short of the quota established for Maryland tobacco for that year, i.e., 5,000 hogsheads "fit for smoaking."[20]

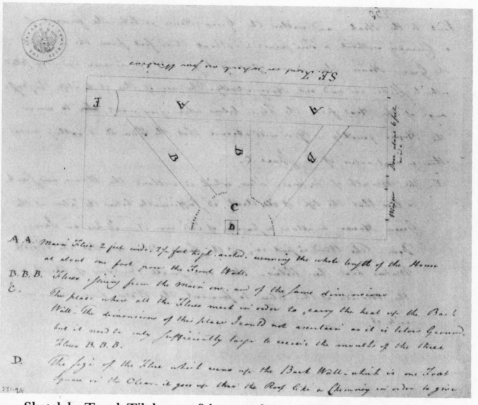

Sketch by Tench Tilghman of the greenhouse at Mount Clare, home of Mrs. Charles Carroll, widow of Charles Carroll, barrister, and Tilghman's sister-in-law, sent to Washington at the latter's request in order to facilitate the rebuilding of the greenhouse at Mount Vernon.
Courtesy: Library of Congress.

In all, Tench Tilghman & Company shipped 3,029 hogsheads of tobacco to France for Morris's account, the last shipments totalling 224 hogsheads leaving Baltimore on three separate vessels, i.e., *Philadelphia* on 18 April 1786—the day of Tilghman's death—with 20 hogsheads aboard and two days later *Bache and Lee* with 200 and *Independence* with 4.

Morris, who by shrewd manipulation of the price had created for himself on this side of the water a tobacco monopoly matching that of the French, brought down upon himself anguished howls from the Virginia growers, leading Thomas Jefferson to intercede on their behalf. Jefferson "won the right to have other American merchants import an additional 15,000 hogsheads into France in 1786 and probably was instrumental in preventing a renewal of Morris's contract in 1788."[21]

In at least two accounts in family papers[22] the statement is made that Morris's ultimate bankruptcy caused the failure of Tench Tilghman & Company. There seems to be no basis for this; chronology alone would seem to rule it out. There may have been other local, more restricted considerations to hamper the smooth execution and probate of Tench's estate, but it is highly unlikely that Morris's failure, knowledge of which Tilghman was happily spared, contributed in any substantial degree to the demise of Tilghman's business. If Carey was affected, it was as an individual. In the Tilghman Papers in the Maryland Historical Society are two Administration of Estate renderings by "Carey and Tilghman" (James Carey and Thomas Ringgold Tilghman, one of Tench's younger brothers, who took over the operation and/or liquidation of Tench Tilghman & Co. upon the death of Tench) which bear this out. In neither instance, particularly in the document dated 1803, is there any evidence of distributions made to claimants brought in by Morris's failure.[23] On the contrary, to Morris went only those sums due him in accordance with the fifty-fifty agreement which created the partnership between Tilghman and Morris but which by scope and practice was limited to operations in Baltimore, entirely outside Morris's broader financial horizons emanating from Philadelphia.

From 1781 to 1789, prior to the adoption of the Constitution, the struggling national government was operating under the Articles of Confederation. The resulting lack of central authority compounded the difficulties of the postwar reconstruc-

War Office 2nd December 1785

Dear Sir

I have to acknowledge the receipt of your favor of the 21st ultimo

The board of treasury at my instance will remit you immediately an order for the sum of four hundred dollars on their Agent in Maryland

I will thank you to inform me of the receipt of the sum that I may have the pleasure of writing you an official letter on the occasion

I expect in the course of a month or two to receive all the swords which were voted by Congress as testimonies of their special approbation, upon receiving them I shall have the pleasure of transmitting yours

I am
Dear Sir
With great sincerity
Your affectionate
Humble Servant
Knox

Col.
Tench Tilghman

Letter from Henry Knox, First Secretary of War, to Tench Tilghman regarding the "elegant sword" voted him by Congress, dated 2 December 1785. Courtesy: Anderson House Museum, Society of The Cincinnati.

tion period, as the states were joined together only loosely and had no chief executive. Fearful of substituting another form of tyrannical government for the one they had just overthrown, the Americans were leery of vesting great power in a central government. It was not a situation to Tilghman's liking. He wrote to Matthew Tilghman, his uncle, father-in-law, and the undisputed father of Maryland's Constitution, to express his sentiments in the most vigorous of terms. The letter was dated 5 February 1786.

> It is a melancholy truth, but so it is that we are at this time the most contemptible and abject nation on the face of the earth. We have neither reputation abroad nor union at home. We hang together merely because it is not the interest of any other power to shake us to pieces, and not from any well-cemented bond of our own. How should it be otherwise? The best men we have are all basking at home in lucrative posts, and we send the scum to represent us in the grand national council. France has met us there on equal terms. Instead of keeping a man of rank as minister at our court, she sends a person in quality of *charge d'affaires* who was but a degree above a domestic in the family of our late minister. All joking apart, I view our Federal affairs as in most desperate straits. I have long been convinced that we cannot exist as republics. We have too great a contrariety of interests ever to draw together. It will be a long time before any one man will be hardy enough to undertake the task of uniting us under one head. I do not wish to see the time.[24]

He did not. His health, frail since his departure from military service, was failing rapidly even at the time the letter was written. Some months earlier, in a letter to his brother William, he had informed the latter that

> I was confined yesterday to my Room and Bed by one of those fevers which generally make one attack upon me in the fall. I immediately administered Tartar and Bark and have today no other feelings but those of great lassitude.[25]

On 31 January 1786, five days before Tench wrote to his father the melancholy letter quoted above, Robert Morris had written to Tench from Philadelphia, entreating him to pay close attention to his health.

> I am very sorry to perceive by Your letter of the 24th ins[t]. that you have anything of the Complaint You mention, it is of a most

dangerous kind, requires care & attention, therefore for Godsake do not Neglect it, leave business and everything else to the care of Your People & do not run a risque of your Health or Life for any Consideration.

Again from Morris on 12 April 1786: "I am very happy to find your health is returning, pray take care & do not expose yourself to take cold again."[26]

In February Tench recuperated slightly after a severe attack of what is now believed to have been hepatitis, but his strength was waning steadily. His sister Molly expressed her concern in a letter written to Polly Pearce from Chestertown over a period of several days in April 1786, the first part written on Thursday the 13th:

When my father left Baltimore my Brother (Tench) was better, tho' still too far from being well. I can only say I am not so uneasy about him as I was. Tomorrow we shall hear from him. God grant the accounts may be favorable. Little Peggy (Tench's daughter) was inoculated two days before Papa came home.

Then the following, added on Tuesday, April 18th:

Alas my dear Polly I am too unhappy about poor Tench to write you more than that we had Letters on Saturday, which inform'd us that he was no better but rather had lost strength. My God what his situation this moment may be. Indeed, I fear he is in great danger. My father went over this Morning, and alone, and a prey to every melancholy conjecture in your affectionate   M. T.[27]

Tilghman died that same day, in his 42nd year. He was buried in the old burial ground surrounding Saint Paul's Church. On 21 April 1786 the *Maryland Journal* carried his obituary:

Yesterday evening were interred in Saint Paul's Church Yard with the greatest mark of respect, the remains of the late Colonel Tench Tilghman, an eminent merchant of this town; he departed from this life on Tuesday evening, after having languished a long time under a most distressing illness, in the forty-second year of his age—In publick life his name stands high as a Soldier and Patriot, his political conduct during the late war having entitled him to the noblest praise, that of an independent, honest man; and his services in the honourable and confidential character of aid-de-camp [sic] to his Excellency, General Washington in the course of the glorious contest for Freedom and Independence deservedly obtained the approbation of his chief and his country; as a private character, the deep affection of his family, the sorrow of his friends, and the universal regret of his fellow citizens, show their sense of the heavy loss they have suffered in the death of this worthy man.

Public notice of Tilghman's death was in no wise restricted to Maryland. As far away as Massachusetts eulogies appeared in the papers of the day. The *Massachusetts Centinel* of 6 May 1786 gave this account:

> Lately departed this life at Baltimore, in the State of Maryland, aged 42, Tench Tilghman, Esq., a gentleman no less distinguished for publick than for private virtues: Of the former, it is enough to say, that he was during the late war, the confidential secretary and aid-du-camp [sic] to the illustrious commander in chief of the American forces—of the latter, his punctuality, integrity, and regularity as a merchant—his excellent deportment as a citizen, a parent, and a friend—and his general benevolence as a man, will long remain the precious testimonials—He bore the rank of Lieut. Col. in the army from April, 1777, to its being disbanded—he received the last publick acknowledgment of esteem from his great chief, on the 19th of October, 1781, on the occasion of the surrender of the Lord Cornwallis and his army—an event which he was sent to notify to Congress—who thereupon, on the 29th of the same month, voted him their plaudit of his merit and abilities; but a short time did he live, to enjoy the glories he had so well earned in the field—or the amiable character he had sustained in every part of life.

Washington in particular was unsparing in his eulogistic pronouncements, feeling a genuine sense of loss from the death of his constant wartime comrade. To Thomas Ringgold Tilghman, Tench's younger brother, from Mount Vernon on 10 May 1786:

> As there were few men for whom I had a warmer friendship, or greater regard, than for your brother, while living; so with much truth I can assure you that there are none whose death I more sincerely regret . . .

And to James Tilghman, on 5 June 1786, also from Mount Vernon:

> Of all the numerous acquaintances of your lately deceased son, and amidst all the sorrowings that are mingled on that melancholy

occasion, I may venture to assert (that excepting those of his nearest relatives) none could have felt his death with more regret than I did because no one entertained a higher opinion of his worth, or had imbibed sentiments of greater friendship for him than I had done.

But it was to Thomas Jefferson, later in that same summer, that Washington penned the accolade most often repeated in illustrations of the esteem in which Washington viewed his late and lamented aide-de-camp.

You will probably have head of the death of Genl Greene before this reaches you, in which cause you will, in common with your Countrymen, have regretted the loss of so great and so honest a man. Genl McDougall, who was a brave Soldier and a disinterested patriot, is also dead . . . Colo. Tilghman, who was formerly of my family, died lately and left as fair a reputation as ever belonged to a human character. Thus some of the pillars of the Revolution fall.[28]

On 11 October 1786, six months after Tench's death, Anna Maria Tilghman Tilghman gave birth to their second daughter and only other child, christened Elizabeth Tench. In the following May, with a generosity matching his wealth, Matthew Tilghman bought—as a haven for his widowed daughter and his two infant grandchildren—Plimhimmon, a substantial plantation adjacent to Oxford, Maryland. The owner at the time was Charles Markland, of Liverpool, who was paid £4,000 for it. The brick manor house, to which a two-story clapboard wing has been added by subsequent owners, is thought to have been built in the early 1700s by Captain John Coward, master of the clipper ship *Integrity*, who lived at Plimhimmon while his ship lay in port on its return voyages from England. Here the widowed Mrs. Tilghman, a woman of remarkable intellect, raised her two children, managed her own affairs astutely and led a life devoted to her family and to charitable works. And it was here that she entertained Lafayette during his 1824-25 visit to America. When invited to visit adjacent Queen Anne's County, Lafayette is quoted as saying:

It is my eager and affectionate wish to visit the Eastern Shore of this State. I anticipate the pleasure to recognize there several of my companions in arms, and among the relations of my departed friends to find the honored widow of a dear brother in General Washington's family, Colonel Tilghman . . .[29]

Anne Maria Tilghman did not die until 13 January 1843, a span of life remarkable even by twentieth century standards, much less the eighteenth or nineteenth. On being informed of her death her nephew-in-law, Judge Nicholas Brice, wrote:

> By letter of the date of the 16th January 1843 received this morning, the death of this excellent lady is announced as having taken place at Ottwell the residence of N. Goldsborough, Esq., her son-in-law, without a struggle and in full possession of her interlects at 9 o'clock on the 13th inst. in the 88th year of her age. No eulogium that I could confer would do full justice to her merits, as a wife, mother, mistress, neighbor and Christian. I will only say in addition that she was an accomplished lady of the old school of which few now remain.

To which his brother John added: "From a long acquaintance with this lady I feel myself authorized to bear with my brother the same testimony."[30]

PART FOUR

EPILOGUE

30 NOVEMBER 1971

CHAPTER 14

Epilogue

In Memory of Col. Tench Tilghman . . .
—Tilghman's epitaph

When Tench Tilghman died in April of 1786 he was buried in the graveyard which adjoined Saint Paul's Church, then as now located on the corner of Charles and Saratoga streets, in Baltimore. The original church building to occupy the site was replaced by a second in 1784,[1] only to be torn down and replaced by a third—the present edifice still in use—in 1817.[2] Referred to as "Old Saint Paul's" by virtue of the age of the parish, it continues to attract a sizeable and loyal congregation. By 1800, however, the surrounding graveyard had clearly become an unacceptable obstacle to the orderly expansion of the rapidly growing parish and city, forcing the vestry to seek a new location for the burial of the dead.[3]

For the new site the vestry chose a large vacant lot on the corner of Freemont and Lombard streets, not far from where Tench had lived. In the years between 1804 and 1817, all the bodies buried at the original site at Charles and Saratoga streets were also removed to the new location. By the standards of those days, the new burial site was still far removed from the city center.

It was inevitable, however, that once again the growth of the city would overtake the good intentions of the church fathers, and by the outbreak of the Civil War the graveyard was surrounded by industrial buildings on the south and east and by workers' housing on the north and west. Despite the deteriorating neighborhood the graveyard remained in active use until the

198

early 1920s. Meanwhile the industrialization of the area continued, and vandalism, despite the best efforts of the church
authorities and the police, became an increasingly serious prob-
lem. It was discovered at one point that several homeless men
had broken into one of the mausoleums and were actually living
there. Moreover the contemplated construction of an East-West
Expressway posed still another threat to the earthly remains of
the buried dead.[4]

By the mid-1960s the deplorable conditions led several of
Tench's descendants[5] to undertake the seemingly impossible task
of obtaining the written permission of *all* of his descendants once
again to remove his remains—this time to be interred in the
Oxford Cemetery, in Talbot County, which had had its beginnings as the private burial ground for the Tilghmans at Plimhimmon. The threat, which fortunately did not materialize, of the
extension of the superhighway through the western end of the
city-bound cemetery gave added impetus to the undertaking. It
was not until seven years later, however, with favorable replies in
hand from some seventy-odd adult lineal descendants, including
several French and Australian nationals, that the vestry of Old
Saint Paul's felt they had met the legal requirements imposed
by Maryland law and granted permission for the removal and
reinterment.

Thus it was that on Tuesday, 30 November 1971, in the
presence of thirty-five of his descendants, Colonel Tench Tilghman returned home. His earthly remains were buried beside
those of his wife, and the flat eighteenth century gravestone,
brought earlier from Old Saint Paul's Cemetery and restored to
its original condition, was placed on his grave. Washington himself had approved the inscription:[6]

In Memory of
Col. Tench Tilghman
Who died April 18, 1786
In the 42nd year of his age,
Very much lamented.
He took an early and active part
In the great contest that secured

The Independence of
The United States of America.
He was an Aide-de-Camp to
His Excellency General Washington
Commander in Chief of the American Armies,
And was honored
With his friendship and confidence,
And
He was one of those
Whose merits were distinguished
And
Honorably rewarded
By the Congress
But
Still more to his Praise
He was
A good man.

APPENDICES

Tilghman Correspondence

1. From Richard Tilghman II to Abraham Tilghman II.

Chester river in Maryland
2 July 1734

Dr. Sir

I received your letter by Mr. Blake with much Joy for I really
thought our names were extinct in England not having but one letter
now since your Father returned from the vituling office into the
Country tho I wrote several and directed them as he desired. I gladly
imbrace the opportunity of renewing a correspondence with you perhaps it may be some Satisfaction to you to know when and in what
manner one of your names and family wandered into this remote part
of the world (for then it was so esteemed) be pleased therefore to be
informed that in the year 1660 my father Richard Tilghman who was
brend a Surgeon with my mother a son and daughter came into this
province and brough₁ with him a tolerable fortune and settled in the
place where I now live they had many children but all the males died
before marriage excepting myself I was born in the year 1672 and my
father died in 75 my Mother lived a widow 20 odd years In the year
1700 I married Anna Maria one of the daughters of Capt Philemon
Lloyd who is now living we have eight children 5 sons and 3 daughters
My daughters are all married Mary married Mr. James Earle she is 32
years old has 3 sons 2 daugts. Henrietta Maria to Mr. George Robins
she is 27 years of age and has 2 daugts Anna Maria to Mr. William
Hemsley she is 25 years of age has one Son & 3 daughts My son Richard
is 29 William 23 Edward 21 James 18 and Mathew near 16. not any of
them married I praise God my children are dutiful and behave de-
cently to all then—I am now one of the Ld Proprietary Council of State
have been possest of several posts of honour but few of profit the latter
is generally given to such who can strongly solicit and make large
promises for which I have no talent. I am very thankful to you for your

kind invitation to any of my Sons that may come to England and do not doubt your Friendship to any of them if an opportunity should offer at present I have no prospect of crossing the Ocean for the politer parts of the world for some of them may have inclinations to that [any?] of them I am not of ability to bear the Expence and make a decent provision for them here however (I praise God) I am content I can make desires conform to my circumstances I can eat my bread with thankfulness and take my rest in peace I have by me an old imperfect manuscript where in among many trifling affairs I find the names of many of my name and family in the year 1540 I find William Tilghman the Elder with the arms of William Tilghman drawn with a pen and William the younger had a male in 1542 Edward and in 1543 Henry who died in 1576 I find Wheternal[1] Tilghman in 1579 Oswald in 1582 Charles in 1584 Lambert but who is the father of these I am at a loss to know for it dos not seam probable that it should be William the younger because of the distance of time between the birth of Henry and Wheternal besides there is a difference in the hand writing it is most probable that Edward was the Son of William the younger in the year 1555 he was bound prentince to serve eight years in 1561. William Tilghman the younger stood Godfather to Alexander son of Edward Tilghman Wheterhall Tilghman married Ellen his Wife in the year 1607 and his issue Mary Samuel Isaac Nathanial Susan Joseph James and Samuel Bengimin, Samuel Tilghman son of Wheternall was married to Allice Cox the 17th day of May 1645 My Fathers name was Richard born in the year 1626 Sn of Oswald Tilghman which I suppose was Brother to Wheternall their dwelling places were Snodland & East & West Malling if by the parish funds of Snodland or any other you could come to a clear Knowledge of our family we should be very much oblidge to you for the information

This Sir is the last information I can give of descent I am mistaken if your father did not inform me that he descended from Whetehall Tilghman As you goe to London sometimes I shall take it a favor if you please to take the trouble to get me the coat of arms of our family when and by whom obtained and what else may be nesary on such occasion the charge that arises thereupon I desire Mr. Samuel Hyde Merchant in London to pay and charge to my account my wife and children joyn with me in our kindest respects to you and yrs & that you may all Injoy health and prosperity is the fervent prayer of yr affectionate Humble Servt RT

Inclose yr letters directed to me to Mr. Samuel Hyde Mercht in London as they will come safe to hand.[2]

2. Tench Tilghman to his father, James Tilghman, 30 September 1768.

It gave us great pleasure to hear from your last Letter, dated at Connaughgahen, that your Journey had turned out so much to your Satisfaction, as far as that place, and we sincerely wish that you may be as agreeably disappointed in the latter as in the former part of your Tour. I shall first inform you of what you will be most anxious to hear, that is of the good Health of my Mother and the rest of the Family. My Brother is not yet come from Maryland nor do we expect him till M^r. Dulany leaves Baltimore.—Publick Affairs remain pretty much as you left them, here, but Things in Maryland have taken a Strange turn. Col^o. Eden is appointed Governor in M^r. Sharpes room, Allen has lost his Agency, which is given to my Uncle Matthew, and my Lord has made Jordan a present of Connegocheauge Manor. No one knows the Reason of these Sudden Changes, as none of the parties had the least Notice of them.—M^r. Shippen was married last Night to Miss Galloway. M^r. Laurence a few days ago to Miss Bond, and M^r. Cadwallader last Sunday to Miss Lloyd. Beveridge is under Suspicion of Matrimony with Miss Emlen, but if it is really so, is not yet made publick. The gentlemen of the Turf are much chagrined at the poor shew of Horses, and the prospect of bad Weather at our approaching Races, they seem heartily sick of the Jocky Club, and determined never to spend more of their time or Money to so little purpose.—
M^r. Penn sails with Friend in about a fortnight, M^r. Moore has taken his passage also, but we shall not be sure he has gone, till we hear of the Ship's leaving New Castle with him on Board.—These little Matters may serve to amuse you and let you know what's passing among us.—My good Mother and the rest of the Family join in Wishes for your Health and safe return with your most dutiful & Affectionate Son

Tench Tilghman[3]

3. Tench Tilghman to his father, James Tilghman, 15 October 1768. The letter is addressed to "James Tilghman, Esq. at Fort Stanwix, to be forwarded from Albany."

By Ennis, we had the pleasure of hearing of your safe Arrival at Fort Stanwix, but are sorry to find that you will be delayed there longer

205

than you expected, by waiting the Assemblage of the Indians.—My Mother and all the Family continue to enjoy the most perfect Health, she is now entirely relieved from that Anxiety she laboured under on your Account, by hearing from yourself and others, that this Journey, instead of impairing your Constitution is likely to be of Service to it.—As I wrote you last, a New Govr: is certainly appointed for Maryland, but the Appointment of my Uncle Matthew for the Agency is not so well confirmed, for tho' the Report gains ground, yet he has never had any regular advices from Home.—

Dicky Tilghman has at length been prevailed on to take a ride this way, he spent the Week of the Races with us, and is now on a Tour to Lancaster, Reading & Bethlehem in Company with M^r. Hemsley. When he came here he was very much reduced by the Ague, which had hung on him for a Twelve Month, but on taking the Bark properly he broke the Fit, and Soon mended in a most Surprizing Manner. I doubt not but this Jaunt will perfectly re-establish his Health. By our last Accounts from my Uncle, Hazens Affairs had taken some unfavourable Turn, as he was then negotiating a final Settlement with him some where about 15/ in the pound. He has compleated his purchase of the Vine Yard at £4 St^g P Acre, which is a great Bargain, the profits of it will go a good Way towards making up his heavy Loss.—

Be kind enough to present my Comp. to my Uncle Tubby and be assured I am most dutifully and Affect^y y^r.

Tench Tilghman[4]

4. Tench Tilghman to his father, "James Tilghman, Esq. If not return'd from Fort Stanwix to be forwarded from Albany," 29 October 1768.

We were much disappointed in Seeing the Governor and M^r. Chew return without you, but we hope your Business will permit you to follow them Soon.—I am Surprized that you were so long in receiving any of my Letters, as I wrote one or two before that of the 30th: Septem^r: which was the first that got to hand; they must have miscarried between Albany and Fort Stanwix. It gives me great pleasure to be still able to inform you of the perfect Health of all the Family, my Mother has only had one very slight Fit of the Head Ache Since you went away. M^r. Hemsley rec. a Letter from Jordan the other day in which he gives him certain information of my Uncles Appointment to the Agency, and of my Lord's presentation to him (Jordan) of Conuicheague Manor with 7000 Acres of Land adjacent. These Matters cause much Speculation below, they have already provided all our Family with Offices of profit. Jimmy Tilghman Att^y Genl. M^r. Hemsley Surveyor Genl. and so on. We have a Change among us that gives Offence to many people, that is the Appointment of P. Jones to the Treasury instead of Doc^r. Moore. There were some Slight Attempts to make Isaac Hunt Clk of the House, but the party found that was a pill too bitter to force even their own led Captains to Swallow. By our last Accounts from my Uncle, he was quite uncertain as to his time of leaving England, we may see him in a Week or two, and perhaps not this Fall.—We hear nothing from R——, except by the different Captains, who all have seen him upon Change and in different parts of London in good Health and Spirits. My poor Aunt is much distress'd, she thinks that by his not writing, he is again in Confinement, or left England, and that we conceal the Truth from her. My Grandmother is well and desires her Love to yourself and my Uncle Turbutt.—We look for you every day, and earnestly wish we may not be disappointed in seeing you soon return to us all and Y^r. dutiful and Affectionate Son

Tench Tilghman[5]

5. From James Tilghman (Philadelphia) to Henry Wilmot Esq. (England), 2 October 1774.

The Affair's of America are now in such a Situation and seem to be big with such important Consequences, that I cannot avoid troubling you with a few Thoughts upon a Subject of the Highest Concern. My Liberty, my Fortune and perhaps my Life may be involved in the Matters now in Agitation on this and your Side of the Water.

I wrote you heretofore that the Cause of Boston was taken up as the Cause of all America, It has brought on a Meeting of Deputies from South Carolina to New Hampshire inclusive, and the Congress hath been sitting at this place for about a Month. They profess to aim at a security of their Liberties, and in that Way to restore the wished for Harmony between the Mother Country and the Colonies. And I hope they are in general sincere. Their Deliberations do not perspire but in a small Degree. One of my Brothers, the Speaker of the Maryland Assembly, is of this Congress and lodges with me, And yet I know nothing of what's going. He can neither divulge, nor I inquire, consistent with the principles of Honor, You'll give me the Liberty in this private Way, to say, he is a man of steadiness and Moderation, and of the strictist Virtue, and utterly averse from all violent Measures. And yet I can find that he is not without Apprehensions of Consequences fatal to the Repose of both Mother Country and the Colonies, should the Parliament or the Ministry, which is the same thing persist in their present system. The Congress have already published a Request to the Merchants to import no more British or indeed European Goods. And I believe it is resolved on, that no Importaton shall be allowed but of Goods shipped, on or before the first of November. And I am told a non-exportation of Lumber to the West Indies immediately, and of every thing else to great Britian, to take Place at a future Day, is in Contemplation . . . .

I am no Politician, but my plan shou'd be to do away the present Causes of Discontent, and to give a Continental Assembly to transact the general Affairs of America or at least of the Continent, This wou'd make a constitutional Union, better in my opinion than these kind of occasional voluntary ones, which however offensive they may be at home, cannot be prevented. I have for the present done with this important disagreeable Subject, and sincerely wishing for better Prospects

I am yr most hb^le & with great
regard most obed^t Servt
1774 James Tilghman

P. S. I have kept my letter by me till now in expectation that I might have something material to inform you of the deliberations of the Congress but there is no intelligence to be depended on, I can collect from general Conversation that there is a moderate and a intemperate party amongst them but which is like to prevail does not transpire, My Brother seems exceedingly tired of the business and I believe thinks upon the whole there is too much heat amongst them, His plan is to keep off all violent proceeding's and to make a firm and respectful remonstrance containing the reasons of non importation and other modes of opposition, He is a firm stickler for the Liberties of America under a proper subordination to and connexion with the Mother Country.[6]

6. Tench Tilghman to his father, James Tilghman, 15 August 1776.

I can assure you your Anxiety on my Account is groundless on the score of Expence, Company & Habit of Idleness. As to the first I live at

less in proportion than at Philad. the second my acquaintance is confined to two or three young Gentlemen of the Generals Family, and to
the last you cannot conceive what a constant scene of Business we are
engaged in. My intent is not to stay with the Army longer than the
active part of the Campaign as I had taken a military part, I could not in
honour withdraw or hold myself back, when I found that contrary to all
Faith and Expectation the Olive Branch was presented accompanied
with Terms most ignominious. When you say "bear with me this once
and I will say no more on the Subject," you seem to hint as if you
thought, that your advice would be disagreeable or set hard upon me,
but indeed you are mistaken, I know it proceeds from your Regard to
me and from no other motive. We are told that the whole of General
Howe's forces are now arrived, and from the movement of yesterday
we expected an attack this morning, but it has rained very hard all
Night and that perhaps has hindered them[7]

7. Tench Tilghman to General Cadwalader, 18 January 1778.

. . . In the underhand political there is a deal of jugling. But I trust the
Storm will break upon the Heads of those who attempt to raise it. Great
pains are taking to swell the Character of the Northern Heroe and to
depreciate that of our worthy General. Who is at the bottom of this you
I dare say will easily guess. But that you may not be in doubt, it is a
Gentleman who resigned important offices at a critical time. Several
letters under the signature of a foreigner have already made their
appearance in the papers all tending to extol G[ates] as the first soldier
in the World, giving him the Credit of all the Northern successes and
not saying a syllable of the Merits of Lincoln or Arnold. The letters are
well wrote, but the Cloven foot is too plain, not to be discerned by the
most common Eye.

This damned faction founded solely upon the Ambition of one
Man, for G[ates] is but a puppet, is so fraught with every mischief, that
every honest Man ought upon the first discovery to give the Alarm, as
he would upon the discovery of a fire which if suffered to gethead,
would destroy one of our most valuable Arsenals. Many of our best
officers have already taken the Alarm and will speak in very plain terms
if matters require it. I cannot say that I am in the least uneasy. I am so
conscious that every action of the General's will bear the light, [from
the commencement of the War to this day,] that I wish they may be
called to view. I am certain that their splendor will confound all those

who like Moses work in the dark, and would wish to undermine the Men that they dare not attack by day. I know you so well, and know the regard you have for the General so well also, that I need not ask you to speak when there is occasion, and to paint matters in their true lights. This is the way to stop the poison that they are attempting to instill into the minds of the people thro' the Channel of a Newspaper—Conway is made Superintendant General with the Rank of Major General. He has come down full of his own importance and wrote the General a letter for which he deserved to be kicked. He treated it with the contempt it deserved, and sent a Copy of it to Congress, who I think must clip his Wings or affront the General direct. The Major's and Brigadier's General have all remonstrated against his extraordinary promotion from youngest Brigadier to Major General. Conway is of the Junto and M[ifflin's] right hand Man. If matters are pushed much farther, a scene will open that few people know any thing about. Arnold will speak and shew who oblige'd Burgoine to strike. I will give you a part of the secret History. Upon the 7th. October, Arnold seeing an advantage sent to Morgan to begin the engagement and pawned his honor to support him. Morgan attacked accordingly, and Arnold advanced his Way. Gates sent Arnold word to halt, he returned for answer, he had promised Morgan to support him and support him he would by G-d.—Victory crowned the Work, and the surrender was the Consequence of it. There are other matters also of a like nature, which would never have been known had not one man have attempted to have robbed all the rest of their share of the Glory . . . I have said enough to set you on fire, but be moderate—

Adieu my good Friend and believe me

Yrs. sincerely
Tench Tilghman

Make free with my Sentiments and with my Name if you have occasion—As Arnold said to Morgan—I will support you—[8]

8. Tench Tilghman to Robert Morris, 2 February 1778.

But I have another and more forcible reason [to wish you to be in Congress] which I will mention to you in confidence. Perhaps these regulations may meet with opposition from a certain quarter because they come from the General. You must have seen and heard some thing of a party forming against him. Publications under the signature of Delisle point out plainly his successor, and the unaccountable behaviour of the late Q^r M^r G^l does not leave a doubt in my mind that he is at the bottom of it. What are his inducements God only knows, but I am sure no man stood higher in the General's good Opinion. Our Enemies have already heard of and exult at this appearance of division and faction among ourselves, and the Officers of the Army who have been all of them at one time or another under his command are exasperated to the highest degree, at a thought of displacing him. I have never seen any stroke of ill fortune affect the General in the manner that this dirty underhand dealing has done. It hurts him the more because he cannot take notice of it without publishing to the World that the spirit of faction begins to work among us. It therefore behoves his Friends to support him against the malicious attacks of those who can have no reason to wish his removal but a desire to fill his place.

Altho' your Business may not admit of your constant attendance upon Congress I hope you will have an Eye towards what is doing there. If the General's conduct is reprehensible let those who think so make the charge and call him to account publickly before that Body to whom he is amenable. But this rascally method of calumniating behind the curtain ought to be held in detestation by all good Men . . .[9]

9. Tench Tilghman (Philadelphia) to James McHenry (Middlebrook) 25 January 1779.

Dear Mac -

I believe I am two or three letters in your debt, which I think is no great deal considering you love scribbling, and have time to indulge it. I have hunted in vain for Justamonds translation of Abbe Reynell. I have seen a copy in the hands of a private Gentleman, but am told there is not a set for sale in the city. I suppose you think we must be, by this time, so wedded to sweet Phila. that it will break our hearts to leave it. Far from it I assure you my Friend. I can speak for myself, and I am pretty certain I can answer for all, when I say that we anxiously wait for the moment that gives us liberty to return to humble Middle Brook. Philada. may answer very well for a man with his pockets well lined, whose pursuit is idleness and dissapation. But to us who are not in the first predicament, and who are not upon the latter errand, it is intolerable. We seem to work hard, and yet we do nothing; in fact we have no time to do anything and that is the true reason why a great assembly do so little. A morning visit, a dinner at 5 o'clock—Tea at 8 or 9—supper and up all night is the round *die in diem*. Does not the Republic go on charmingly? By the Body of my father as honest Sancho used to swear, we have advanced as far in luxury in the third year of our Indepeny. as the old musty Republics of Greece and Rome did in twice as many hundreds: But we Americans are a sharp people. And we are in more senses than one; and if we do not keep a sharp look out we shall be little the better for the profusion of money and no small quantity of Blood that has been spent. All cry out that nothing but economy can save us, and yet no one allows that he or she is extravagant. I will not touch upon politics. They are too valuable to trust to paper and Wax. You shall hear much when we fill the sociable bunks, where all is under the secure lock and key of Friendship . . ."[10]

10. Tench Tilghman to his father, James Tilghman.
Head Quarters Valley Forge
31st May 1778

Hon[d]. Sir

I recd. yours by General Cadwalader and by Gen[l] Dickinson. I cannot say they gave me pleasure because at the time of writing them you seem to have been under very great uneasiness. —I will not undertake to dictate, but I wish for your own sake, that of your family, and the preservation of your fortune, you would think seriously of conforming to the law of the Country in which you are obliged to live. If you thought the Measures which have been pursued, wrong, you have done everything in your power to oppose them, not by acting, but by speaking your sentiments moderately and in such a manner, that even those of a different opinion have not blamed you. A majority of people upon this Continent are determined to support the independency of America, and a great European Power has acknowledged and determined also to support them in it. Great Britain has herself in fact acknowledged the independency, for Sir Henry Clinton has this day informed the General that he is charged with dispatches from Lord Howe the Kings Commissioner to Congress. What these dispatches contain I do not know. But formerly they foolishly disdained to mention the name of Congress but in the most contemptuous manner. Things being thus circumstances, it is no more derogatory to your honour and Consicence to take an Oath of fidelity to the form of Government under which you live, than it is for a Member of any representative Body to take an Oath which he had opposed in the House. He takes it because the Majority think it right—A few days ago M[r]. Secretary Matlock inclosed me your parole, and desired me to forward it to you, informing you that you were discharged from it and at liberty to act as you should judge best. I take it for granted that you have seen the law of the State of Pennsylvania which affects you, but lest you should not, I inclose you a single sheet which has the two material sections N°. 8 and 9. As you are out of the province, you may take time to consider well of it, and if you chuse to conform, which I hope in God you will, you may do it any time within ten days after you come in. The folly of the British Ministry in sending out terms after they knew we had concluded an Alliance with France, crowns all their former acts of Madness. The terms of our Alliance with France are generous to the highest degree, we are not even bound to give them an exclusive trade. We only engaged to assist them should they be drawn into a War with England on our Account. You always treated my intelligence of the intentions of France as chimerical. I could not speak plainer than I did consistent with my duty and the confidence which is reposed in me. But you may be assured, that not only France but the whole of her Connection are determined to support America ag^t. Great Britain and whether she will be able to overpower us backed by such powerful Advocates you may judge from the Struggles we have heretofore made alone.[11]

11. Tench Tilghman to his father, James Tilghman, 12 June 1778.

You will receive a letter with this, that has been wrote some days, but no opportunity has offered of sending it. The Commissioners have arrived since. They are Earl Carlisle, Govr. Johnstone and M^r. W. Eden. Their Secretary Doc^r. Ferguson. Whether their powers are any greater than expressed in the Acts of parliament I do not know, but I suspect not, from the letters that Govr. Johnstone and M^r. Eden have wrote to the General. They are full of compliment and even adulation, but they regret that they are not likely to have a personal acquaintance with him. Congress you know had, upon the Rec^t. of the Copies of the Acts of Parliament determined not to negotiate but upon two Conditions, acknowledgment of Independene, or withdrawing of the Army . . . It seems agreed on all hands that the American War cannot be supported in conjunction with a french one. The arrival of the Commissioners has postponed the evacuation of Philad^a a little while, but I imagine it will soon take place. Under the present Situation of Affairs let me again press you to follow a step which several of your friends in similar circumstances to yourself has taken. M^r. Hamilton has taken the Oaths, and Charles Stewart told me to day that M^r. Chew would take them as soon as he came into the Province. He says M^r. Penn only hesitates because he thinks he might involve young M^r. Penn. How this would be in law I do not know. But to see you at peace with and conforming to what is now the establishment of this Country would give me greater pleasure than anything I have experienced in a Contest, in which I have faithfully laboured, and by which I flatter myself I have assisted my friends and have gained some reputation to myself. I am Dear and Hon^d. Sir

Y^r. most dutiful and Affec^t. Son
Tench Tilghman[12]

12. Tench Tilghman to his father, James Tilghman, 27 February 1778.

You ask me if I ever think of my private affairs and what situation they are in? I have the pleasure to inform you that I have taken all possible care of them and that I believe few people's considering the times are in so good. I have collected and secured in good hands about £8000. and for the greatest part of the remainder of our debts have Bonds and real securities. The partnership of F. & T. has only one debt in England something upwards of £1000 Sterling due to the Estate of M^r. Heate which shall be discharged the Moment there is a possibility of remitting money to Europe. Part of the £8000 before mentioned belongs to S. C. & Co. for goods sold upon their account and part of the outstanding debts are likewise upon their accounts. My poor Uncle has indeed suffered cruelly and wantonly by the waste of war. I have not seen him, but he has given me a lively picture of his distress. Till he felt the stroke, he would not, like many others believe, that a British Army could carry desolation with them. He had always by his own Expences and paying my Grandmothers annuity and some other matters, drawn his full proportion of the profits of our Business and I believe, something more . . . The provision you intend to make for my Sisters is highly pleasing to me. I never could bear the thought of a woman being left in such a situation (if it could be avoided) as to be obliged to accept of an unworthy and disagreeable match for want of subsistance. What you have done for Phil [The reference is to his younger brother Philemon.] shall be most solemnly observed by me, but how ardently I wish that there had never been any occasion for so doing, and that the time may be far off before the trust devolves upon me—His first act was a boyish trick and might have been overlooked. But thank God he has chosen a service that will never throw him in my way as an Enemy—I will endeavor to forward a letter to him, if you send it to me.[13]

13. Tench Tilghman to his father, August 1778.

Let matters get a little settled and I will engage to bring my rash and childish Brother home in safety provided he will return—surely he will not wish to remain in a Service, in which, void of friends to push his future he may attain a Lieutenancy at the end of his life. His was the inconsiderate action of a Boy and as such I dare say I can get it overlooked, provided he does not persevere till he becomes a Man.[14]

14. Tench Tilghman to his father, 2 January 1779.

Hon^d Sir

I was much disappointed at finding your letter at this place instead of yourself . . . The moment I heard that Phil was on board the *Somerset* when she stranded, I wrote to him, and put my letters under cover to Genl. Gates that there might be no miscarriage. I desired him to write to you and to me, and to inform me whether he wanted any assistance in money matters, which I imagine he will not, as the Captains and all the Officers are together, and can have Credit for what they want. I have rec^d. no answer, and am therefore fearful that the letters may have been in a mail from Boston which was taken a little time ago by a set of Villains who infest the mountains in Morris County, and carried into New York.[15]

15. Tench Tilghman to George Washington, 27 October 1781.

Sir:

I arrived at this place early Wednesday morning, although I lost one whole night's run by the stupidity of the skipper, who got over on Tangier shoals, and was a whole day crossing, in a calm, from Annapolis to Rock Hall. The wind left us entirely on Sunday evening, thirty miles below Annapolis. I found that a letter from Count de Grasse to Gouvernour Lee, dated the 18th, had gone forward to Congress, in which the Count informed the Gouvernour that Cornwallis had surrendered. This made me the more anxious to reach Philadelphia, as I knew both Congress and the public would be uneasy at not receiving dispatches from you; I was not wrong in my conjecture, for some really began to doubt the matter. The fatigue of the journey brought back my intermittent fever, with which I have been confined almost ever since I came to town.

A Committee, consisting of Mr. Randolph, Mr. Carroll and Mr. Boudinot, were appointed to inquire of me the several matters of a particular kind, which were not included in your dispatches. They not only went into these, but into the motives which led to the several articles of the capitulation. And I have the pleasure to inform you that they were perfectly satisfied with the propriety and expediency of every step which was taken; and so, indeed, were the whole body of Congress, except the South Carolinians, whose animosities carry them to that length, that they think no treatment could have been too severe for the garrison, the officers, and Lord Cornwallis in particular. One of them, whose name I will mention when I have the pleasure of meeting your excellency, made a motion that the officers should be detained until the further order of Congress. This was unanimously rejected as an affront upon you, a violation of the capitulation, a violation of our national honor, and that of our ally, whose Admiral and General were parties. Upon the whole, Sir, you may be assured that the capitulation is considered by every unbiased person, both in and out of Congress, as highly honorable to the arms, and beneficial to the interests of both nations.

I shall set out, as soon as I am well enough to ride, to Chestertown, at which place I propose waiting until I hear the route which your Excellency intends to take. You will, therefore, be good enough to let one of the gentlemen direct a line for me, to the care of Gouvernour Lee, with a desire to send it immediately over to Rock Hall, where I will leave orders to have it forwarded to me. I can, by making use of this little interval, pay a short visit to my friends, and look into my private affairs, which much want my inspection.

Whenever I am acquainted with your determination, I shall, without delay, join you. I am too much attached, by duty and affection, to remain a moment behind, when I think my presence can render any service or assistance to your Excellency. I beg you to be assured that I am, with the utmost sincerity, your Excellency's

Most obedient and most humble servant.

Tench Tilghman[16]

16. Tench Tilghman to Anna Maria Tilghman, 6 August 1782.

By waiting for public dispatches, I have gained a reprieve of a day, and I will dedicate it, as I would were it the last of my life, to thee, in whom my Heart and Soul delighteth.

I am rich beyond expression—a Day—twelve long hours are my own—I have taken leave of my friends—I have settled my little worldly affairs, and for that period of Bliss, I donate myself to Anna—

I divest myself of mortality - I call for the Spirit of my beloved— She comes—She comes!—Her soul meets mine—we embrace—we unite—We are one—and tho' our bodies are separated, we enjoy a happiness, of which none can partake, but those who are susceptible of the purest and most disinterested Love—

Are we not one? Are we not joined by heaven?

Each interwoven with the other's fate?

How different my feelings? How solid—how substantial my happiness compared to that which I experienced some years ago, when engaged in a pursuit of a similar nature? All then was tumult—distrust and jealousy, and if there was a momentary Calm, it but portended a cruel storm—The scene is changed—Conscious of loving and confident of being loved, my cares, save only those which love creates, are lulled to rest - my Anna's bosom is a sea of bliss, which knows not guileful rocks nor sands, and on which I'll boldly venture, pilotted by love alone Tho' the poor boy is blind.

I have seen Count Deuxponts—Capt. Lynch—& young Dillon—I enquire of them all whether they have been at the Mount [Mount Clare, the Baltimore home of Charles Carroll, Barrister.]—They have—I ask, who did you see there?—My eager soul flies out of my eyes, and before they can answer, I say or seem to say—my Anna—was she there? She was—and she was well. My joy betrays me, and too plainly confirms the report which I find they all have heard—Well—as the old song says "I care not that the whole World knows

How dearly I love Anny O?"

I am every day more and more satisfied with myself, because . . . I approach nearer and nearer to that state, which I ought to be in . . . of a union with you . . . You are the bright star by which I am guided and directed—I will never lose sight of it until I have gained that happy port for which I steer, and in which I am sure of finding a reward for all my pains and toil and trouble—

And now once more my dearest life farewell—How light when I return will seem the heavy miles which now I am about to tread—'Till that time may Heaven bless and protect my love, and may it defend for her sake if not for his her most sincerely affectionate

Tench Tilghman[17]

17. George Washington to Tench Tilghman, 10 January 1783.

I have been favored with your letters of the 22d. and 24th. of last Month from Philadelphia, and thank you for the trouble you have had with my small Commissions. I have sent Mr. Rittenhouse the Glass of such Spectacles as Suit my Eyes, that he may know how to grind his Christals.

Neither Du Portail nor Gouvion[18] are arrived at this place. To the latter, I am refer'd by the Marqs. de la Fayette for some matters which he did not chuse to commit to writing. The sentiments however which he has delivered (with respect to the negociations for Peace accord precisely withe Ideas I have entertained of this business, ever since the Secession of Mr. Fox; viz; that no Peace would be concluded before the meeting of the British Parliament, and that if it did not take place within a month afterwards, we might lay out Accts. for one more Campaign, at *least* . . .

Mrs. Washington has received the Shoes you ordered for her and thanks you for your attention to her request. I receive with great sensibility and pleasure your assurances of affection and regard. It would be but a renewal of what I have often repeated to you, that there are few men in the world to whom I am more sincerely attached by inclination than I am to you. With the cause, I hope, most devoutly hope, there will soon be an end to my Military Services. When, as our places of residence will not be far apart, I shall never be more happy than when I see you at Mount Vernon . . .[19]

18. Tench Tilghman to George Washington, 18 August 1784.

Enclosed you wil find answers to your Several Queries respecting the Green House in the order in which they were put, and that you may the better understand the construction of Mrs. Carroll's, I have made a rough plan of the Manner of conducting the Flues—your floor being 40 feet long Mrs. Carroll recommends two Flues to run up the Back Wall, because you may then increase the number of Flues which run under the Floor, and which she looks upon as essential—the Trees are by that means kept warm at the roots—She does not seem to think there is any occasion for the Heat to be conveyed all round the Walls by means of small Vacancies left in them. She has always found the Flues mark'd in the plan sufficient for her House—

She recommends it to you to have the upper parts of your window sashes to pull down, as well as the lower to rise—you then give Air to the Tops of your Trees—

Your ceiling she thinks ought to be arched and at least 15 feet high—she has found the lowness of hers which is but 12 very inconvenient—

Smooth stucco she thinks preferable to common Plaster because dryer—

The Door of the House to be as large as you can conveniently make it—otherwise when the Trees come to any size, the limbs are broken and the fruit torn off by moving in and out—

It is the custom in many Green Houses to set the Boxes upon Benches—But Mrs. Carroll says they do better upon the Floor, because they then receive the Heat from the Flues below to more advantage—

I recollect nothing more—I hope your Excellency will understand this imperfect description of a matter which I do not know much about myself.[20]

19. Charles Willson Peale to William Paca, Governor of Maryland, 7 September 1784.

The portrait of His Excellency Genl. Washington ordered by the Assembly of your state, I have within a few hours labour finished. The likeness of Col. [Tench] Tilghman and the Marquis de la Fayette I have of my own accord introduced in the same piece with his Excellency, which I hope will give pleasure to my countrymen. I had coppyed the likeness of the marquis from a head in my Collection, and the Marquis seeing the picture the other day, generously offered to give me a sitting that it might be made more compleat, and has appointed this morning for that purpose. I have made in the distance a View of York & Gloster with the British army surrendering in the order [in] which it happened. And in the middle distance I have introduced French and American officers with [the] Colours of their nations displayed, between them the British with their Colours cased. These figures serve to tell the story at first sight which the more distant could not so readily do.[21]

Aides-de-Camp

General Washington's Aides-de-Camp and Military Secretaries—with dates of original appointment

Thomas Mifflin, of Pennsylvania	July 4, 1775
Joseph Reed, of Pennsylvania	July 4, 1775
John Trumbull, of Connecticut	July 27, 1775
George Baylor, of Virginia	August 15, 1775
Edmund Randolph, of Virginia	August 15, 1775
Robert Hanson Harrison, of Virginia	November 5, 1775
	May 16, 1776 (Secretary)
Stephen Moylan, of Pennsylvania	March 5, 1776
William Palfrey, of Massachusetts	March 6, 1776
Caleb Gibbs, of Massachusetts	May 16, 1776
George Lewis, of Virginia	May 16, 1776
Richard Carey, of Virginia	June 21, 1776
Samuel Blatchley Webb, of Connecticut	June 21, 1776
Alexander Contee Hanson, of Maryland Assistant Secretary	June 21, 1776
William Grayson, of Virginia Assistant Secretary	June 21, 1776
Tench Tilghman, of Maryland Volunteer Aide	August 8, 1776
Pierre Penet, of France By Brevet	October 14, 1776
John Fitzgerald, of Virginia	November -, 1776
George Johnston, of Virginia	January 20, 1777
John Walker, of North Carolina Extra Aide	February 19, 1777

AIDES-DE-CAMP

Alexander Hamilton, of New York	March 1, 1777
Richard Kidder Meade, of Virginia	March 12, 1777
Peter Presley Thornton, of Virginia Extra Aide	September 6, 1777
John Laurens, of South Carolina Volunteer Extra Aide	September 6, 1777
James McHenry, of Maryland Assistant Secretary	May 15, 1778
David Humphreys, of Connecticut	June 23, 1780
Richard Varick, of New York Recording Secretary	May 25, 1781
Johathan Trumbull, Jr., of Connecticut Secretary	June 8, 1781
David Cobb, of Massachusetts	June 15, 1781
Peregrine Fitzhugh, of Virginia Extra Aide	July 2, 1781
William Stephens Smith, of New York	July 6, 1781
Benjamin Walker, of New York	January 25, 1782
Hodijah Baylies, of Massachusetts Extra Aide	May 14, 1782

Source: Francis B. Heitman, *Historical Register of Officers of the Continental Army*, Washington, D. C., 1914 and John C. Fitzpatrick, ed., *Calendar of Correspondence of General Washington with Congress*, Washington, D. C., 1906.

Tilghman's Uniform

Measurements of Lieut. Colonel Tench Tilghman's Continental uniform

Coat

back, seam at neck to estimated waistline	22″
middle of neck to bottom of sleeve (over shoulder)	30″
interior of cuffs	9¾″
inside measurement of coat, when hooked at collar	18″
back, sleeve seam to sleeve seam	13½″
depth of coat vent	18″

Waistcoat

chest	38″
back of waistcoat, neck to hem	25″

Breeches, split-fall style

drawstring adjustment in back at waistline	
waist	31½″
waistline to bottom of breeches	23″
circumference of lower leg	14″
inseam	16″

These measurements were taken at the Maryland Historical Society on 24 May 1976 by Ms. Judy Coram, of the Society's staff, and the author.

The Duc de Lauzun

The Duc de Lauzun carries the news of the surrender of Cornwallis to the French Court

Despite the honor accorded him, Armand-Louis de Gontaut-Biron, Duc de Lauzun (1747-93) was, in fact, a reluctant messenger to his King. In his *Memoires* he states: "M de Rochambeau selected me to carry the great news to France and sent for me. I advised him to send M. de Charles, by which he would make his peace with M. de Castries, and perhaps secure the better treatment for his army. I could not persuade him; he said to me that I had been first in action and to me it fell to carry the news; Count de Charles never forgave him or me either . . ."[1]

Armand-Louis de Gontaut-Biron was the epitome of everything that was extravagant, reckless, gallant, and charming. After his mother died in childbirth, he was brought up in the boudoir of Madame de Pompadour, to whom his father was utterly devoted. By the age of twelve he had entered into a regiment of the Guards and at eighteen he married Mme. de Boufflers, an heiress picked out for him by his father. She brought an enormous dowry, but for perhaps understandable reasons he never cared for her, and they separated almost immediately. From then on he flitted from one mistress to another, and the list of his conquests, as reported in his *Memoires,* grows tiresome. Among them, however, were Lady Sara Bunbury, Princess Czartoryska, Madame de Coigny, and even, according to rumor, Marie Antoinette herself. Nevertheless, in between these indulgences he found time to fashion his regiment into a first-class fighting machine, of which Louis XVI made him not only the colonel but also the owner-proprietor. "Lauzun's Legion" (Volontaires Etrangers de Lauzun), made up largely of German, Polish, and Irish recruits, was created by Royal Edict on 5 March 1780. In addition to Lauzun, colonel-proprietor-inspector, the staff included the Vicomte d'Arrot, commanding colonel, and Comte Robert-Guillaume Dillon, second colonel.

Sufficiently in favor at court, Lauzun won for himself and for his legion a place in Rochambeau's army. Landing in Rhode Island in July 1780, he spent the winter of 1780-81 at Lebanon, Connecticut, and commanded the left column of the army on the march to Virginia. During the siege of Yorktown he was stationed at Gloucester.

Rochambeau's dispatch to M. de Segur, the French Minister of War, was written as follows: "Camp before Yorktown, 20 October 1781. Sir—I have the honor to send to you the Duc de Lauzun who is bringing to the King the news of the capture of Lord Cornwallis and his corps of troops. Comte Guillaume de Deux-Ponts will bring the duplicate and the recommendations for *graces*. These are the two superior officers who have performed the two most distinguished feats, as you will see in the journal that will inform you of all the details . . ."

The frigate *Surveillante*, commanded by Cillart de Villeneuve, made the crossing in twenty-two days, arriving at Brest on the evening of 15 November. Lauzun lost no time in reaching Versailles where, according to his *Memoires* (Vol. 2, page 300): "My news caused great joy to the King; I found him in the Queen's apartments; he asked me many questions and had many kind words for me. He asked me if I intended to return to America; I replied that I did; he added that I might assure his army that it would be well rewarded, better than any other ever had been. M. de Segur ws present . . ." The *Surveillante* also brought the navy's courier, Chef d'Escadre Louis-Guillaume de Parscau du Plessix, who had distinguished himself aboard the *Languedoc* in the Battle of the Chesapeake, bearing Admiral de Grasse's dispatches to the Marquis de Castries, Minister of Marine.

The Duc de Lauzun rejoined the French army in America in September 1782, taking command of the detachments left there after the departure of the main body of Rochambeau's army. His account of his experiences in America lacks the precision of other journals written by French officers, but it is a lively and highly personal document that sheds much light on the actors in the drama. The good fortune of his years in America did not follow him after his return to France in 1783. He was guillotined ten years later at the hands of the Committee of Public Safety during the French Revolution.

The Articles of Capitulation

Yorktown, Virginia, 19 October 1781

Four contemporary copies of the Articles of Capitulation are known to exist, two of which are unsigned:

1) The first is a rough copy, or draft, of Articles 1, 2, 4, 5, and part of Article 6 only. It is in the handwriting of Major Ross, one of the British commissioners, and is in the manuscript collection of the Pierpont Morgan Library, New York City.[1] Obviously unsigned, its many corrections and strikeovers simply served as the model for the two final drafts prepared back at Washington's headquarters following the long deliberations at Mr. Moore's house between the commissioners for the opposing sides on 18 October.

2) The second known copy, i.e., that carried by Colonel Tilghman to the Continental Congress and now in the Library of Congress, is acknowledged to be in the hand of Jonathan Trumbull, Jr.[2] We have Washington's own word that it was made "in the morning early" on 19 October. On the night of 18 October, when the negotiating session in the Moore house broke up, the British representatives, Colonel Dundas and Major Ross, obviously took back with them to Cornwallis's headquarters in the Nelson house a rough draft of what Cornwallis would be forced to sign the following morning. This seems apparent from the speed with which the signing was accomplished—a deduction again stemming from Washington's diary.[3] Consequently after Trumbull had completed his copy for the Congress, another had to be made for Cornwallis.

3) This third copy is now in the Public Record Office, Chancery Lane, London, folio 18-134. In Tilghman's clear hand, the copy assumes additional importance due to several little appreciated circum-

stances. It is, for example, the only copy signed not only by Cornwallis, Symonds, and Washington, but also by Rochambeau and de Barras as well, the latter "en mon nom et celui du Comte de Grasse." The Cornwallis copy served as the prototype for early printings of the document with all five signatures. It is of interest, in the present context, to note that the instrument to which the French representatives put their signatures was in English; there was no parallel French text, although Laurens and Tilghman - as well as a number of French officers present - were capable of preparing it. This was done later by the French staff and a small 8-page pamphlet, *Articles de la Capitulation*, was printed shortly after the event, perhaps on the printing press aboard the *Ville de Paris*, de Grasse's flagship then riding at anchor off the Virginia Capes. Copies are in the Rochambeau Papers, Library of Congress, Vol. 3, page 28, and also in the Papers of the Vicomte d'Arrot, in the manuscript collection of the Colonial Williamsburg Foundation.

4) There is a fourth manuscript copy in the Papers of Sir Henry Clinton in the Clements Library at the University of Michigan. Of it Mr. John C. Dann, Curator of Manuscripts, said in a letter to the author dated 16 April 1976: "Our copy of the Articles of Capitulation is not an official copy. It is the one which Clinton had in his papers - presumably drawn up by a British clerk in Yorktown and transmitted to him." Obviously it is without signatures.

Notes

Full citations for books, periodicals, and manuscripts appear in the Bibliography.

Chapter 1. A Prelude to Victory

1 Custis, *Recollections and Private Memoirs of Washington*, 237.
2 The George Washington Papers, S4, P4. Library of Congress. See also Fitzpatrick, *The Diaries of George Washington*, vol. 2, 261n.
3 Names of naval officers listed in the catalogue of the 1976-78 tour in the United States of *Souvenirs de L'Independance Americaine Dans Les Chateaux Francais*, a photographic exhibition presented by "Vieilles Maisons Francaises," under the patronage of the Ambassador of France in the United States and with the sponsorship of French Alliances in the United States, New York City.
4 Tilghman's Yorktown Diary, entry for 22 September 1781. Original in the manuscript collection of the Society of The Cincinnati, Anderson House Museum, Washington, D. C., and herein quoted by permission.
5 Third Maryland Regiment under Lieut. Colonel Peter Adams, as identified in Fitzpatrick, *The Diaries of George Washington*, vol. 2, 261n.

Chapter 2. The Tilghmans in England and America

1 A seat known to have belonged to one Henry de Holweye in the reign of Henry III. Remained in the possession of that family until passing into the hands of the Tilghmans under Edward III. Ireland, *History of the County of Kent*, 584.
2 *Harleian Society Publications, Visitation of Kent 1619*, vol. 42, 37.
3 Another example: in a reprint of the records of Saint Dionis Backchurch, London, 1538-1754, the following appears among the burials: "1661 Oc-

tober 9. A child of Mr. Tilmans, the Chirurgion." *Harleian Society Publications, Register Series,* vol. 3, 233.

4 Johnston, "The Tilghman Family," 184.
5 *Harleian Society Publications, Marriage Licenses of London 1611-1628,* vol. 26, 8.
6 Ibid., vol. 25.
7 Berry, *Kent Genealogies,* 70.
8 Johnston, "The Tilghman Family," 290. See also Wagner, *English Genealogy,* 263.
9 A facsimile copy is among the Tilghman papers at the Historical Society of Pennsylvania.
10 Hanson, *Old Kent,* 230.
11 Scharf, *History of Maryland,* vol. 1, 217.
12 *Archives of Maryland,* vol. 3, 475.
13 Johnston, "The Tilghman Family," 184.
14 Calvert Papers, No. 205, Maryland Historical Society.
15 *Archives of Maryland,* vol. 4, 55.
16 Scharf, *History of Maryland,* vol. 1, 120-24.
17 Johnston, "The Tilghman Family," 280.
18 Hanson, *Old Kent,* 231.
19 Skirven, "Seven Pioneers," 411.
20 Johnston, "The Tilghman Family," 280.
21 Ibid.
22 *Archives of Maryland,* vol. 2, 244.
23 Ibid., 269.
24. Johnston, "The Tilghman Family," 280.
25 Skirven, "Seven Pioneers," 244.
26 Ibid., 411. The inscription, now obliterated by the passage of time, reads as follows: Vale/Ita Dixit/Richardus Tilghmanus, BM./In artique chirugi magister qui/sub hoc tumulo sepultus est Obit. Janu 7 mo. Anno 1675.
27 Bordley, *Hollyday Families,* 256.
28 Ibid.
29 Ibid.
30 Ibid.
31 Ibid.
32 *Archives of Maryland,* vol. 6, 52.
33 Bordley, *Hollyday Families,* 257.
34 Tilghman, Harrison, "Letters of the Tilghman Family," 148-75. In 1697 there began a correspondence between the English and American branches of the family which lasted until 1764. The extant letters appear to be copies, dating from about 1790. Assuming that they were copied correctly—and there is no reason to believe otherwise—they are most revealing. The first of the series is from England, written by Abraham Tilghman The Elder (to distinguish him from his son) to Richard Tilghman II at The Hermitage. Dated 24 October 1697 it indicates that Samuel Tilghman, Admiral of

NOTES

Maryland, 1658, had left sons surviving him, but that they in turn were dead without surviving male issue at the time the letter was written.

While there were undoubtedly other letters between Richard Tilgh-man II and Abraham Tilghman The Elder, the next known letter is dated 2 July 1734, thirty-seven years later. It was written from Maryland by Richard Tilghman II to Abraham Tilghman II. (See Appendix I: Tilghman Cor-respondence.) It is obvious from this letter that Richard Tilghman II, the first of his line to be born in Maryland and already in his sixty-second year, was unfamiliar with the records in the registers of All Saints Church, Snodland, Kent; otherwise he would not have been "at a loss to know" whether William Tilghman (The Younger) was the father of "Wheternal," Oswald, Charles, and Lambert Tilghman, since the baptismal records make it clear that such was the case in each instance. He is referring to the family register brought to Maryland by his father. See page 12 of this chapter.

35 Johnston, "The Tilghman Family," 281.
36 Ibid.
37 Ibid.
38 Hanson, *Old Kent*, 296. He had also been paying court to Elizabeth, whose family lived at nearby Otwell. For unspecified reasons the Turbutts op-posed marriage, resulting in an elopement by the young couple to White Marsh Church, also in Talbot County, on 29 December 1724. Hearing of the elopement, Elizabeth's relatives dashed after them and arrived at the church just as the minister was saying, "If any man has just cause to forbid this marriage . . ." Whereupon Tench Francis drew his sword and declared, "If any man gainsayeth this marriage I will run him through with my sword." The wedding proceeded without interruption.
39 Ibid.
40 Johnston, "The Tilghman Family," 369.
41 Montgomery, *A History of The University of Pennsylvania*, 47.
42 Cabeen, "Society of The Sons of Saint Tammany," 448.
43 The Hollyday Papers (MS No. 1317, 1740-56) in the Maryland Historical Society contain an original patent from Frederick, Lord Baltimore, to James Tilghman for 50½ acres called "Fausley Meadow," obviously adja-cent to Fausley. The patent is dated 17 February 1755.
44 Johnston, "The Tilghman Family," 369.
45 "Diary of James Allen," 178.
46 Delaplaine, Edward S., "Life of Thomas Johnson," 56.
47 *Archives of Maryland*, vol. 14, 160.
48 *Archives of Pennsylvania*, Second Series, "Officers Of The Province of Penn-sylvania," vol. 9, 625.
49 Tilghman, *Memoir*, 9.
50 *Archives of Pennsylvania*, vol. 10, 180-81.
51 Bordley, *Hollyday Families*, 260. Also Cadwalader, "A Diary of Trifling Occurrences," 441n.
52 Ibid.
53 *Appleton's Cyclopaedia of American Biography*, vol. 6, 116.
54 Ibid.
55 Johnston, "The Tilghman Family," 369.

Chapter 3. Youth and Early Training

1 Tilghman's uniform is on public display at the Maryland Historical Society. Other than Washington's uniform which is preserved in the Smithsonian Institution, this is the only Revolutionary officer's uniform known to exist today. See Appendix II.

2 Whiteley, *Washington and His Aides-de-Camp*, 25.

3 Tilghman, *History of Talbot County*, vol. 1, 42.

4 Ives, *Washington's Headquarters*, 218-19.

5 Johnston, "The Tilghman Family," 369.

6 Ives, *Washington's Headquarters*, 260.

7 Johnston, "The Tilghman Family," 369.

8 Swem, "Historical and Genealogical Notes," 212.

9 Tilghman, *Memoir*, 11.

10 Johnston, "The Tilghman Family," 374.

11 Ibid.

12 University of Pennsylvania, *Biographical Catalogue*, 18.

13 Bordley, *Hollyday Families*, 262.

14 Ibid.

15 Ibid.

16 Ibid.

17 *Dictionary of American Biography*, vol. 18, 546. McKean was himself Chief Justice of the State from 1777 to 1799, and together with Tilghman, John Bannister Gibson, and Jeremiah S. Black is generally included among those possessing the great legal minds in American jurisprudence in the late eighteenth and early nineteenth centuries. His contributions to the affairs of his native Pennsylvania as well as to the new nation which he helped produce were wide ranging and significant, from the outbreak of the Revolution to the eve of the War of 1812. Aggressive, perhaps even stubborn, McKean was an enigmatic, complex character with an indomitable nature and a quick temper. His life story is filled with anecdotes which reveal his Scotch-Irish background. His appointment of William Tilghman as Chief Justice was not a popular one and some of his political associates were quick to so inform him. McKean listened to their objections with patience then "with a profound bow and mock courtesy, asked what the great Democracy desired. 'The appointment of a man,' they said, 'more in accordance with our wishes.'

'Indeed,' said McKean; 'inform your constituents that I bow with submission to the will of the great Democracy of Philadelphia, but by God! William Tilghman shall be Chief Justice of Pennsylvania.'" Fisher, *The Making of Pennsylvania*, 181.

18 University of Pennsylvania, *Biographical Catalogue*, 18.

19 *Dictionary of American Biography*, vol. 18, 546.

20 Hanson, *Old Kent*, 256.

21 Ibid. Lord Byron, the English poet, married a close cousin, Anne Isabella

Milbanke. Lady Byron's father was Sir Ralph Milbanke, the elder brother of Admiral Mark Milbanke. Thus Harriet Milbanke Tilghman was the first cousin of Lady Byron's father.

22 Johnston, "The Tilghman Family," 369.
23 Ibid.
24 Walsh and Fox, *Maryland - A History*, 35.
25 Tilghman, *History of Talbot County*, vol. 1, 8.
26 Barker, *Background of the Revolution*, 183.
27 McGrath, *Pillars of Maryland*, 491.
28 Ibid.
29 Land, *Letters From America*, 54-55.
30 Fisher, *Men, Women and Manners*, 209.
31 Wertenbaker, *The Golden Age of Colonial Culture*, 86.

Chapter 4. The Education of a Revolutionary

1 Fisher, *Men, Women and Manners*, 365.
2 Wertenbaker, *The Golden Age of Colonial Culture*, 75.
3 McGrath, *Pillars of Maryland*, 457.
4 Sellers, *Charles Willson Peale*, 29.
5 Gillespie, "Early Fire Protection," 252.
6 Wertenbaker, *The Golden Age of Colonial Culture*, 70.
7 *History of The Schuylkill Fishing Company*, 407-9.
8 Montgomery, *A History of The University of Pennsylvania*, 122.
9 Ibid., 210. Known as the University of the State of Pennsylvania in 1780. The name was changed to the University of Pennsylvania in 1791.
10 Ibid., 238.
11 Ibid., 239.
12 Chamberlain, *The University of Pennsylvania*, 78.
13 "Peters discovered that Benedict Arnold was applying to his own use funds placed in his hands for the purchase of clothing and subsistence for the army, and an attempt on Peter's part to stop this robbery produced between him and Arnold an open quarrel. In a letter to a friend he wrote; 'I did not conceal, but wrote to headquarters my want of confidence in Arnold. When his traitorous conduct at West Point became public neither Colonel Pickering nor myself were the least surprised.'" *Appleton's Cyclopaedia of American Biography*, vol. 4, 743.
14 *Dictionary of American Biography*, vol. 6, 31.
15 Heitman, *Historical Register of Officers*, 12.
16 *Biographical Congressional Directory*, 728-29.
17 Hamilton, *Sir William Johnson and The Indians of New York*, 31.
18 Ibid.
19 Letter dated 2 February 1769, in the manuscript collection of the Massachusetts Historical Society.

Chapter 5. The Mohawk Spawns Another Treaty

1 Tilghman, *Memoir*, 124-25.
2 *American Archives*, Fourth Series, vol. 1, 1347-49.
3 Ibid., vol. 2, 661.
4 Van Every, *Forth To The Wilderness*, 281.
5 Ibid.
6 Graymont, *The Iroquois In The American Revolution*, 16.
7 Ibid., 50.
8 *American Archives*, Fourth Series, vol. 3, 50.
9 Ibid., 473-96.
10 Ibid., 489-90.
11 Tilghman's Indian Journal, entry for 8 August 1775. Original in the manuscript collection of the Society of The Cincinnati, Anderson House Museum, Washington, D. C., and herein quoted by permission.
12 Tilghman's Journal, 10 August 1775.
13 Ibid., 11 August 1775.
14 The Reverend Samuel Kirkland and Mr. James Dean were both present as interpreters. Graymont, *The Iroquois In The American Revolution*, 71.
15 Tilghman's Journal, 14 August 1775.
16 *American Archives*, Fourth Series, vol. 3, 474.
17 Tilghman's Journal, 15 August 1775.
18 *American Archives*, Fourth Series, vol. 3, 474.
19 Tilghman's Journal, 15 August 1775.
20 Ibid., 16 August 1775.
21 *American Archives*, Fourth Series, vol. 3, 489.
22 Ibid., 243.
23 Ibid., 490.
24 Ibid., 489.
25 Hendrickson in *Hamilton I*, 249-52, related that Alexander Hamilton and Tilghman on occasion traded off to each other their respective sweethearts including Betsy Schuyler and Kitty Livingston, as well as a certain "Polly," otherwise unidentified, an early Hamilton mistress.
26 There are no figures to substantiate the statement, but it would be safe to say that four of the richest men in America at the outbreak of the Revolution were George Washington, Philip Schuyler, John Hancock, and Charles Carroll of Carrollton. All were pronounced patriots, two of them signing the Declaration of Independence. Schuyler as well as Washington was a general in the Continental Army.
27 Mrs. Huger, Mrs. Lynch, Mrs. Cuyler and Miss Lynch. Tilghman's Journal, 20, 23 August 1775.
28 Tilghman's Journal, 24 August 1775.
29 Ibid., 26 August 1775.
30 Ibid., 30 August 1775.
31 Ibid.
32 Ibid.

33 *American Archives,* Fourth Series, vol. 3, 494.
34 Ibid., 488.
35 Ibid., 489.

Chapter 6. The Long Road Begins

1 Lecky, *History of England,* vol. 3, 414.
2 James Tilghman to Henry Wilmot. This letter in its entirety may be found in "Letters from the Penn Papers," 457; a longer portion of it appears in Appendix I.
3 Stille, *Life and Writings of John Dickinson,* vol. 1, 156.
4 Tilghman, *Memoir,* 14.
5 Tilghman so inscribes himself on the title page of his own copy of *The Military Guide For Young Officers,* by Thomas Simes, now in the collection of the Historical Society of Talbot County, Maryland.
6 Stille, *Life and Writings of John Dickinson,* vol. I, 156.
7 Steuart, *A History Of The Maryland Line,* 5.
8 Tilghman, *Memoir,* 124-25.
9 Heitman, *Historical Register of Officers,* 400.
10 Ibid., 12.
11 I, 16. This work, first published in 1915, was compiled principally from voluminous notes, accounts, and documents left by Oswald Tilghman's late father-in-law, Dr. Samuel Alexander Harrison (1822-90), an historian of considerable reputation who wrote extensively on people and events connected with Maryland's Eastern Shore.
12 Bordley, *Hollyday Families,* 273. A portrait of Judge James Tilghman hangs in the ceremonial dining room at Stratford, the Lee home in Virginia.
13 Fitzpatrick, *George Washington: Colonial Traveller,* 341. From Mount Vernon on 23 March 1773 Washington wrote to James Tilghman, father of Tench, asking him specifically to "come down and stay with us a day or two," as Governor Eden would be there. Fitzpatrick, *Writings of Washington,* vol. 3, 126.
14 Ibid., 364.
15 Ibid., 380.
16 Ibid., 381.
17 Whiteley, *Washington And His Aides-de-Camp,* 26.
18 Ibid.
19 Tilghman, *Memoir,* 131.
20 Dangerfield, *Chancellor Robert R. Livingston of New York,* 465.
21 Tilghman, *Memoir,* 128.
22 Ibid.
23 These letters remained in the hands of a Tilghman descendant until the latter part of the last century when they were sold at auction. They may be read in their entirety, as well as the Committee's replies, in *Revolutionary Manuscripts and Portraits.*
24 Hendrickson, *Hamilton I,* 126.

25 Tilghman, *Memoir*, 134.

26 Colonel at Germantown, Brigadier General 1779, Commanding 2nd Maryland Brigade. Heitman, *Historical Register of Officers*, 192.

27 *Maryland and North Carolina In The Campaign of 1780-1781.*

28 Balch, *Papers Relating Chiefly To The Maryland Line*, 65-66.

29 Tilghman, *Memoir*, 137.

30 Reed, *Life and Correspondence of General Joseph Reed*, vol. 1, 237.

31 Ibid., 238.

32 Tilghman, *Memoir*, 139.

33 Reed, *The Life and Correspondence of General Joseph Reed*, vol. 1, 238.

34 New York Historical Society, St. James Chronicle, 7-9 November 1776, 275.

35 *American Archives*, Series 5, vol. 2, 182.

36 Ibid., 193.

37 Tilghman, *Memoir*, 139-40. Thomas Fleming, an historian who has written extensively on the Revolutionary era, in an article in *New York Magazine*, 14 July 1975, makes a compelling case for the theory that American patriots, under the leadership of Nathan Hale, did indeed put the torch to New York, quoting this letter from Tilghman as proof of Washington's complicity. Fleming lays particular emphasis on Tilghman's statement that "Some were executed next day upon Good grounds." In the light of Tilghman's earlier disclaimer (in the same letter) of Washington's or any other commanding officer's responsibility, and since many historians repeatedly portray Tilghman as privy to Washington's innermost secrets, it would appear - at least to this observer - that the reference is to persons who were indeed acting as incendiaries but totally on their own.

38 Reed, *Life and Correspondence of General Joseph Reed*, vol. 1, 231.

39 Tilghman, *Memoir*, 143.

40 Ibid., 144.

41 *American Archives*, Fifth Series, vol. 3, 521.

42 Tilghman, *Memoir*, 149.

43 *American Archives*, Fifth Series, vol. 3, 1058ff.

44 Philemon Dickinson (1739-1809), a fellow native Marylander, born in Talbot County. Colonel, Hunterdon County Battalion, New Jersey Militia, later Major General in command of all New Jersey Militia. Acted as second to General John Cadwalader in his duel with General Thomas Conway, 4 July 1778.

45 Tilghman, *Memoir*, 149.

46 Bill, *The Campaign of Princeton 1776-1777*, 40.

47 Tilghman, *Memoir*, 150.

48 Whiteley, *Washington and His Aides-de-Camp*, 37.

49 Thayer, *Nathanael Green, Strategist of The American Revolution*, 152.

Chapter 7. Enter Lafayette

1 Letter from London dated 1 January 1777, quoted in *Freeman's Journal*, Portsmouth, New Hampshire, 22 March 1777.

2 *Dictionary of American Biography,* vol. 5, 173.

3 Boatner, *Encyclopedia of The American Revolution,* 515.

4 Marie Joseph Paul Yves Roch Gilbert du Motier, the Marquis de Lafayette. From 1789 onwards Lafayette wrote his name in one word, the form now used almost universally by historians. Prior to that time he had spelled it "La Fayette." La Fuye and Babeau, *Lafayette: The Apostle of Liberty,* 11.

5 *Dictionary of American Biography,* vol. 3, 497.

6 Emory, *History of Queen Anne's County,* 451. See also "Mission of William Carmichael to Spain," 5-6, and Gottschalk, *Lafayette Comes to America,* 162.

7 "Letters of William Carmichael to John Cadwalader, 1777," 1.

8 Ibid.

9 deKalb had been in America and spoke fluent English. Zucker, *General De Kalb, Lafayette's Mentor,* 67.

10 The officer referred to is Colonel De Lesser. See Kite, "Lafayette and His Companions On The *Victoire,*", 9-10.

11 Captain (Brevet Colonel) de Volfort. Ibid. See also Balch, *The French In America,* 243.

12 The late Louis R. Gottschalk, in his *Lafayette Comes To America* (1935), states (p. 21) that a photostat copy of this letter is in the collection of W. P. Gardner, of Jersey City, N. J. A typescript copy also appeared in the *New York Sun,* 1 June 1902.

13 Among the Lafayette papers in the Olin Library at Cornell University is a letter dated 30 July 1825 from Tench Tilghman (1782-1827), son-in-law of Lieut. Col. Tench Tilghman, inviting Lafayette to visit Plimhimmon, the Tilghman homestead in Talbot County, Maryland, where Anna Maria (Tilghman) Tilghman, widow of Lieut. Colonel Tench Tilghman, was still living. The visit was subsequently made.

14 It now hangs in the Old Senate Chamber in the Maryland State House in Annapolis.

15 Waln, *Life of The Marquis de La Fayette,* 13.

16 Latzko, *Lafayette: A Life,* 41.

17 Kite, "Lafayette and His Companions On The *Victoire,*" 11-12.

18 Whitlock, *Lafayette,* vol. 1, 69.

19 Heitman, *Historical Register Of Officers,* 12, 257.

20 Fitzpatrick, *Writings of Washington,* vol. 1, xliii-xlvii.

21 Tilghman, *Memoir,* 148.

22 Ibid., 153.

23 Fitzpatrick, *Writings of Washington,* vol. 26, 29.

24 Ibid., 358.

25 Scharf, *History of Maryland,* vol. 2, 309.

26 Desmond, *Sword and Pen For George Washington,* 56.

27 Fitzpatrick, *Writings of Washington,* vol. 7, 495.

28 Tilghman, *Memoir,* 158.

29 William Alexander (1726-1783) came from a prominent New York family. He served in the French and Indian War and as a Major General in the Revolution. Despite his failure to gain official British recognition for his

claim to the Scottish earldom of Stirling he was known as Lord Stirling in
  America. He and Tilghman were close friends.

30 Trevelyan, *The American Revolution*, vol. 3, 249.

31 Harrison, *Annals*, 177.

32 Thayer, *Nathanael Greene*, 199.

32 Brigadier General Agnew; Ward, *The War of The Revolution*, vol. 1, 371.
    General Agnew commanded the 4th Foot Brigade under Major General Sir
    William Howe. Katcher, *Encyclopedia of Army Units, 1775-1783*, 134.

33 Tilghman, *Memoir*, 166.

34 Alden, *The American Revolution*, 127.

35 *Private Papers of James Boswell*, vol. 14, 229.

36 American Antiquarian Society, *Isaiah Thomas Collection of Broadside Ballads*,
    reproduced by permission.

37 Cooke, "Tench Coxe: Tory Merchant," 48.

38 Ward, *The War of The Revolution*, vol. 2, 543ff.

39 Thane, *Washington's Lady*, 168.

40 Marshall, *Life of Washington*, vol. 3, 339.

41 Greene, *Life of Nathanael Greene*, vol. 1, 552.

42 *Confidential Correspondence of Robert Morris*, 164.

43 Boatner, *Encyclopedia Of The American Revolution*, 277.

44 Freeman, *Washington*, vol. 4, 547.

45 Beveridge, *Life of John Marshall*, vol. 1, 121.

46 Butterfield, *Letters Of Benjamin Rush*, vol. 1, 159-61.

47 Tilghman, *Memoir*, 156.

48 Scharf, *History of Maryland*, vol. 2, 342.

49 Leonard, *Life of Charles Carroll of Carrollton*, 151.

50 Smith, *Charles Carroll of Carrollton*, 172.

51 Ibid., 176-80.

52 Fitzpatrick, *Writings of Washington*, vol. 10, 362n.

53 Ibid.

54 Leonard, *Life of Charles Carroll of Carrollton*, 172.

55 Fitzpatrick, *Writings of Washington*, vol. 10, 362-403.

56 Smith, *Charles Carroll of Carrollton*, 180.

57 Papers of Joseph Reed, Box 4, New York Historical Society.

58 Smith, *Charles Carroll of Carrollton*, 180.

59 Garden, *Anecdotes of The Revolutionary War In America*, 431. One account of
    this incident has General Conway turning to his opponent and saying good-
    humoredly, "You fire, General, with much deliberation, and certainly with a
    great deal of effect."

60 Boatner, *Encyclopedia Of The American Revolution*, 278.

Chapter 8. The Hottest Day . . .

1 Freeman, *George Washington*, vol. 5, 27.

2 Tilghman, in *Lee Papers*, New York Historical Society, vol. 3, 80.

3 Ibid., 81.

4 Tucker, *Mad Anthony Wayne and The New Nation*, 126.

5 Fisher, *The Struggle For American Independence*, vol. 2, 185.

6 Ibid., 63. An interesting sidelight is to be found in the memoirs of Colonel Israel Shreve's son, Lieutenant John Shreve, who also fought at Monmouth. The reliability of the memoirs, however, has to be open to some question since John Shreve's account of the battle was not written until he had reached the advanced age of ninety-three. For the most part details of the battle agree with other accepted accounts. He had the following to say about Lee. "General Lee disobeyed the orders and suffered the English rearguard, with not half the number of men that Lee had, to drive him. The British general then knew that Washington was not there, he went out north and met Washington late in the afternoon. After being engaged nearly half an hour the enemy retreated, and left their dead and wounded on the field. Washington sent his aid-de-camp three times to know why Lee did not press on the enemy. Lee said, 'Tell the General I am doing well enough.' My father heard him say it." Allen, *Genealogy and History of the Shreve Family*, 626. If true, it is obvious that the encounters between the aide-de-camp, probably Hamilton, and Lee preceded that between Washington and Lee.

7 Freeman, *George Washington*, vol. 5, 29.

8 Tilghman, in *Lee Papers*, New Historical Society, vol. 3, 82.

9 Hughes, *George Washington*, vol. 3, 376.

10 Stryker, *Battle of Monmouth*, 218.

11 Freeman, *George Washington*, vol. 5, 28n.

12 Really Lt. Colonel Thomas Henderson, a physician whose house had been burned by the British the day before. He was not in uniform and Washington did not recognize him. Stryker, *The Battle of Monmouth*, 175.

13 New York Historical Society, *Lee Papers*, 79-82.

14 Fitzpatrick, *Writings of Washington*, vol. 12, 128.

15 Steiner, *The Life and Correspondence of James McHenry*, 25-26.

16 Tilghman, *Memoir*, 157.

17 Ibid., 164.

18 Ibid., 169.

19 Land, *The Dulanys of Maryland*, 256-57.

20 Tilghman, *Memoir*, 165.

21 Miller, *The Founding Finaglers*, 88.

22 Myers, ed., *Sally Wistar's Journal*, 20 June 1778.

23 Flexner, *The Traitor and The Spy*, 252.

24 Todd, *The Real Benedict Arnold*, 201.

25 Van Doren, *Secret History*, 187.

26 Todd, *The Real Benedict Arnold*, 213.

27 Tilghman, *History of Talbot County*, vol. 1, 27.

28 Ibid.

29 Tilghman, *Memoir*, 123.

30 Tilghman, *History of Talbot County*, vol. 1, 27.

31 Boatner, *Encyclopedia Of The American Revolution*, 747.

32 Ibid.

33 Manuscript collection of the Connecticut Historical Society. Letter dated 16 December 1779.
34 Manuscript Collection, National Park Service, Morristown National Historic Park.
35 Fitzpatrick, *Writings of Washington,* vol. 17, 327-75.

Chapter 9. The Aides-de-Camp

1 In two volumes. First printed in London; reprinted in 1776 in Philadelphia by J. Humphreys, R. Bell, and R. Aitken.
2 Quoted from Tench Tilghman's own copy, now in the collection of the Historical Society of Talbot County.
3 Fitzpatrick, *The Spirit Of The Revolution,* 60.
4 John Trumbull, the artist, became an aide-de-camp on 27 July 1775. As stated, he was on the staff for only a few weeks and left the army entirely in 1777, resigning his commission. Despite choosing to include Tilghman in the center grouping of his detailed painting, "The Capture of The Hessians at Trenton," Trumbull probably did not know Tilghman during this period of his life - perhaps not at all - as the painting, which now hangs in the Yale University Art Gallery, was not even undertaken until 1787 and not completed until 1794.
5 Ford, *Writings of Washington,* vol. 5, 195, 499n.
6 Heitman, *Historical Register of Officers,* 12.
7 Hendrickson, *Hamilton I,* 122.
8 Fitzpatrick, *Writings of Washington,* vol. 1, xliv.
9 In contrast, think of the headquarters of a division, corps, or army in the U. S. Army today. Organized strictly in accordance with the General Staff concept developed by Field Marshal Gneisnau, a brilliant tactician who served under Frederick the Great as well as with German mercenaries in the American Revolution, the headquarters of a U. S. army (two or more corps) will be commanded by a general of four-star rank - certainly three - who will have under him as his Chief of Staff another general with a rank related to that of his superior, i.e., one less star. The Chief of Staff in turn will be supported by a bevy of colonels, designated as G-1 (Personnel), G-2 (Intelligence), G-3 (Operations), and G-4 (Supply). In World War II Eisenhower added a G-5 Section, composed of officers especially trained in the administration of occupied enemy territory, including art conservators. Moreover there will be a Secretary to the General Staff (and an accompanying secretariat) to serve the several general staff sections and to keep the paper work flowing smoothly. Parallel to and complementing this General Staff one finds a Special Staff, embracing Public Relations, Special Services, Information and Education Officers, Billeting and Mess Officers, civilian Red Cross personnel, as well as scores of clerk-typists, communications clerks, messengers, orderlies, pilots of indigenous aircraft, and chauffeurs. Furthermore all generals, down to and including brigadiers, are entitled to

aides-de-camp, the rank and number of which are determined by the rank of the general whom they serve.

10 Hendrickson, *Hamilton I*, 121.
11 Fitzpatrick, *Writings of Washington*, vols. 5 to 22 inclusive.
12 Fitzpatrick, *Writings of Washington*, vol. 11, 458-60. For extensive corrections made by Tilghman to a first draft by Washingto, see the latter's letter to the President of Congress, 8 April 1781, vol. 21, 429-31.
13 General Orders, 14 July 1775. See also Fitzpatrick, *The Spirit of The Revolution*, 120.
14 Lodge, *Works of Alexander Hamilton*, vol. 9, 232.
15 Fitzpatrick, *Writings of Washington*, vol. 22, 70-72.
16 Tilghman, *History of Talbot County*, vol. 1, 18.
17 Syrett, *The Papers of Alexander Hamilton*, vol. 2, 165.
18 Ibid., vol. 2, 600. The "My Lord" reference is to Lord Stirling, whose propensity for the bottle was well-known.
19 Tilghman, *Memoir*, 147.
20 Simms, *Army Correspondence of Colonel John Laurens*, 59.
21 Chastellux, *Travels In North America*, "translated from the French By An English Gentleman who Resided In America At That Period." Originally published in London in 1797, the excerpt is from the reprint edition (Arno Press - 1968), 113-14. The meeting took place at Washington's Headquarters at New Windsor on 23 December 1780.
22 Townsend, *An American Soldier*, 247.
23 Marshall, *Life of George Washington*, vol. 4, 587.

Chapter 10. Rochambeau . . .

1 Willcox, ed., *The American Rebellion*, 208.
2 Charles Louis d'Arsac, Chevalier de Ternay (1722-1780). He died at Newport of natural causes 12 December 1780.
3 *Program of the Washington-Rochambeau Celebration 1780-1955*, 19.
4 Fitzpatrick, *Writings of Washington*, vol. 20, 43.
5 Ibid., 79-81.
6 Ibid., 93.
7 This quotation can be found in two source references, i.e., Rush, *Occasional Productions*, 79-80, and Commager, *The Spirit of 'Seventy-Six*, 757.
8 Manuscript Collection, New York Historical Society.
9 Fitzpatrick, *Writings of Washington*, vol. 20, 91.
10 As quoted in Callahan, *The Tories of The American Revolution*, 236.
11 Syrett, *The Papers of Alexander Hamilton*, vol. 2, 441-42. See also Van Doren, *The Secret History*, 187, 200.
12 Lutnick, *The American Revolution and The British Press*, 168.
13 Fitzpatrick, *Writings of Washington*, vol. 21, 16, 19.
14 Ibid., 162.
15 Now in the manuscript collection of Mr. Paul Mellon, Upperville, Virginia.

16 Fitzpatrick, *Writings of Washington,* vol. 21, 403-10.

17 Ibid., vol. 22, 388.

18 Manuscript Collection, Library of the Morristown National Historical Park; quoted by permission.

19 Syrett, *The Papers of Alexander Hamilton,* vol. 2, 563-64.

20 Steiner, *The Life and Correspondence of James McHenry,* 35.

21 Thane, *Washington's Lady,* 218.

22 Fitzpatrick, *Writings of Washington,* vol. 21, 331.

23 Frederick R. Kirkland, Pennsylvania State Historical Society, as quoted in the *Philadelphia Evening Bulletin,* 11 April 1941.

24 Hornor, "Notes and Documents," 364, fn 22.

25 Ibid., 364-65.

26 Ibid., 367.

27 Ibid., 368.

28 Fitzpatrick, *Writings of Washington,* vol. 21, 385.

29 Ibid., 331.

30 Depuy and Hammerman, *People and Events Of The American Revolution,* 395. James Rivington, the publisher of the *Gazette,* started the war as a Loyalist but by 1781 had switched sides, becoming an American secret agent. His biggest achievement was the theft of the British Navy's entire signal book, which was turned over to Admiral de Grasse.

31 Ferguson, *The Papers of Robert Morris,* vol. 1, 74.

32 George Washington Papers, 15, LC.

33 Fitzpatrick, *The Diaries of George Washington,* vol. 2, 23 May 1781. The draft of the circular is in George Washington Papers, LC. It is printed in Ford, *Writings of Washington,* vol. 9, 256.

34 Tilghman, *Memoir,* 174.

35 Ibid., 175.

36 Ferguson, *The Papers of Robert Morris,* vol. 1, 175.

37 *Program of the Washington-Rochambeau Celebraton 1780-1955,* 17.

38 Manuscript Collection of The Historical Society of Talbot County, quoted by permission. The letter, written from New Windsor, is to Robert Morris and is dated 4 June 1781. Youngs Ledyard (1751-1781) of Groton, Connecticut, Captain in a company under the command of his uncle Colonel William Ledyard (1738-1781) was the bearer of the information.

39 Garden, *Anecdotes of The American Revolution,* 80. This secret mission, though lost in history, does not depend on Garden's brief account or McLane's unsupported word. In the McLane Papers in the New York Historical Society is McLane's own journal in which is recorded, with maddening brevity, the success of this vital mission: "Visited Cap Francois [now Cap Haitien] in July, was examined by Count de Grasse in Council of War aboard the *Ville de Paris,* gave as [my] considered opinion that Count de Grasse could make it easy for Genl Washington to reduce the British Army in the South if he proceeded with his fleet and Army to the Chesapeake." Moreover one finds in the same collection a corroborating affidavit—obtained by McLane in April 1820, when he was contemplating writing his memoirs (which he never got around to, more's the pity!)—from Richard

O'Brien, a lieutenant on the *Congress* during the historic voyage to de Grasse. This document substantiates in minute detail McLane's account of his voyage except for some minor confusion about the identity of the French flagship. The reference to McLane in *The Dictionary of American Biography* (vol. 12, 113) touches briefly on McLane's trip to see de Grasse. Three bound volumes of letters and papers of McLane, including autobiographical notes, are in the New York Historical Society. They have been neither edited nor indexed.

40 Ward, *The War Of The Revolution*, vol. 2, 882.
41 Ibid.
42 Washington to Lafayette, 31 May 1781; Papers of Sir Henry Clinton, William L. Clements Library, University of Michigan.
43 Wertenbaker, *Father Knickerbocker Rebels*, 241.
44 *Archives of Maryland*, vol. 47, 486. The Mr. Hollyday mentioned was probably the Honorable James Hollyday (1728-1788) of Readbourne, Queen Anne's County. He studied law in the Middle Temple and became a member of the Governor's Council. He did not marry. Bordley, *Hollyday Families*, 265, and Pleasants, "The Letters of Molly and Hetty Tilghman," 30n.
45 Tower, *The Marquis de La Fayette In The American Revolution*, vol. 2, 435. Brevet Colonel Jean-Baptiste Gouvion (1747-1792) was one of four French military engineers sent to America at the request of Congress. He helped plan and construct fortifications at West Point; participated in the Yorktown campaign. An intimate friend of Lafayette's, he accompanied him on a tour of Germany and Austria in 1785. He was killed in action in the War of The First Coalition.

Chapter 11. Yorktown . . .

1 Fitzpatrick, *Writings of Washington*, vol. 23, 243.
2 Tilghman's Yorktown Diary, Manuscript Collection, Society of The Cincinnati, Washington, D. C. Quoted by permission.
3 Kennett, *The French Forces In America*, 137.
4 Ibid., 145.
5 Boatner, *Encyclopedia Of The American Revolution*, 1242.
6 Fitzpatrick, *The Diaries of George Washington*, 17 October 1781.
7 Thinking of everything, Tilghman had drafted a letter to de Grasse, dispatched on the 17th over Washington's signature: "I should be anxious to have the honor of your Excellency's participation in the treaty, which will according to present appearance shortly take place. I need not add how happy it will make me to welcome your Excellency in the name of America on this shore, and embrace you upon an occasion so advantageous to the interests of the common cause, and on which it is so much indebted to you. Should naval reasons deprive me of this happiness, by requiring your Excellency's presence on board, I entreat that you will be pleased to appoint an officer to represent you, and take charge of the capitulation to be signed by your Excellency."

8 Lee, *Memoirs of The War In The Southern Department*, 512.

9 Kennett, *The French Forces in America*, 151.

10 "Notes and Queries," 125.

11 Tilghman's Yorktown Journal, Manuscript Collection, Society of The Cincinnati, Washington, D. C.

12 There has been much speculation about the size and type of boat used by Colonel Tilghman on this leg of his journey. Tilghman's use of the term *skipper* (see Tilghman to Washington, 27 October 1781, George Washington Papers, LC.) could indicate a crew of more than one, whereas if he had said *boatman* his meaning would have been much clearer. Under any circumstance it is odd that the other person or persons on board have not left behind some record of the occurrence.

      A present-day fictionalized account of this trip, Fry *What Did They Say To Each Other?*, would have us believe that Tilghman embarked a horse as well at Yorktown. Several factors lead this author to doubt the story: 1) Being fully aware of the regular packet service between Annapolis and Rock Hall, Tilghman's undoubted destination on leaving Yorktown was Annapolis, where he knew he could obtain a suitable horse for the next leg of his journey—having obtained two on the march down by levy against the Council of Safety. (*Archives of Maryland*, vol. 47, 486.) 2) Also, being thoroughly familiar with the upper Eastern Shore and well-known personally in the area (his father, two sisters, and a brother were then living in Chestertown, Maryland), he rightly figured he could get additional horses there on demand; and 3) with the size of the boat on which Tilghman embarked at Yorktown, beyond question small and probably open and sloop-rigged, it would be impossible to tack with a horse on board. It could be done if the mainsail were rigged without a boom, but the list of the boat induced when shifting from a port to starboard tack or vice versa could cause a fractious horse to panic and even to jump overboard. Moreover fresh water, feed, and forage for a horse on such a trip—undertaken with speed as a primary consideration—would be so bulky as to be counter-productive.

13 *Archives of Maryland*, vol. 45, 651.

14 Ibid., vol. 47, 486.

15 Tilghman to Washington, 27 October 1781, George Washington Papers, LC.

16 On his own initiative Governor Lee had de Grasse's letter copied and forwarded to Philadelphia. The route taken by de Grasse's courier from Yorktown to Annapolis is not known; beyond Annapolis he took the same route as Tilghman. Little attention has been given to the fact that the elapsed time it took both messengers to reach Philadelphia was the same, i.e., four days. Had wind and tide not been against him, Tilghman would have reached Philadelphia a day earlier, thereby gaining a full day on de Grasse's man, who left Yorktown two days ahead of him.

17 *Maryland Journal*, 13 November 1781.

18 Johnson, *General Washington*, 266.

19 "A Loyalists Account of Certain Occurrences in Philadelphia After Cornwallis's Surrender," 104.

20 *Pennsylvania Packet,* 1 November 1781.
21 Hunt, *Journals,* 1082-83.
22 For the details of the interrogation, plus Tilghman's answers, see Ibid.
23 George Washington Papers, LC.
24 Hunt, *Journals,* vol. 21, 1082-83.
25 Eberlein, *Diary of Independence Hall,* 285-86.

Chapter 12. Marriage . . . and a Partnership

1 Fitzpatrick, *Writings of Washington,* vol. 26, 422.
2 Ibid., vol. 27, 177.
3 Ibid., vol. 23, 357n.
4 Ibid., vol. 24, 87n.
5 Ibid., vol. 25, 2n.
6 Freeman, *George Washington,* vol. 5, 408.
7 Tilghman, *History of Talbot County,* vol. 1, 27.
8 Papers of Dr. Samuel A. Harrison, Manuscript Collection, No. 432, Maryland Historical Society, Biographical Annals, vol. 1, 66-70.
9 Tilghman, *History of Talbot County,* vol. 1, 29.
10 Ibid., 30.
11 Bordley, *Hollyday Families,* 262.
12 Fitzpatrick, *Writings of Washington,* Vol. 25, 2n.
13 Ibid., vol. 25, 433n.
14 While a lieutenant-colonelcy under normal circumstances cannot be considered a rank of great seniority, it must be remembered that from 1781 onward no promotions to the rank of colonel were made in the American army. (Fitzpatrick, *Writings of Washington,* vol. 22, 388.) Consequently the most senior of Washington's aides remained as lieutenant-colonels to the war's end. This fact, coupled with the intimate association which Tilghman enjoyed with his commander in chief, qualified him as a front-runner for honors in the postwar era.
15 Tilghman, *Memoir,* 50.
16 Burnett, *Letters of Members of The Continental Congress,* vol. 7, 190-91.
17 On Morris's appointment as Superintendent of Finance, Washington wrote: "I have great expectations of the appointment of Mr. Morris, but they are not unreasonable ones; for I do not suppose that by art magick, he can do more than recover us, by degrees, from the labyrinth in which our finance is plunged." Washington to General Nathanael Greene, 27 February 1781, George Washington Papers, LC.
18 Tilghman, *History of Talbot County,* vol. 1, 31.
19 Papers of Dr. Samuel A. Harrison, Manuscript Collection, No. 432, Maryland Historical Society, Biographical Annals, vol. 4, 43.
20 Tench Tilghman to George Washington, 15, 27 July 1784, George Washington Papers, LC.
21 Bruchey, *Robert Oliver,* 29-32.
22 Ver Steeg, *Robert Morris,* 190.

23 Papers of Tench Tilghman, Manuscript Collection, No. 1445, Maryland Historical Society.
24 *Map of Baltimore*, 1784, Map Collection, Peale Museum, Baltimore. Also Hawkins, *Life and Times of Elijah Stansbury*, 235-41.

Chapter 13. The Shadows Lengthen . . .

1 Greene, *Baltimore: An Illustrated History*, 46.
2 *Diary of Nathanael Greene*, October 1783.
3 Greene, *Baltimore: An Illustrated History*, 50.
4 MHM, vol. 1, 280ff.
5 LaFuye and Babeau, *Lafayette: The Apostle of Liberty*, 69.
6 Gottschalk, *Lafayette Between The American and The French Revolution*, 730.
7 Scharf, *The Chronicles of Baltimore*, 237.
8 Ibid., 238.
9 Gottschalk, *Lafayette Between The American and The French Revolution*, 435.
10 From the original Institution of the Society. Anderson House Museum, Washington, D. C.
11 Metcalf, *Original Members And Other Officers Eligible To The Society of The Cincinnati*, unnumbered page in Introduction.
12 Scharf, *The Chronicles of Baltimore*, 279.
13 Griffith, *Annals of Baltimore*, 102-19.
14 Hume, *George Washington's Correspondence Concering The Society of The Cincinnati*, 188.
15 Ibid., 195.
16 A case in point is that of John Rawlins, a stucco worker or plasterer, originally from England. Washington wrote to Tilghman on 30 November 1785 to recruit Rawlins, after an inspection of his work at Perry Hall, to decorate what Washington referred to as his New Room at Mount Vernon. Articles of Agreement were signed by Rawlins and Tilghman on 25 February 1786. George Washington Papers, LC.
17 George Washington to Tench Tilghman, 11 August 1784, George Washington papers, LC.
18 Willing, Morris, and Swanwick Papers, 23 February, 24, 29 March, 3, 10 May, and 27 July 1784, F. Folder, Division of Archives and Manuscripts, Pennsylvania Historical and Museum Commission, Harrisburg.
19 Papenfuse, *In Pursuit of Profit*, 198.
20 Ibid.
21 Ibid., 196n. As a sidelight it is interesting to note that so highly had the qualities of Maryland tobacco been rated by the cigarette smokers of France that the French government kept a full-time office in Baltimore until the middle 1960s for the sole purpose of insuring an adequate supply to the cigarette manufacturers of that nation.
22 Memoranda (typescript) About My Maternal Family, Related To Me By My Maternal Uncle, John Bozman Kerr, Josiah Bayly Done and The Papers of

Dr. Samuel A. Harrison, Volume 4, Biographical Annals, both in the Maryland Historical Society.

23 Acct. of Sales of Sundry Merchandize Belonging To The Estate of Tench Tilghman & Co. and Sold by Carey and Tilghman 13 July 1786-26 December 1791 and Dr. Robert Morris's Stock Account With Tench Tilghman & Co., Phila., 9 March 1803.

24 Tilghman, *Memoir*, 56-57.

25 Letter dated 2 September 1785 to William, still in Chestertown with James, father of both. Location of letter unknown. Quotation taken from photoprint of original.

26 Both letters from the manuscript collection of a Tilghman descendant who wishes to remain anonymous.

27 Pleasants, "Letters," 123-49.

28 Washington to Jefferson, 1 August 1786; Fitzpatrick, *Writings of Washington*, vol. 25, 506.

29 As quoted in Emory's *History of Queen Anne's County*, 451, from the Easton Star of 11 January 1825. Also found in Bordley's *Hollyday Families*, 161. In the Dean Manuscript Collection, Cornell University Library, American Correspondents of Lafayette, is a letter dated 30 July 1825 from Tench Tilghman (son of Peregrine Tilghman of Hope) informing Lafayette of the steamboat schedules from Baltimore and Annapolis to Oxford in anticipation of this visit.

30 Nicholas Brice married Anna Maria Margaret Tilghman, the eldest daughter of Richard Tilghman IV, brother of Anna Maria Tilghman of Plimhimmon. John Brice was the older brother of Nicholas. Extracted from Brice family records, written by John Brice in 1844, now in the hands of Mrs. Charles G. Linder, Annapolis, Maryland.

Chapter 14. Epilogue

1 Beirne, *St. Paul's Parish, Baltimore*, 30.
2 Ibid., 77.
3 Ibid., 59.
4 Ibid., 141.
5 Mrs. William D. Waxter, Jr., L. G. Shreve, and John Frazer, Jr.
6 Fitzpatrick, *Writings of Washington*, vol. 29, 101.

Appendix I. Tilghman Correspondence

1 Variations in the spelling of proper names appear throughout the transcripts, and have been retained.
2 Tilghman, "Letters Between the English and American Branches of the Tilghman Family," 155-57.
3 In the collection of a member of the Tilghman family who wishes to remain anonymous.

4 This letter was written after Tench had received a letter from his father in Philadelphia. In the collection of a member of the Tilghman family who wishes to remain anonymous.

5 In this letter Tench took note of the return of Governor John Penn and Judge Benjamin Chew and spoke candidly of political developments which might run counter to family interests. In the collection of a member of the Tilghman family who wishes to remain anonymous.

6 "Letters from the Penn Papers," 457.

7 Tilghman, *Memoir,* 132.

8 "Military Papers of General John Cadwalader," 167-70.

9 Original in the collection of Mr. John F. Reed, King of Prussia, Pennsylvania, and herein quoted by permission.

10 Steiner, *The Life and Correspondence of James McHenry,* 25-26.

11 Tilghman, *Memoir,* 167-68.

12 Ibid., 173.

13 Ibid., 164.

14 Ibid., 169.

15 Ibid., 172.

16 George Washington Papers, LC.

17 Manuscript Collection, Mrs. W. D. Waxter, Jr., Baltimore, Md.

18 Chevalier Louis le Begue de Presle Duportail was a French volunteer who contributed significantly to American independence. Brigadier General and Chief of Engineers 17 November 1777 at Valley Forge; played a vital role in siege operations at Yorktown; and promoted to Major General in 1781. Jean Baptiste Gouvion; intimate of Lafayette; one of four French military engineers sent to America at the request of Congress was at Yorktown, accompanied Lafayette on his trip to Austria following the American Revolution, and was killed in action in War of the First Coalition.

19 Fitzpatrick, *Writings of Washington,* vol. 26, 27-29.

20 George Washington Papers, LC. Excavations at Mount Clare were undertaken as a first step in the restoration of its greenhouse in 1981. Copies of the Washington-Tilghman correspondence on this subject, discovered in the custodial library at Mount Vernon by the author and unknown to the restoration architects, have been turned over to them to form the cornerstone of the rebuilding of the greenhouse, referred to more frequently as The Orangery.

21 Charles Willson Peale Letter Books, American Philosophical Society, as quoted in Sellers, *Charles Willson Peale,* vol. 1, 235.

In addition to Trumbull's historic painting there are three other known likenesses of Colonel Tilghman, all by Charles Willson Peale. The one herewith described hangs now, as it has since the day it was turned over by Peale to the ownership of the State of Maryland, in the Old Senate Chamber in the State House at Annapolis. Of heroic proportions it is probably Tilghman's best known portrait and has been widely reproduced. The figure of Washington is identical in every respect to his portrait which hangs in the State Capitol at Williamsburg, with Tilghman and Lafayette eliminated. Peale's "Washington and His Generals at Yorktown" was painted, in all likelihood, later than either of the two mentioned above, and can now be seen at the Maryland Historical Society. In it Tilghman is depicted in the precise pose as in the one at Annapolis, except that he is hatted. In both paintings the Articles of Capitulation appear in his left hand, somewhat less tightly rolled in the latter. The third likeness is a miniature on ivory, now in the hands of a descendant, Richard Tilghman Smyth, Wolcott, Vermont 05680.

Appendix IV. The Duc de Lauzun

1 *Magazine of American History,* vol. 6, No. 1 (Jan. 1881), 51-53.

Appendix V. The Articles of Capitulation

1 Fitzpatrick, *Writings of Washington,* vol. 23, 242n.
2 George Washington Papers, LC.
3 Fitzpatrick, *The Diaries of George Washington,* entries for days indicated.

Bibliography

I. MANUSCRIPTS

A. *Collections*

American Antiquarian Society, Worcester, Massachusetts
  Isaiah Thomas Collection of Broadside Ballads
Anderson House, Headquarters and Museum of The Society of the
 Cincinnati, Washington, D. C.
  The Diary and Journal of Tench Tilghman
William L. Clements Library, University of Michigan, Ann Arbor,
 Michigan
  The Papers of Sir Henry Clinton
  The Shelbourne Papers
Library of Congress, Manuscript Division, Washington, D. C.
  The George Washington Papers
Maryland Historical Society, Baltimore, Maryland
  The Calvert Papers
  Carmichael Family Genealogy, No. E71 C287
  The Papers of Dr. Samuel A. Harrison
  The Hollyday Papers
  The Papers of Tench Tilghman
  Tench Tilghman's Ride by B. Howell Griswold, Jr., prepared
   for delivery before the Eastern Shore Society of Baltimore,
   1931
New York Historical Society, New York, New York
  The Papers of Allan McLane
New York Public Library, New York, New York
  The Papers of Robert Morris
Olin Library, Cornell University, Ithaca, New York
  Dean Manuscript Collection
Historical Society of Pennsylvania, Philadelphia, Pennsylvania
  The Papers of William Tilghman

BIBLIOGRAPHY

Pennsylvania Historical and Museum Commission, Harrisburg, Pennsylvania
     Willing, Morris, and Swanwick Papers
Public Record Office, London, England
     The Articles of Capitulation, 19 October 1781

B. Individual items of Tilghman correspondence or documents

American Philosophical Society, Philadelphia, Pennsylvania
Connecticut Historical Society, Hartford, Connecticut
Houston University Library, Houston, Texas
Huntington Library, San Marino, California
Maine Historical Society, Portland, Maine
Morristown National Historical Park, Morristown, New Jersey
Historical Society of Talbot County, Easton, Maryland
Talbot County Free Library, Easton, Maryland
Western Reserve Historical Society, Cleveland, Ohio

C. Collections in private hands

Mr. John Frazer, Jr., Annapolis, Maryland
Mr. Tench Frazer, Philadelphia, Pennsylvania
Mr. Paul Mellon, Upperville, Virginia
Mr. John F. Reed, King of Prussia, Pennsylvania
Mr. Ronald von Klaussen, New York, New York
Mrs. William D. Waxter, Jr., Baltimore, Maryland

II. BOOKS

AND PUBLISHED DOCUMENTS CITED

Alden, John Richard. *The American Revolution, 1775-1783.* New York, 1954.

Alexander, Holmes. *To Covet Honor: A Biography of Alexander Hamilton.* Belmont, Massachusetts, 1977.

Allen, Luther Prentice. *The Genealogy and History of The Shreve Family.* Greenfield, Illinois, 1901.

American Archives. 9 vols. Edited by Peter Force. Washington, D. C. 1837-53.

Appleton's Cyclopaedia of American Biography. 6 vols. Edited by James Grant Wilson and John Fiske. New York, 1889.

Archives of Maryland. 72 vols. Edited by William Hand Browne. Baltimore, 1883-1972.

Archives of Pennsylvania, 1st Series. 12 vols. 1852. 2nd Series. 19 vols. Edited by Samuel Hazard. Harrisburg, Pennsylvania 1852-56.

Armes, Ethel. *Nancy Shippen: Her Journal Book.* Philadelphia, 1935.

Bakeless, John. *Turncoats, Traitors and Heroes.* Philadelphia, 1959.

Balch, Thomas Willing. *The French In America During The War of Independence of The United States.* Philadelphia, 1895.

————. *Letters and Papers On The Provincial History of Pennsylvania.* Philadelphia, 1855.

————. *Papers Relating Chiefly To The Maryland Line.* Philadelphia, 1857.

Barker, Charles Albro. *The Background of The Revolution in Maryland.* Hamden, Connecticut, 1967.

Beirne, Francis F. *Saint Paul's Parish, Baltimore: A Chronicle of The Mother Church.* Baltimore, 1967.

Berry, Thomas. *Hampshire Genealogies.* London, 1833.

————. *Kent Genealogies.* London, 1886.

Bill, Alfred Hoyt. *The Campaign of Princeton 1776-1777.* Princeton, 1948.

Biographical Congressional Directory (1911).

Boatner, Mark Mayo, II. *Encyclopedia of The American Revolution.* New York, 1966.

Bordley, James, Jr. *The Hollyday and Related Families of The Eastern Shore of Maryland.* Baltimore, 1962.

Boylan, Brian Richard. *Benedict Arnold: The Dark Eagle.* New York, 1973.

Brown, Anne S. K. *The American Campaigns of Rochambeau's Army,* with Howard Crosby Rice. Princeton, 1972.

Bruchey, Stuart Weems. *Robert Oliver, Merchant of Baltimore 1783-1819.* Baltimore, 1956.

Burnett, Edmund C., ed. *Letters of Members of the Continental Congress.* 8 vols. Washington, 1928.

Busch, Noel F. *Winter Quarters: George Washington And The Continental Army at Valley Forge.* New York, 1974.

Butterfield, Lyman H., ed. *The Letters of Benjamin Rush.* Princeton, 1951.

Cabeen. "Society of the Sons of Saint Tammany of Philadelphia," *Pennsylvania Magazine of History and Biography,* vol. 25 (1901).

Cadwalader, Sophia, ed. "A Diary of Trifling Occurrences - Philadelphia 1776-1778," *Pennsylvania Magazine of History and Biography,* vol. 82 (1958), 441n.

Callahan, North. *The Tories of The American Revolution*. New York, 1963.

Chamberlain, Joshua L. *The University of Pennsylvania*, 2 vols. Boston, 1901.

Chastellux, Francois Jean. *Travels In North America In The Years 1780, 1781 and 1782*, 2 vols. London, 1787.

Coe, Samual Gwynn. *The Mission of William Carmichael To Spain*. Baltimore, 1928.

Commanger, Henry Steel. *The Spirit of 'Seventy-Six*. New York, 1967.

Confidential Correspondence of Robert Morris. Auction Catalogue, Henkels, Philadelphia, 1917.

Cooke, Jacob E. "Tench Coxe: Tory Merçhant," *Pennsylvania Magazine of History and Biography*, vol. 96 (1972).

Custis, G. W. Parke. *Recollections and Private Memoirs of Washington*. Philadelphia, 1867.

Dallett, James Francis. *Guide To The Archives of The University of Pennsylvania From 1740 to 1820*. Philadelphia, 1978.

Dangerfield, George. *Chancellor Robert R. Livingston of New York 1746-1813*. New York, 1960.

Delaplaine, Edward S. "Life of Thomas Johnson," *Maryland Historical Magazine*, vol. 14 (1919).

Desmond, Alice Curtis. *Sword and Pen For Washington*. New York, 1964.

"Diary of James Allen," *Pennsylvania Magazine of History and Biography*, vol. 9 (1885).

Dictionary of American Biography. 20 vols. and Index. Edited by Allen Johnson and Dumas Malone. New York, 1928-1937.

Dupuy, Trevor N. *People and Events of The American Revolution*, with Gay M. Hammerman. Dunn Loring, Virginia, 1974.

Eberlein, Harold Donaldson, and Hubbard, Courtland Van Dyke. *Diary of Independence Hall*, Philadelphia, 1948.

Emory, Frederick William. *History of Queen Anne's County*. Baltimore, 1950.

Ferguson, James E., ed. *The Papers of Robert Morris*. 4 vols. Pittsburgh, 1973-1978.

Fisher, Sydney George. *The Making of Pennsylvania*. Philadelphia, 1896.

———. *Men, Women and Manners In Colonial Times*. Philadelphia, 1900.

———. *The Struggle For American Independence*. 2 vols. Philadelphia, 1908.

Fitzpatrick, John C. *George Washington: Colonial Traveller 1732-1775*. Indianapolis, 1927.

———. *The Spirit of The Revolution*. New York, 1924.

Fitzpatrick, John C., ed. *The Diaries of George Washington 1748-1799*. 4 vols. Boston, 1925.

————. *The Writings of George Washington From The Original Manuscript Sources*. 39 vols. Washington, 1931-1944.

Fleming, Thomas J. *Beat the Last Drum: The Siege of Yorktown*. New York, 1963.

Flexner, James T. *The Traitor and The Spy: Benedict Arnold and John Andre*. New York, 1953.

Ford, Worthington C. *The Writings of Washington*. 14 vols. New York, 1889-1893.

Freeman, Douglas Southall. *George Washington: A Biography*. 7 vols. New York, 1948-1957.

French Alliances in the United States. *Souvenirs de L'Independence Americaine Dans Les Chateaux Francais, Catalogue of the American Tour of the Photographic Exhibit, 1976-1978*. New York, 1976.

Frye, Harriet. *What Did They Say To Each Other?* Kilmarnock, Virginia, 1975.

Garden, Alexander. *Anecdotes of The Revolutionary War In America*. Charleston, 1822 (1st series), 1828 (2nd series).

Gillespie. "Early Fire Protection and Use of Fire Marks," *Pennsylvania Magazine of History and Biography*. vol. 46 (1922).

Gottschalk, Louis R. *Lafayette: A Guide To The Letters, Documents and Manuscripts in The United States*, with Phyllis S. Pestieau and Linda J. Pike. Ithaca, 1975.

————. *Lafayette Joins The American Army*. Chicago, 1937.

————. *Lafayette and The Close of The American Revolution*. Chicago, 1942.

————. *Lafayette Comes to America*. Chicago, 1935.

————. *Lafayette Between The American and French Revolution*. Chicago, 1950.

Graydon, Alexander. *Memoirs of His Own Time*. Philadelphia, 1846.

Graymont, Barbara. *The Iroquois In The American Revolution*, Syracuse, 1972.

Green, V. H. H. *The Later Plantagenets*. London, 1955.

Greene, George W. *Life of Nathanael Greene*. 3 vols. Boston, 1846.

Greene, Suzanne Ellery. *Baltimore: An Illustrated History*. Woodland Hills, California, 1980.

Griffith, Thomas W. *Annals of Baltimore*. Baltimore, 1824.

Gummere, Richard M. *Seven Wise Men of Colonial America*. Cambridge, 1967.

Hamilton, John C., ed. *The Works of Alexander Hamilton,* 7 vols. New York, 1850-1851.

Hamilton, Milton W. *Sir William Johnson and The Indians of New York*. Albany, 1967.

Hanson, George A. *Old Kent: The Eastern Shore of Maryland*. Baltimore, 1876.

Harleian Society Publications. 114 Vols. Edited by Joseph Jackson Howard and George John Armitage, London 1869.

Harleian Society Publications, Register Series. 47 Vols. Edited by Granville W. G. Leveson Gower, London 1887.

Harrison, Mary. *Annals of The Ancestry of Charles Curtis Harrison and Ellen Waln Harrison.* Philadelphia, 1932.

Hawkins, Archibald. *The Life and Times of Elijah Stansbury.* Baltimore, 1874.

Heitman, Francis B. *Historical Register of Officers of The Continental Army.* Washington, 1914.

Hendrickson, Robert. *Hamilton I (1757-1789).* New York, 1976.

History of the Schuylkill Fishing Company of the State of Schuylkill 1732-1888. Philadelphia, 1889.

Horner, Marian Sadtler. "Notes and Documents," *Pennsylvania Magazine of History and Biography,* vol. 65.

Hughes, Rupert. *George Washington.* 3 vols. New York, 1930.

Hume, Edgar Erskine. *George Washington's Correspondence Concerning The Society of The Cincinnati.* Baltimore, 1941.

Hunt, Gaillard, ed. *Journals of the Continental Congress.* 34 vols. Washington, 1904-1937.

Ireland, W. H. *History of the County of Kent.* London, 1829.

Johnson, Bradley T. *George Washington.* New York, 1894.

Johnston, Christopher. "The Tilghman Family," *Maryland Historical Magazine,* vol. 1 (1906).

Katcher, Philip R. N. *Encyclopedia of British, Provincial, and German Army Units 1775-1783.* Harrisburg, 1973.

Kennett, Leo. *The French Forces in America 1780-1783.* Westport, 1977.

Kite, Elizabeth S. "Lafayette and His Companions on the *Victoire,*" *Records of the American Catholic Historical Societey,* vol. 45 (1934).

Klinger, Robert L. *Sketch Book '76: The American Soldier, 1775-1781,* with Richard A. Wilder. Arlington, 1967.

La Fuye, Maurice, and Babeau, Emile. *Lafayette: The Apostle of Liberty.* London, 1956.

Land, Aubrey C. *The Dulanys of Maryland.* Baltimore, 1968.

Land, Aubrey C., ed. *Letters from America, William Eddis.* Cambridge, 1969.

Larrabee, Harold A. *Decision At The Chesapeake.* New York, 1974.

Latzko, Andreas. *Lafayette: A Life.* New York, 1936.

Lecky, W. E. H. *History of England In The Eighteenth Century.* 8 vols. London, 1878-1890.

Lee, Henry. *Memoirs of The War In The Southern Department of The United States.* New York, 1869.

Leonard, Lewis A. *Life of Charles Carroll of Carrollton.* New York, 1918.

"Letters from the Penn Papers," *Pennsylvania Magazine of History and Biography*, vol. 31 (1907).

"Letters of William Carmichael to John Cadwalader, 1777," *Maryland Historical Magazine*, vol. 44 (1949).

Lodge, Henry C. *The Works of Alexander Hamilton.* 12 vols. New York, 1903.

"A Loyalists Account of Certain Occurrences in Philadelphia After Cornwallis's Surrender," *Pennsylvania Magazine of History and Biography*, vol. 16 (1892).

Lutnick, Solomon. *The American Revolution and The British Press.* Columbia, Missouri, 1967.

McGrath, F. Sims. *Pillars of Maryland.* Richmond, 1950.

Marshall, John. *Life of Washington*, 5 vols. Philadelphia, 1805.

Maryland and North Carolina in the Campaign of 1780-1781, Maryland Historical Society Fund Publication No. 33, 1893.

Mayo, Katherine. *General Washington's Dilemma.* New York, 1938.

Metcalf, Bryce. *Original Members And Other Officers Eligible To The Society of The Cincinnati.* Strasburg, Virginia, 1938.

Miers, Earl Schenck. *Blood of Freedom: The Story of Jamestown, Williamsburg and Yorktown.* New York, 1958.

"Military Papers of John Cadwalader," *Pennsylvania Magazine of History and Biography*, vol. 32 (1908).

Miller, Nathan. *The Founding Finaglers.* New York, 1976.

"Mission of William Carmichael to Spain," *Johns Hopkins Studies in Historical and Political Sciences*, vol. 46 (1928), 5-6.

Montgomery, Thomas Harrison. *A History of The University of Pennsylvania From Its Foundation to A. D. 1770.* Philadelphia, 1900.

Morant, Philip. *History and Antiquities of The County of Essex.* London, 1768.

Myers, Albert C., ed. *Sally Wistar's Journal: Being A Quaker Maiden's Account of Her Experiences With Officers Of The Continental Army, 1777-1778.* Philadelphia, 1902.

New York Historical Society. *Collections:* St. James Chronicle, 7-9 November 1776. vol. 1 (1870).

———. *Collections: The Lee Papers, 1754-1811.* 4 vols. (1872-1875).

"Notes and Queries," *Pennsylvania Magazine of History and Biography*, vol. 22, 125, fn 9.

Papenfuse, Edward C. *In Pursuit of Profit: The Annapolis Merchants In The Era of The American Revolution.* Baltimore, 1975.

Pleasants, J. Hall, ed. "The Letters of Molly and Hetty Tilghman," *Maryland Historical Magazine.* vol. 21, 30n.

Private Papers of James Boswell from Malahide Castle. Privately printed, W. E. Rudge, Mount Vernon, New York in 18 vols. 1928-1934.

Index and revised edition published by Oxford University Press, 1937.

Program of the Washington-Rochambeau Celebration, 1780-1955. Preservation Society of Newport County, Rhode Island, 1955.

Reed, W. B. *The Life and Correspondence of General Joseph Reed.* 2 vols. Philadelphia, 1847.

Revolutionary Manuscripts and Portraits. Auction Catalogue No. 683. Thomas Birch's Sons, Philadelphia, 1892.

Rivington, James. A Candid Examination of The Mutual Claims of Great Britain and The Colonies, With A Plan of Accommodation On Constitutional Principles. New York, 1775.

Rush, Richard. *Occasional Productions: Political, Diplomatic and Miscellaneous.* Philadelphia, 1860.

Scharf, J. Thomas. *The Chronicles Of Baltimore.* Baltimore, 1874.

————. *History of Maryland: From The Earliest Period To The Present Day,* 3 vols. Baltimore, 1879.

Schouler, James. *Americans of 1776.* New York, 1906.

Sellers, Charles Coleman. *Charles Willson Peale.* New York, 1969.

Semmes, Raphael. *Baltimore As Seen By Visitors 1783-1800.* Baltimore, 1953.

Simes, Thomas. *The Military Guide For Young Officers.* London, 1776.

Simms, William Gilmore. *Army Correspondence of Colonel John Laurens, 1777-1778.* New York, 1867.

Sizer, Theodore. *The Works of Colonel John Trumbull.* New Haven, 1967.

Skirven. "Seven Pioneers of the Colonial Eastern Shore," *Maryland Historical Magazine,* vol. 15 (1920).

Smith, Ellen Hart. *Charles Carroll of Carrollton.* Cambridge, 1942.

Steiner, Bernard Christian. *The Life and Correspondence of James McHenry.* Cleveland, 1907.

Steuart, Rieman. *A History of The Maryland Line in The Revolutionary War 1775-1783.* Towson, Maryland, 1969.

Stille, Charles Janeway, ed. *The Life and Writings of John Dickinson.* 2 vols. Philadelphia, 1891.

Stryker, William S. *The Battles of Trenton and Princeton.* Boston, 1898.

————. *The Battle of Monmouth.* Princeton, 1927.

Swem, Earl Gregg, ed. "Historical and Genealogical Notes and Queries," *Virginia Magazine of History and Biography,* vol. 13 (1905-6).

Syrett, H. C., ed. *The Papers of Alexander Hamilton,* 25 vols. New York, 1961-62.

Thane, Elswyth. *Washington's Lady.* New York, 1960.

Thayer, Theodore George. *Nathanael Greene: Strategist of The American Revolution.* New York, 1960.

Tilghman, Harrison, ed. "Letters Between the English and American Branches of the Tilghman Family," *Maryland Historical Magazine*, vol. 33 (1938).

Tilghman, Oswald. *History of Talbot County, Maryland, 1661-1861*. 2 vols. Baltimore, 1925.

———. *Memoir of Lieut. Colonel Tench Tilghman*. Albany, 1876.

Tillman, Stephen F. *The Tilghman/Tillman Family*. Washington, 1962.

Todd, Charles Burr. *The Real Benedict Arnold*. New York, 1903.

Tower, Charlemagne. *The Marquis de La Fayette In The American Revolution*, 2 vols. Philadelphia, 1895.

Townsend, Sarah B. *An American Soldier: The Life of John Laurens*. Raleigh, 1958.

Trevelyan, George O. *The American Revolution*, 6 vols. London, 1909-1914.

Tucker, Glenn. *Mad Anthony Wayne and The New Nation*. Harrisburg, 1973.

University of Pennsylvania. *Biographical Catalogue of The Matriculates 1749-1893*. Philadelphia, 1894.

Van Doren, Carl. *The Secret History of The American Revolution*. New York, 1941.

Van Every, Dale. *Forth To The Wilderness: The First American Frontier*. New York, 1961.

Ver Steeg, Clarence L. *Robert Morris: Revolutionary Financier*. New York, 1972.

Wagner, Anthony B. *English Genealogy*. London, 1960.

Wallace, Willard M. *Traitorous Hero: The Life and Fortunes of Benedict Arnold*. New York, 1954.

Waln, Robert, Jr. *The Life of The Marquis de La Fayette*. Philadelphia, 1825.

Walsh, Richard, and Fox, Lloyd. *Maryland: A History 1632-1972*. Baltimore, 1974.

Ward, Christopher. *The War Of The Revolution*. 2 vols. New York, 1952.

Wertenbaker, Thomas Jefferson. *Father Knickerbocker Rebels*. New York, 1948.

———. *The Golden Age of Colonial Culture*. New York, 1942.

Whiteley, Emily Stone. *Washington And His Aides-de-camp*. New York, 1936.

Whitlock, Brand. *Lafayette*. 2 vols. New York, 1929.

Willcox, William B., ed. *The American Rebellion, Sir Henry Clinton's Narrative of His Campaigns, 1775-1782, With An Appendix of Original Documents*. New Haven, 1954.

Young, Eleanor. *Forgotten Patriot: Robert Morris*. New York, 1950.

Zucker, Adolph Eduard. *General de Kalb, Lafayette's Mentor*. Chapel Hill, 1966.

Index

257